Commercial Design
Using Revit® Architecture 2009

Daniel John Stine

ISBN: 978-1-58503-464-2

PUBLICATIONS

Schroff Development Corporation

www.schroff.com

Foreword

To The Student:
The intent of this book is to provide the student with a well-rounded knowledge of tools and techniques for use in both school and industry.

It is strongly recommended that this book is completed in lesson order. Most exercises utilize project content created in previous lessons.

You will find "video" symbols (example at right) throughout the book which indicate a short **video** on that subject can be found on the DVD. Note the number in the icon and view that video file from the DVD. Be sure to check out the DVD for several bonus videos on topics not even covered in this textbook!

To the Instructor:
This book was designed for the architectural student using Revit Architecture 2009. Throughout the book the student develops a three story office building. The drawings start with the floor plans and develop all the way to photo-realistic renderings similar to the one on the cover of this book.

Throughout the book many Revit tools and techniques are covered while creating the office building model. Also, in a way that is applicable to the current exercise, industry standard conventions are covered.

An Instructor's resource guide is available with this book. It contains:
- Answers to the questions at the end of each chapter
- Outline of tools and topics to be covered in each lesson's lecture
- Suggestions for additional student work (for each lesson)

About the Author:
Dan Stine is a registered Architect with seventeen years experience in the architectural field. He currently works at LHB (a 170 person multidiscipline firm; www.LHBcorp.com) in Duluth Minnesota as the CAD Administrator (providing training, customization and support for two regional offices). Dan has worked in a total of four firms. While at these firms, Dan has participated in collaborative projects with several other firms on various projects (including Cesar Pelli, Weber Music Hall – University of Minnesota - Duluth). Dan is a member of the *Construction Specification Institute* (CSI) and the *Autodesk Developer Network* (ADN) and also teaches *AutoCAD* and *Revit Architecture* classes at Lake Superior College, for the Architectural Technology program; additionally, he is a Certified Construction Document Technician (CDT). Mr. Stine has also written the following textbooks (published by SDC Publications):
- *Residential Design using Revit Architecture 2009*
- *Residential Design using AutoCAD 2009*
- *Commercial Design using AutoCAD 2009*

You can contact the publisher with comments or suggestions at **schroff@schroff.com**.
Please do not email with Revit questions unless they relate to a problem with this book.

Thanks:
I could not have done this with out the support from my family; Cheri, Kayla & Carter.

Many thanks go out to Stephen Schroff and Schroff Development Corporation for making this book possible!

Table of Contents

Design Option Set

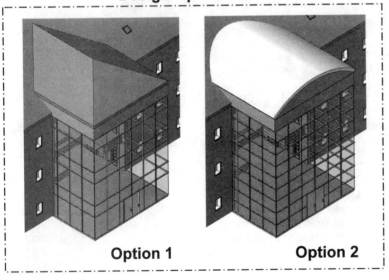

Option 1   Option 2

Image from pg. 7-24
This image shows the two design options that are developed in Lesson 7. Also developed in this book are the:

♦   Floor Plans
♦   Elevations
♦   Sections
♦   Curtainwall Design
♦   Renderings
♦   Doors & Windows
♦   Text & Dimensions
♦   Schedules

Lesson 1
Getting Started with Revit Architecture 2009::

This chapter will introduce you to Revit Architecture 2009. You will study the User Interface and learn how to open and exit a project and adjust the view of the drawing on the screen. It is recommended that the student spend an ample amount of time learning this material, as it will greatly enhance your ability to progress smoothly through subsequent chapters.

Exercise 1-1:
What is Revit Architecture 2009?

What is Revit Architecture 2009 used for?
Revit Architecture 2009 is the world's first fully parametric architectural design software. This revolutionary software, for the first time, truly takes architectural computer aided design beyond simply being a high tech pencil. Revit Architecture 2009 is a product of Autodesk, makers of AutoCAD, AutoCAD Architecture, Autodesk Maya and Autodesk 3DS Max. The Autodesk company web site (www.autodesk.com) claims more than 8 million users in 106 countries. Autodesk's thousands of employees create products available in 18 languages.

What is a parametric building modeler?
Revit is a relatively new program designed from the ground up using state-of-the-art technology. The term parametric describes a process by which an object is modified in one view and automatically updated in all other views and schedules. For example, if you move a door in an interior elevation view, the floor plan will automatically update. Or, if you delete a door, it will be deleted from all other views and schedules. You can even delete a door from the door schedule and the drawings will instantly be revised to reflect the change.

A major goal of Revit is to eliminate much of the repetitive and mundane tasks traditionally associated with CAD programs to allow more time for design and visualization. For example; all sheet numbers, elevation targets and reference bubbles are updated automatically when changed anywhere in the Project. It is impossible to have a miss-referenced detail tag.

The best way to understand how a parametric model works is to describe the Revit project file. A single Revit file contains your entire building project. Even though you mostly draw in 2D views, you are actually drawing in 3D. In fact, the entire building project is a 3D model. From this 3D model you can generate 2D elevations, 2D sections and perspective views. Therefore, when you delete a door in an elevation view you are actually deleting the door from the 3D model from which all 2D views are generated (and automatically updated).

Why use Revit?

Many people ask the question, why use Revit versus other programs? The answer can certainly vary depending on the situation and particular needs of an individual or organization.

Generally speaking, this is why most companies use Revit:
- Many designers and drafters are using Revit to streamline repetitive drafting tasks and focus more on designing and detailing a project.
- Revit is a very progressive program and offers many feature for designing buildings. Revit is constantly being developed and Autodesk provides incremental upgrades/patches on a regular basis; this version was released less than a year after the previous version.
- Revit was designed specifically for architecture and includes features like:
  - Mental Ray's Photo-realistic renderer
  - Phasing (which makes Revit a 4D tool)
  - Pantone digital color
  - Vectoral Shadows (real-time shadows)
  - Design Options

The future is limitless.

We can expect some amazing advancements in the program as it develops. For example, with the building being a 3D model, we will see building code analyzers with plug-in modules for state and local codes, similar to tax programs like TurboTax. We are starting to see structural, mechanical and electrical engineers designing in the same model as the architects (using Revit Structure 2009 and Revit MEP 2009). This is helping to eliminate conflicts found in many drawings.

Exercise 1-2:
Overview of the Revit User Interface

Revit is a powerful and sophisticated program. Because of its powerful feature set it has a measurable learning curve, though its intuitive design makes it easier to learn than other CAD programs. However, like anything, when broken down into smaller pieces, we can easily learn to harness the power of Revit. That is the goal of this book.

This section will walk through the different sections of the User Interface (UI). As with any program, understanding the user interface is the key to using the program's features.

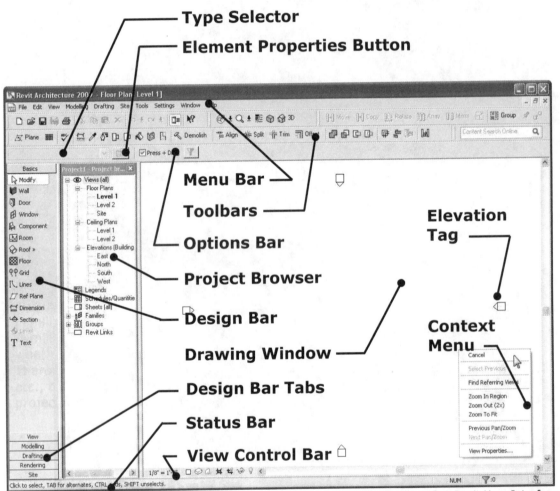

Figure 1-2.1 Revit User Interface

The Revit User Interface:

Menu Bar: Like all Windows programs, Revit has a series of pull-down menus across the top of the screen. Click on each of the menus to explore their contents. Many of these commands are graphically represented by Toolbars and the *Design Bar*.

Toolbar – Standard: The *Standard* toolbar contains commands found in most Windows programs. Some examples are: Open, Save, Cut, Copy, Paste, Undo, Redo and Print.

new   open save save* print   cut   copy paste delete undo redo   browser what's this

Toolbar – View: This toolbar allows you to adjust the current drawing windows view. You can Zoom in and out, Pan and switch to 3D Views.

steering   zoom   thinlines show mass 3D view

Toolbar – Edit: Contains commands that modify objects in the drawings, i.e., Move, Mirror, Array, Group, Rotate.

resize   pin Create
similar

Toolbar – Tools: Contains common commands that modify objects in the drawings, i.e., Trim, Split, Offset, Tape Measure.

work plane, spelling tape measure, match type, linework, show/remove hidden lines, paint, split ...

Toolbar – Worksets: This toolbar allows you to manage and work with Worksets. Worksets allow multiple users to work on the same project (i.e., same project file). This toolbar is not visible by default; you can turn it on by: *Window → Toolbar → Worksets* via the *Menu Bar*.

Toolbar –
  Design Options   This toolbar allows you to manage various Design Options in your project. One Design Option might be a hip vs. a gable roof. This toolbar is not visible by default; you can turn it on by: *Window → Toolbar → Design Options* via the *Menu Bar*.

Toolbar –
  Content Search   This toolbar allows you to type in a keyword and search via the *Autodesk Seek* site. Try typing "toilet" and press Enter; then narrow the search to RFA file types and you will have access to several toilets that can be used in your BIM. Ideally, over time most manufacturers will have their products readily available here.

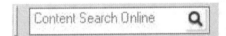

Options Bar: This "toolbar" dynamically changes to show options that complement the current operation.

Options Bar example with Wall tool active:

type selector   properties draw pick- pick- wall height
                                          lines faces

Project Browser: The *Project Browser* shows all the views, families, sheets, legends, schedules and groups available in the current project. A view is a floor plan, elevation or ceiling plan of the model.

Design Bar:	This area is like an enhanced *Menu Bar*. Each tab (see *Design Bar Tabs* next) displays commands related to the tab title. This area also dynamically changes to show options related to the current operation.
Design Bar Tabs:	The *Design Bar Tabs* are groupings of commands in the *Design Bar* area. The current tab is the tab located at the bottom of the top group of tabs. Notice when you select a *Design Bar Tab* (e.g., Structural) that the tabs above it also slide to the top. Think of it like drawers of design tools. **TIP:** *Right-click on a* Design Bar Tab *to see a pop-up menu that allows you to turn on and off various tab groups.*
Status Bar:	This area will display information about the current command or list information about a selected object. **TIP:** *Look here often while you are learning Revit.*

Status Bar example with the Demolish tool active:

Drawing Window:	This is where you design your project and generate views and schedules.
Type Selector:	The *Type Selector* lists the available families and types for the current operation. E.g., when inserting doors you can select different door styles and sizes; when inserting walls you can select various wall types to draw. This important feature is actually on the *Options Bar*.
Properties Button:	This button allows you to view the various properties of the selected components or active tool. Many of the properties are editable here as well. This feature is also apart of the *Options Bar*.
View Control Bar:	This is a feature gives you convenient access to tools that control each view's display settings (i.e., scale, shadows, detail level and graphics style).

Context Menu:

The Context Menu appears near the cursor whenever you right-click on the mouse. The options on that menu will vary depending on what tool is active or what is selected.

Context menu example with a wall selected:

Cancel
Flip Orientation
Select Joined Elements
Hide in view ▶
Override Graphics in View ▶
Create Similar
Edit Family
Select Previous
Select All Instances
Delete
Find Referring Views
Zoom In Region
Zoom Out (2x)
Zoom To Fit
Previous Scroll/Zoom
Next Scroll/Zoom
View Properties...
Element Properties...

Elevation Marker:

This item is not really part of the Revit UI, but is visible in the drawing window by default (via the various templates you can start with), so it is worth mentioning at this point. The four elevation markers point at each side of your floor plan and ultimately indicate on which drawing sheet you would find an elevation drawing of that side of the building. All you need to know right now is that you should draw your floor plan generally in the middle of the four elevation markers that you will see in each plan view; and DO NOT delete them.

This concludes our brief overview of the Revit user interface. Many of these tools and operations will be covered in more detail throughout the book.

Exercise 1-3:
Open, Save and Close an existing project

Open **Revit Architecture 2009**.
Start → All Programs → Autodesk →
Revit Architecture 2009
*(Figure 1-3.1 – **NOTE:** Windows XP Start menu shown)*

Revit
Architecture
2009

Or double-click the Revit icon from your desktop.

This may vary slightly on your computer; see your instructor or system administrator if you need help.

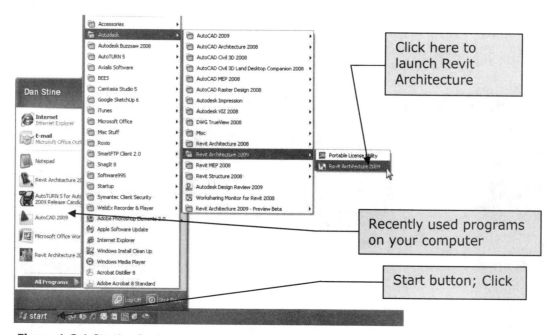

Figure 1-3.1 Starting Revit

Open an existing Revit project:

By default, Revit will open in the *Recent Files* window (which will display thumbnails of recent projects you have worked on; clicking on the preview will open the project).

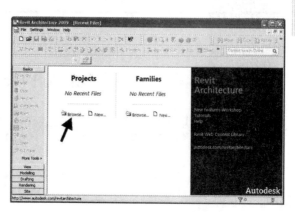

1. Click the **Browse** link (see image to the right).

Next you will open an existing Revit project file. You will select a sample file that was installed with the Revit program.

2. On the left side of the *Open* dialog box, scroll down and click on the **Training Files** icon (Figure 1-3.2):

    a. **TIP:** *If you cannot locate this file substitute "Office Building.rvt" located at the root level of the DVD that came with this textbook.*

    b. **TIP:** *Alternatively you can go to File → Open or browse via My Computer to the training files:* **C:\Documents and Settings\All Users\Application Data\Autodesk\RAC 2009\Training.** *If you do not see the Application Data folder, it may be because your folder is set to "hidden" via My Computer. In My Computer go to Tools → Folder Options → View tab and then check the option: Show hidden files and folders.*

    c. **TIP:** *The training folder may not contain any files depending on how Revit was installed on your computer. You can access the files on Autodesk's website (www.autodesk.com).*

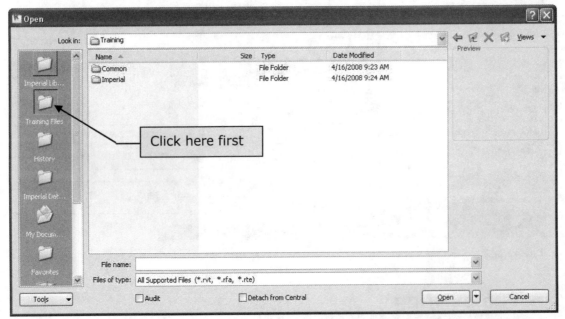

Figure 1-3.2 Open dialog: click Training Files shortcut

3. Double-click (with the left mouse button) the **Imperial** folder.

4. Select the file named **i_Urban_House.rvt** and click **Open**.
    FYI: *Click OK if you get any "room" warnings or upgrade messages.*

The *i_Urban_House.rvt* file is now open and the last saved view is displayed in the Drawing Window (Figure 1-3.3).

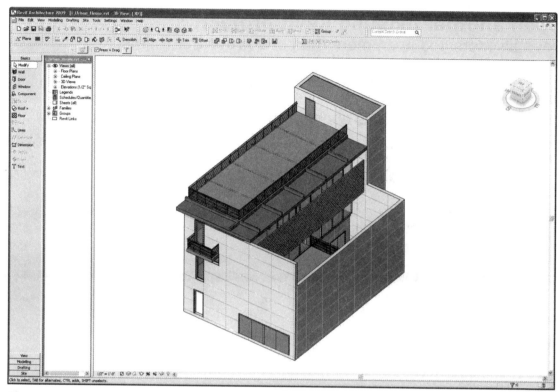

Figure 1-3.3 Training file "i_Urban_House.rvt"

The *Window* pull-down menu on the *Menu Bar* lists the projects and views currently open on your computer.

5. Click **Window** from the *Menu Bar* (Figure 1-3.4).

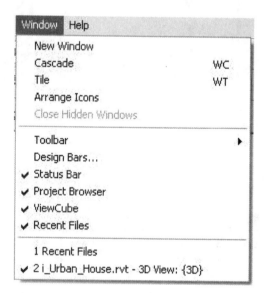

Figure 1-3.4 Window menu

Notice that the *i_Urban_House.rvt* project file is listed. Next to the project name is the name of a view (e.g., floor plan, elevation) open on your computer.

Additional views will be added to the list as you open them. Each view has the project name as a prefix. The current view (i.e., the view you are working in) has a check mark next to it. You can quickly toggle between opened views from this menu.

Open another existing Revit project:
Revit also lets you open more than one project at a time.

6. Click **File → Open** from the *Menu Bar*.

7. Per the instructions above, browse to **Training Files**.

8. In the **Imperial** folder, select the file named **i_Curtain_Walls.rvt** and click **Open** (Figure 1-3.5).

   a. **TIP:** *If you cannot locate this file, substitute "Church Building.rvt" located at the root level of the DVD that came with this textbook.*

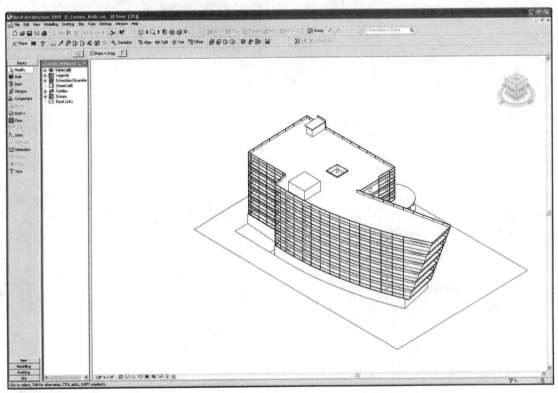

Figure 1-3.5 Training file "i_Curtain_Walls.rvt"

9. Click **Window** from the *Menu Bar* (Figure 1-3.6).

Notice that the *i_Curtain_Walls.rvt* project is now listed along with a view (*3D View: {3D}*).

Try toggling between projects by clicking on *i_Urban_House.rvt – 3D View: {3D}*.

Close a Revit project:

10. Select **File → Close** from the *Menu Bar*.

This will close the current project/view. If more than one view is open for a project, only the current view will close. The project and the other opened views will not close (until you get to the last open view).

11. Repeat step 10 to close the other project file.

Figure 1-3.6 Window menu

If you have not saved your view yet, you will be prompted to do so before Revit closes the view. **Do not save at this time**.

Saving a Revit project:

At this time we will not actually save a project.

To save a Project view, simply select **File → Save** from the file menu. You can also click the save icon from the Standard toolbar.

You should get in the habit of saving often to avoid losing work due to a power outage or program crash.

Closing the Revit program:

Finally, from the *File* pull-down menu select *Exit*. This will close any open projects/views and shut Revit down. Again you will be prompted to save (if needed) before Revit closes the view. **Do not save at this time**.

You can also click the red **X** in the upper right corner of the Revit window. *(The icon is red in Window XP only.)*

Exercise 1-4:
Creating a new project

Open **Revit Architecture**.

Creating a new project file:

The steps required to set up a new Revit Architecture model project file are very simple. As mentioned earlier, simply opening the Revit program starts you in the *Recent Files* window.

To manually create a new project (maybe you just finished working on a previous assignment and want to start the next one):

1. Select **File → New → Project...** from the *File Menu Bar* *or* select the *New* icon from the *Standard* toolbar *or* click the *New...* link from the *Recent Files* window (under Projects).

NOTE: *If you select the* New *icon, a new project is quickly setup using the default template. (This is not recommended as this template lacking.)*

If you select *File → New → Project...* from the *Menu Bar* *or* the *New...* link from the *Recent Files* window, you will get the **New Project** dialog box (Figure 1-4.1).

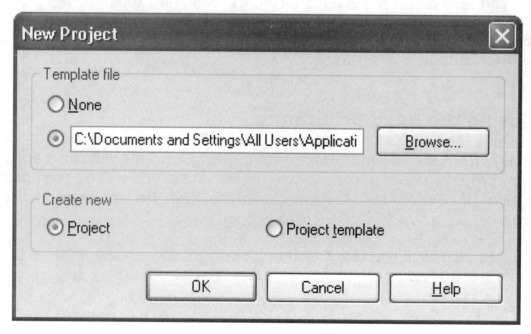

Figure 1-4.1 New Project dialog box

The *New Project* dialog box lets you specify the template file you want to use, or not use a template at all. You can also specify whether you want to create a new project or template file.

2. Leave the **default.Rte** *Template file* selected (you need to click in the text box and "arrow key" to the right to see the template file name), and leave *Create new* set to **Project** (Figure 1-4.1).

3. You now have a new "unnamed" project file.

To name an unnamed project file you simply save. The first time an unnamed project file is saved you will be prompted to specify the name and location for the project file.

4. Select **File → Save** from the *Menu Bar*.

5. Specify a **name** and **location** for your new project file.
   Your instructor may specify a location or folder for your files in this class.

What is a template file?

A template file allows you to start your project with certain settings preset the way you like or need them.

For example, you can have the units set to Imperial or Metric. You can have the door, window and wall families you use most loaded and eliminate others less often used. Also, you can have your company's title block preloaded and even have all the sheets for a project set up.

A custom template is a must for design firms using Revit and will prove useful to the student as he or she becomes more proficient with the program.

Be Aware:
It will be assumed from this point forward that the reader understands how to create, open and save project files. Please refer back to this section as needed. If you still need further assistance ask your instructor for help.

Exercise 1-5:
Using Zoom and Pan to view your drawings

Learning to Pan and Zoom in and out of a drawing is essential to accurate and efficient drafting and visualization. We will review these commands now so you are ready to use them with the first design exercise.

Open **Revit Architecture**.

You will select a sample file from the DVD that came with this textbook.

1.   Select **File → Open** from the *Menu Bar*.

2.   Browse to the **Training Files** area.
     REMINDER: *Click the "Training Files" shortcut icon on the left.*

3.   In the **Imperial** folder select the file named **i_Drawing_exercise.rvt** and click **Open** (Figure 1-5.1).

     a.   ***TIP:*** *If you cannot locate this file substitute "Office Building.rvt" located at the root level of the DVD that came with this textbook.*

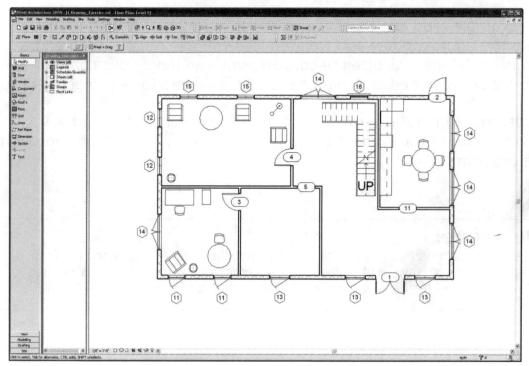

Figure 1-5.1 i_Drawing_exercise.rvt project

If the default view that is loaded is not **Floor Plan: Level 1**, double-click on **Level 1** under **Views\Floor Plans** in the *Project Browser*. Level 1 will be bold.

Using Zoom and Pan tools:

You can access the zoom tools from the **View** toolbar, or the *View* pull-down menu and the *scroll wheel* on your mouse.

View toolbar commands (from left to right):
- Dynamically modify view
- Zoom In *(includes drop-down arrow for additional zoom tools)*
- Thin Lines *(to be covered in a later lesson)*
- Show Mass
- Default 3D view

Zoom In

4. Select the zoom icon by clicking directly on the magnifying glass (not the down arrow).

5. Drag a window over your plan view (Figure 1-5.2).

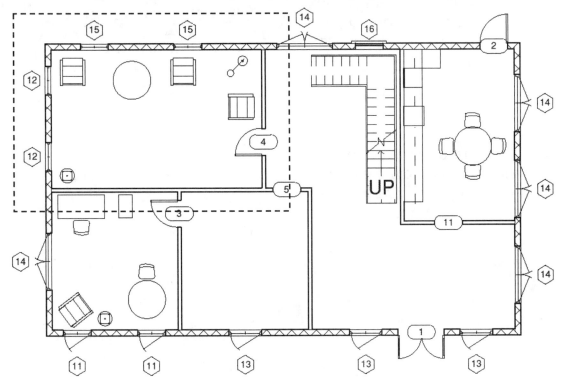

Figure 1-5.2 Zoom In window

You should now be zoomed in to the specified area (Figure 1-5.3).

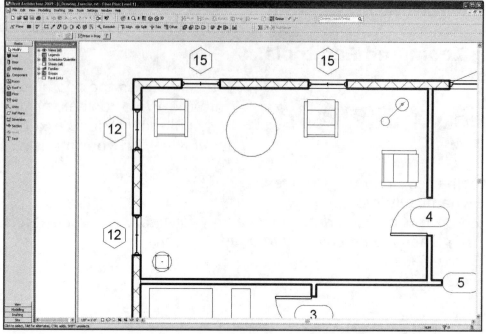

Figure 1-5.3 Zoom In results

Zoom Out

6. Click the down-arrow next to the Zoom icon (Figure 1-5.4). Select **Previous Pan/Zoom**.

You should now be back where you started.

Take a minute and try the other zoom tools to see how they work. When finished, click **Zoom All to Fit** before moving on.

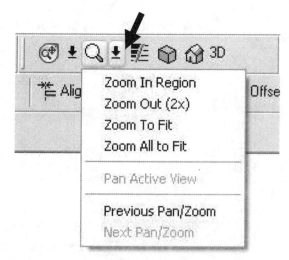

Figure 1-5.4 Zoom Icon drop-down

Default 3D View

Clicking on the *Default 3D View* icon loads a 3D View in another drawing window. This allows you to quickly switch to a 3D view.

7. Click on the *Default* **3D View** icon.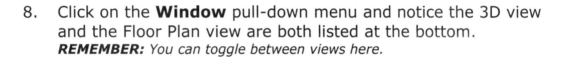

8. Click on the **Window** pull-down menu and notice the 3D view and the Floor Plan view are both listed at the bottom.
   REMEMBER: *You can toggle between views here.*

9. Click the **Esc** key to close the *Window* menu.

ViewCube

The ViewCube gives you convenient view control over the 3D view. This technology has been implemented in many of Autodesk's programs to make the process seamless for the user.

10. You should notice the **ViewCube** in the upper right corner of the *Drawing Window* (Figure 1-5.5). If not you can turn it on by clicking on the *ViewCube* option in the *Window* pull-down menu.

    TIP: *The ViewCube only shows up in 3D views.*

Hovering your cursor over the ViewCube activates it. As you move about the cube you see various areas highlight; if you click you will be taken to that highlighted area in the *Drawing Window*. You can also click and drag your cursor on the cube to "roll" the model in an unconstrained fashion. Clicking and dragging the mouse on the "frisbee" below the cube allows you to spin the model without rolling. Finally, you have a few options in a right-click menu and the Home icon, just above the cube, gets you back to where you started if things get too messed up!

Figure 1-5.5 ViewCube

11. Give the ViewCube a try; click the Home icon when you are done.

SteeringWheel

Similar to the ViewCube, the SteeringWheel aids in navigating your model. With the SheetingWheel you can walk through your model, going down hallways and turning into rooms. Revit is not advanced to the point where the doors will open for you; thus, you walk through closed doors or walls as if you where a ghost!

It is way too early in your Revit endeavors to learn about the SteeringWheel just yet. Once you get to the end of this book you can take a look at the bonus videos on the DVD that came with this book if you want to see this feature in action.

Figure 1-5.6 SteeringWheel

12. **Close** the *i_drawing_exercise* project without saving.

Using the Scroll wheel on the mouse

The scroll wheel on the mouse is one of the best improvements to the computer in recent years. In Revit you can Pan and Zoom without even clicking a zoom icon. You simply **scroll the wheel to zoom** and **hold the wheel button down to pan**. This can be done while in another command (e.g., while drawing walls). Another nice feature is that the drawing zooms into the area near your cursor, rather than zooming only at the center of the *Drawing Window*.

Exercise 1-6:
Using Revit's Help System

This last section of your introductory chapter will give you a quick understanding of Revit Architecture's Help system. This will allow you to study topics in more detail if you want to know how something works beyond the introductory scope of this textbook.

   1. From the *Help* menu select **Revit Architecture 2009 Help**.

You are now in Revit's Help window (Figure 1-6.1). This is a separate program running on the task bar of Windows which allows you to have the Help window open next to (and at the same time as) the Revit program window, which is especially nice if you have a dual-screen computer system. When Revit is closed the Help system will close automatically.

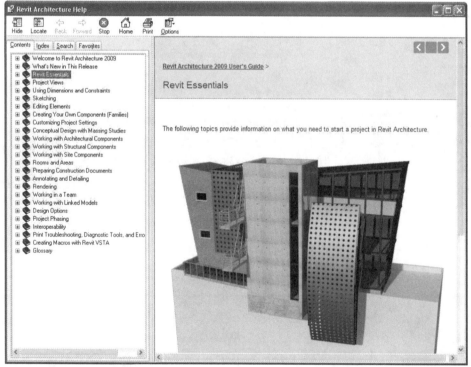

Figure 1-6.1 Help window

Notice the four tabs in the upper left: Contents, Index, Search and Favorites. The first three allow you find information in the *Help* system, each using a different method. As you can see in the image above, the Contents tab groups information by topic/task (think of it as the "yellow pages" of the phone book). The Index tab lists everything in the help system alphabetically, allowing you to look something up like you would in the "white pages" of the phone book. The next tab allows you to type and search.

The best way to understand the difference between these three methods of navigating the *Help* system is to use each to find the same content.

2. On the **Contents** tab, click the "+" symbol next to *Revit Essentials*.

Notice the *Revit Essentials* section expands and the "+" turns into a "-".

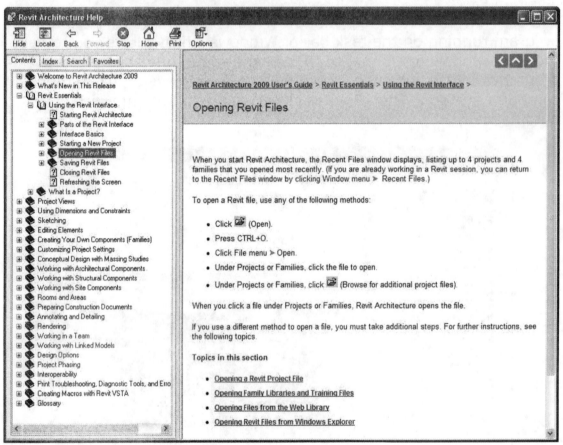

Figure 1-6.2 Help window – Contents tab

3. Click the "+" next to *Using the Revit Interface* and then select **Opening Revit Files**.

You should now see the information shown in Figure 1-6.2.

Now you will find the same information via the Index tab.

4. Click on the **Index** tab (Figure 1-6.3).

5. Start typing "file" and then select "opening" below the work files.

You should now see the same information shown in Figure 1-6.2. Finally, you will use the Search tab to find the same information.

Figure 1-6.3 Help window – Index tab

6. Click the **Search** tab.

7. Type "**open**" and then press *Enter*.

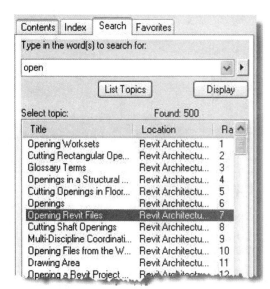

8. Click **Opening Revit Files** in the resultant list (Figure 1-6.4).

Again, you should now see the same information on opening Revit files as originally found via the *Contents* tab.

Figure 1-6.4 Help window – Search tab

The *Favorites* tab allows you to "add" specific help topics to a convenient "quick" access list, which is great if you think you might want to refer back to an item more than once (Figure 1-6.5).

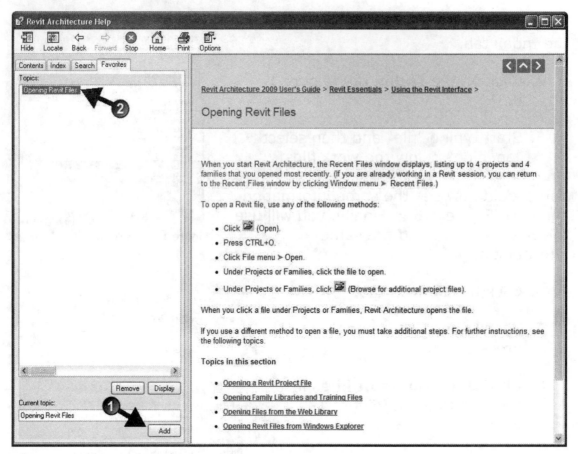

Figure 1-6.5 Help window – Favorites tab

Self-Exam:

The following questions can be used as a way to check your knowledge of this lesson. The answers can be found at the bottom of this page.

1. The *View* toolbar allows you to save your project file. (T/F) _False_

2. You can zoom in and out using the wheel on a wheel mouse. (T/F) _True_

3. Revit is a parametric architectural design program. (T/F) _True_

4. A _____ file allows you to start your project with certain setting preset the way you like or need them. _Template_

5. In the Revit user interface, projects are viewed in the _____ window. _Drawing_

Review Questions:

The following questions may be assigned by your instructor as a way to assess your knowledge of this section. Your instructor has the answers to the review questions.

1. The *Options* toolbar dynamically changes to show options that compliment the current operation. (T/F) _True_

2. Revit is strictly a 2D drafting program. (T/F) _False_

3. The Projects/Views listed at the bottom of the *Window* pull-down menu allow you to see which Projects/Views are currently open. (T/F) _True_

4. When you use the scroll tool you are actually moving the drawing, not just changing what part of the drawing you can see on the screen. (T/F) _False_

5. Revit was not originally created for architecture. (T/F) _False_

6. The icon with the floppy disk picture (🖫) allows you to _Save_ _____ a project file.

7. Clicking on the _____ next to the 'Zoom In' icon will list additional zoom tools not currently shown in the *View* toolbar. _down arrow_

8. You do not see the ViewCube unless you are in a _____ view. _3D_

Notes:

Lesson 2
Quick Start: Small Office::

In this lesson you will get a down and dirty overview of the functionality of Revit Architecture. The very basics of creating the primary components of a floor plan: Walls, Doors, Windows, Roof, Annotation and Dimensioning will be covered. This lesson will show you the amazing "out-of-the-box" powerful, yet easy to use, features in Revit. It should get you very excited about learning this software program. Future lessons will cover these features in more detail while learning other editing tools and such along the way.

Exercise 2-1:
Walls, Grids and Dimensions

In this exercise you will draw the walls, starting with the exterior. Read the directions carefully, everything you need to do is clearly listed.

Exterior Walls:

1. Start a new project named **Small Office** per the following instructions:

    a. **File → New → Project...**

    b. Click **Browse...** (Figure 2-1.1)

    c. Select the template file named **Commercial-Default.rte**. *(You should be brought to the correct folder automatically.)*

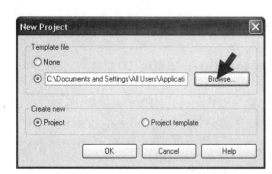

Figure 2-1.1 New Project

    d. Click **Open**.

    e. With the template file just selected and *Create new* "Project" selected, click **OK** (Figure 2-1.1). *See Lesson 1 for more information on creating a new project.*

2. Click on the **Wall** tool under the *Basics* tab in the **Design Bar**. (Figure 2-1.2)

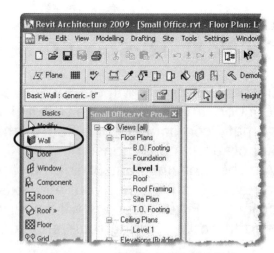

Notice that the *Options Bar* has changed to show settings related to walls. Next you will modify those settings.

FYI: *By default, the bottoms of new walls will be at the current floor level and the tops of the walls are set via the Options Bar as shown in the next step.*

Figure 2-1.2 Wall tool

Figure 2-1.3 Options Bar

3. Modify the **Options Bar** to the following (Figure 2-1.3):
   a. *Type Selector:* Click the down-arrow and select **Basic Wall: Generic – 12"**.
   b. *Height:* Change the height from 20'-0" to **9'-0"**.
   c. *Loc Line:* Set this to **Finish Face : Exterior**.
   d. Click the Rectangle icon. *(This allows you to draw four walls at once [i.e., a rectangle], rather than one wall at a time.)*

You are now ready to draw the exterior walls.

4. In the *Drawing Window*, click in the upper left corner.
   TIP: *Remember to draw within the four elevation markers (image to right).*

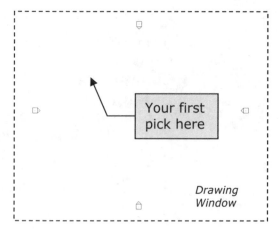

5. Start moving the mouse down and to the right. **Click** when the two temporary on-screen dimensions are approximately **100'** (wide) and **60'** (deep).

Getting the dimensions exact is not important as they will be revised later on.

Your drawing should look similar to Figure 2-1.4 (similar in that the dimensions do not have to be exact right now and the building's location relative to the four elevation tags may vary slightly).

The *Temporary Dimensions* are displayed until the next action is invoked by the user. While the dimensions are displayed, you can click on the dimension text and adjust the wall dimensions. Also, by default the *Temporary Dimensions* reference the center of the wall – you can change this by simply clicking on the grips located on each *Witness Line* (each click toggles the witness line location between center, exterior face and interior face).

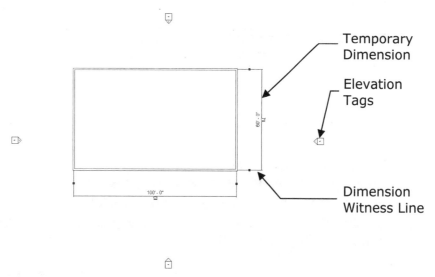

Figure 2-1.4 Exterior walls

In the next few steps you will create grid lines and establish a relationship between the walls and the grids such that moving a grid causes the wall to move with it.

Grids:

Grids are used to position structural columns and beams in a building. Adding a grid involves selecting the *Grid* tool and then picking two points in the drawing window.

6. On the *Basics* tab, select the **Grid** tool. Grid

Next you will draw a vertical grid off to the left of your building. Once you have drawn all the grids you will use a special tool to align the grid with the walls and lock that relationship.

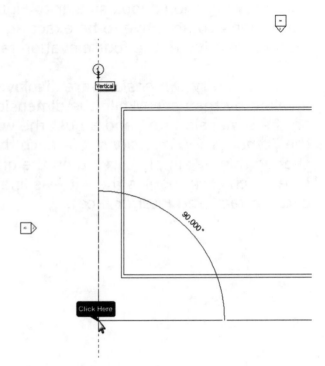

Figure 2-1.5 Drawing a grid

7. [*first pick*] **Click** down and to the left of your building as shown in Figure 2.1-5.

    FYI: 'Click' always means left-click, unless a right-click is specifically called for.

8. [*second pick*] Move the cursor straight up (i.e., vertically) making sure you see a dashed green line (which indicates you are snapped to the vertical plane) and the angle dimension reads 90 degrees. Just past the top edge of the building (as shown in Figure 2.1-5), click.

You have now drawn your first grid line. Next you will quickly draw four more grid lines (two horizontal and two vertical).

NOTE: The Grid tool will remain active until you select another tool or select Modify (which allows you to select previously drawn items).

9. Draw another vertical grid approximately centered on your building. BEFORE YOU PICK THE FIRST POINT, make sure you see a dashed green reference line indicating the grid line will align with the previous grid line (you will see this before clicking the mouse at each end of the grid line), then go ahead and pick both points (Figure 2-1.6).

10. Draw the remaining grid lines shown in Figure 2-1.6. Again, do not worry about the exact location of the grid lines.

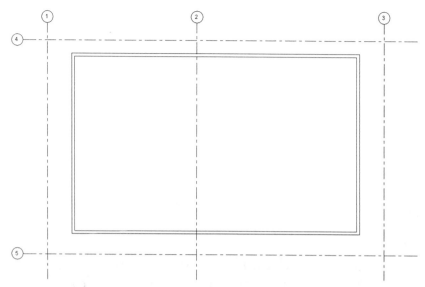

Figure 2-1.6 Grids added

Next you will change the two horizontal grid lines to have letters instead of numbers.

11. Zoom in on the grid bubble for the upper horizontal grid line.

12. [click *Modify* and then] Click on the grid line to select it.

13. With the grid line selected, click on the blue text within the bubble.

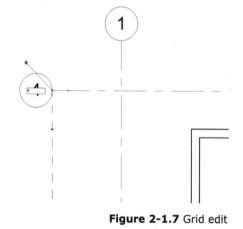

14. Type **A** and press *Enter* on the keyboard. (Figure 2-1.7)

15. Click the **Modify** tool on the *Design Bar*.

Figure 2-1.7 Grid edit

16. Change the other horizontal grid to **B**.

Align:

Next you will use the *Align* tool to reposition the grid lines so they "align" with the exterior face of the adjacent walls. The steps are simple: select the *Align* tool from the toolbar; pick the reference line (i.e., the exterior wall face); and then you select the item to move (i.e., the grid line). This tool works on many Revit objects!

17. Click the **Align** icon from the *Tools* toolbar.   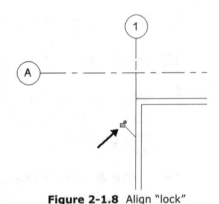 Align

> **TIP:** *Go to* Window *(pull down menu)* → Toolbar *and select a listed toolbar to toggle it on and off if needed.*

18. [*Align: first pick*] With the *Align* tool active (notice the prompt on the *Status Bar*), select **Wall faces** on the *Options Bar* (next to Prefer) and then select the exterior face of the wall adjacent to grid line 1.

19. [*Align: second pick*] Select **grid line 1**. Be sure to see the next step before doing anything else!

The grid line should now be aligned with the exterior face of the wall. Immediately after using the *Align* tool you have the option of "locking" that relationship; you will do that next. The ability to lock this relationship is only available until the next tool is activated. After that you would need to use the *Align* tool again.

20. Click the un-locked **padlock** symbol to "lock" the relationship between the grid line and the wall (see Figure 2-1.8).

21. Use the steps just outlined to **Align** and **Lock** the remaining grid lines with their adjacent walls. Do not worry about the location of grid line 2 (i.e., the vertical grid in the center).

Figure 2-1.8 Align "lock"

Dimensions:

Next you will add dimensions to the grid lines and use them to drive the location of the walls/grids and lock their relationships.

22. Select **Modify** and then **right-click** anywhere within the Drawing Window; click **Zoom To Fit**.

23. On the *Design Bar*, under the *Basics* tab, select the **Dimension** tool.

At this point you are in the *Dimension* tool. Notice the various controls available on the *Options Bar*. You can set things like the dimension style (via the *Type Selector*) and the kind of dimension (linear, angle, radius, etc.) and which portion of the wall to *Prefer* (e.g., face, center, core face).

| Linear Dimension Style : Linear - 3/3: ⌄ | | | | | | | Prefer: Wall centerlines ⌄ | Pick: Individual References ⌄ | Options |

24. With the *Options Bar* set as shown above (which should have been the default settings), **select grid line 1**.

   > **FYI:** *The grid line will pre-highlight before you select it, which helps you know you are about to select the correct item (e.g., the grid line versus the wall).*

25. Now **select grid line 2** and then **select grid line 3**.

Your last pick point is to decide where the dimension line should be.

26. Click in the location shown in Figure 2-1.9 to position the dimension line.

   > **TIP:** *Do not click near any other objects or Revit will continue the dimension string to that item.*

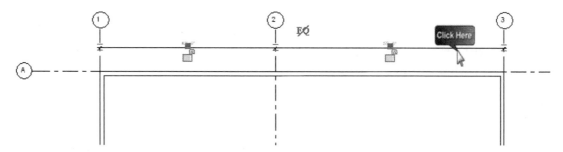

Figure 2-1.9 Adding dimensions

Notice that while the dimension string is selected, you see an EQ symbol with a slash through it. This symbol indicates that the individual components of the dimension string are not equal in length. The next step will show you how easy it is to make these dimensions equal!

27. With the dimension string selected, click the ⌷⌀ symbol located near the middle of the dimension.

The grid lines are now equally spaced (Figure 2-1.10) and this relationship will be maintained until the EQ symbol is selected again to toggle the "dimension equality" feature off. **NOTE:** *The grid line will not move back to its original location; Revit does not remember where the grid was.* Typically, you would not want to click the padlock icons here because that would lock the current dimension and make it so the grid lines could not be moved at all.

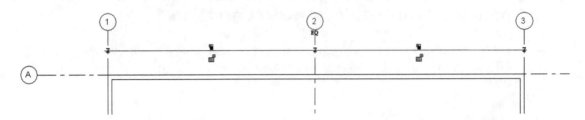

Figure 2-1.10 Toggling dimension equality

Next you will add an "overall building" dimension from grid line 1 to grid line 3. This dimension can be used to drive the overall size of your building (all the time keeping grid line 2 equally spaced).

28. Using the *Dimension* tool, add a dimension from grid line 1 to grid line 3 and then pick to position the dimension line. (Figure 2-1.11)

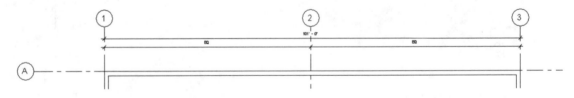

Figure 2-1.11 Overall building dimension added

When using a dimension to drive the location of geometry, you need to select the item you want to move and then select the dimension text to enter the new value. You cannot just select the dimension because Revit does not know whether you want the left, right or both grid lines to move. The only thing you can do, graphically, by selecting the dimension directly is "lock" that dimension by clicking on the padlock symbol and then click the blue dimension text to add a suffix, for example. Next you will adjust the overall building size.

29. Click **Modify** on the *Design Bar* (or press the *Esc* key twice) to make sure you cancel the *Dimension* tool and that nothing is selected.

30. **Select grid line 3**.

31. With grid line 3 selected, click the dimension text and type **101** and then press *Enter*.

    FYI: Notice that Revit assumes feet if you do not provide a foot or inch symbol.

32. Repeating the previous steps, add a dimension between grid lines A and B, and then adjust the model so the dimension reads **68'-0"**.

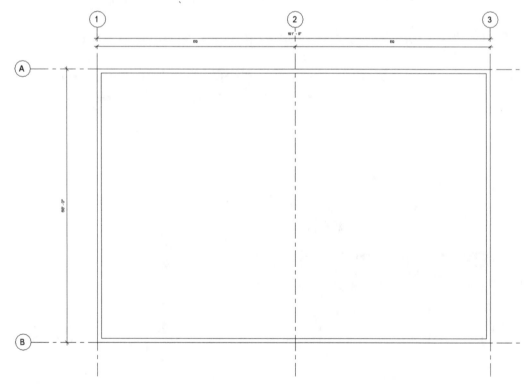

Figure 2-1.12 Building size established

Your project should now look similar to Figure 2-1.12. You should notice that dimensions must "touch" two or more items (the grid lines in this case). Also, because the walls where aligned and locked to the grids, moving the grids causes the walls to move.

The last thing you will do before moving on to the interior walls is to swap out the generic walls with a more specific wall. This would be a common situation in a design firm; a generic wall is added as a "place holder" until the design is refined to the point where the exterior wall system is selected.

The process for swapping a wall is very simple: select the wall and pick a different type from the *Type Selector*. The next steps will do this, but will also show you how to quickly select all the exterior walls so you can change them all at once!

33. Click **Modify** and then hover your cursor over one of the exterior walls so it pre-highlights. (Do not click yet.)

34. *With an exterior wall pre-highlighted,* take your hand off the mouse and press the **Tab** key until all four walls pre-highlight.

    FYI: *The Tab key cycles through the various items below your cursor. The options should include: one wall, a chain of walls, and a grid line.*

35. *With all four walls pre-highlighted,* click to select them.

36. *With all four walls selected:* pick **Basic Wall: Exterior – Brick on CMU** from the *Type Selector* on the *Options Bar*.

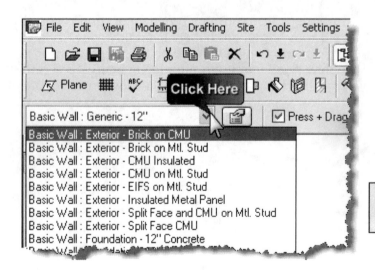

Type Selector with the *Wall* tool active

Detail Level:

Revit allows you to control how much detail is shown in the walls.

37. On the *View Control Bar* (lower left corner of the drawing window), set the *Detail Level* to **Fine**.

As you can see in the two images below, *Course* simply shows the outline of a wall system and *Fine* shows the individual components of the wall (i.e., brick, insulation, concrete block, etc.).

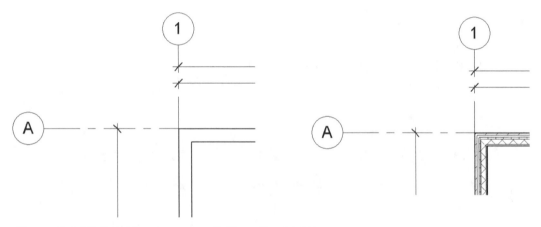

Figure 2-1.13 Detail level – course (left) vs. fine (right)

Now that you have the exterior walls established, the grid lines properly placed, and their relationships embedded in the project, you can now proceed with the layout of the interior spaces.

Interior Walls:

38. With the **Wall** tool selected, modify the **Options Bar** to the following:

   a. *Type Selector:* Click the down-arrow and select **Basic Wall: Interior – 4 7/8" Partition**.
   b. *Height:* **Roof**
   c. *Loc Line:* Set this to **Wall Centerline**.

39. Draw a wall from the west wall (i.e., vertical wall on the left) to the east wall (on the right). See Figure 2-1.14.
   a. Make sure your cursor "snaps" to the wall before clicking.
   b. Before clicking the second point of the wall, make sure the dashed green line is visible so you know the wall will be truly horizontal (relative to the computer screen).
   c. The exact position of the wall is not important at this point as you will adjust it in the next step.
   d. With the temporary dimensions still active, proceed to the next step.

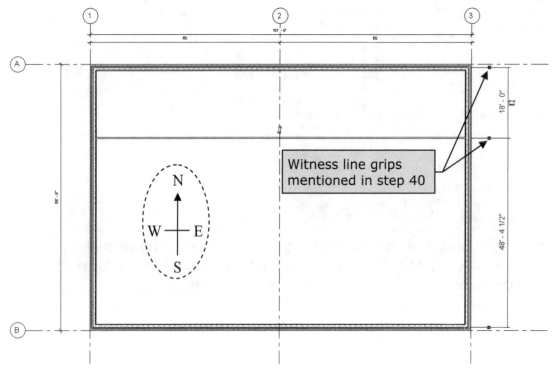

Figure 2-1.14 Adding interior walls – North indicator added for reference only

40. Click the **witness line grips** (see Figure 2-1.14) until the "clear" space of the room is listed (see Figure 2-1.15).

41. Now click the blue text of the temporary dimension, type **22**, and then press *Enter* (Figure 2-1.15).

42. Click **Modify** to finish the current task.

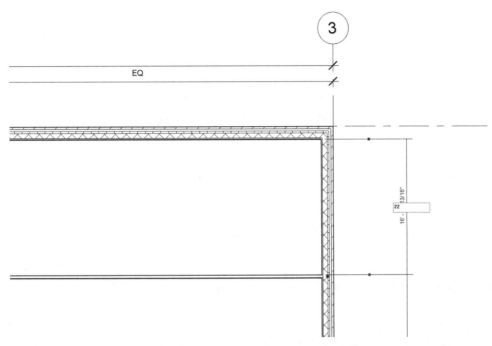

Figure 2-1.15 Repositioning interior wall via temporary dimensions

The clear space between the interior wall and the north wall is now 22'-0". Next you will add additional interior walls to create equally spaced rooms in this area.

43. Using the same settings as the interior wall just added, draw five (5) vertical walls as shown in Figure 2-1.16.
    a. Make sure they are orthogonal (i.e., the dashed green line is visible before picking the walls endpoint).
    b. Make sure you "snap" to the perpendicular walls (at the start and endpoint of the walls you are adding).
    c. Do not worry about the exact position of the walls.
    d. *TIP: Uncheck* Chain *on the* Options Bar.

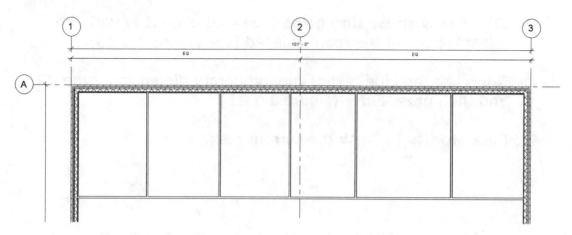

Figure 2-1.16 Adding additional interior walls

In the next step you will use a dimension string to reposition the walls so they are equally spaced. This process is similar to what you did to reposition grid line 2. However, you have to specify which part of the wall you want to dimension to (center, face, core center, core face).

FYI: The "core" portion of a wall system typically consists of the structural element(s) such as the concrete block (in your exterior walls) or the metal studs (in your interior walls).

44. Click the **Dimension** tool on the *Design Bar* (on the *Basics* tab).

45. On the *Options Bar*, select **Wall Faces** next to *Prefer*.

This setting will force Revit to only look for the face of a wall system. You can select either face depending on which side of the wall you favor with your cursor. This feature lets you confidently pick specific references without needing to continually zoom in and out all over the floor plan.

46. Select the interior face of the west (i.e., left) wall to start your dimension string.

The next several picks will need to reference the wall centerlines. Revit allows you to toggle the *Prefer* option on the fly via the *Options Bar*.

47. Change the *Prefer* setting to **Wall Centerlines**.

48. The next five picks will be on the five vertical interior walls. (Make sure you see the dashed green reference line centered on the wall to let you know you are about to select the correct reference plane.)

49. Change the *Prefer* setting back to **Wall Faces** and select the interior face of the east wall.

50. Your last pick should be away from any elements to position the dimension string somewhere within the rooms (Figure 2-1.17).

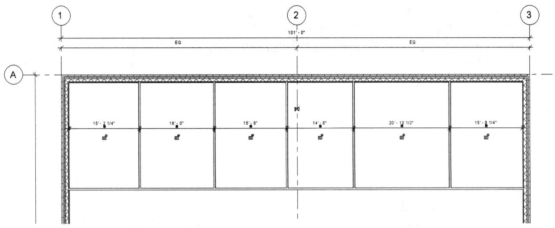

Figure 2-1.17 Adding a dimension string

51. Click the ⌘ symbol to reposition the interior walls.

52. Click **Modify**.

The interior walls are now equally spaced (Figure 2-1.18)!

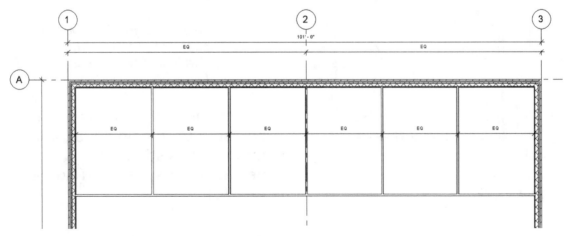

Figure 2-1.18 Enabling dimension equality

53. Add a vertical "clear" dimension to indicate the depth of the rooms. (Set *Prefer* to **Wall Faces** for both ends of the dimension line.) See Figure 2-1.19.

54. Click the **padlock** symbol (🔓) to tell Revit this dimension should not change. (Figure 2-1.19)

55. Click **Modify**.

Next you will adjust the overall building dimensions and notice how the various parametric relationships you established cause the model to update!

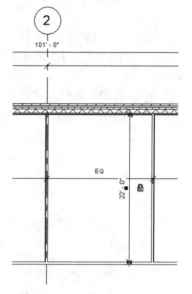

Figure 2-1.19
Locking dimensions

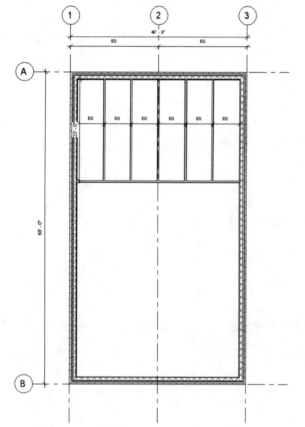

Figure 2-1.20 Adjusting dimensions

56. Click grid line 3 and change the overall dimension (by clicking on the dimension text) from 101 to **40** and then press *Enter*.

    TIP: *When adjusting the building footprint via the dimensions, you need to select the grid line, not the east wall, because the dimension references the grid line.*

Notice the interior walls have adjusted to remain equal, and grid line 2 is still centered between grids 1 and 3 (Figure 2-1.20).

57. Change the 40'-0" dimension to **110'-0"**.

58. Select grid line A and change the 68'-0" dimension to **38'-0"**.

Your model should now look similar to Figure 2-1.21. Notice the interior wall maintained its 22'-0" clear dimension (because the interior wall has a dimension which is locked to the exterior wall, and the exterior wall has an alignment which is locked to grid line A).

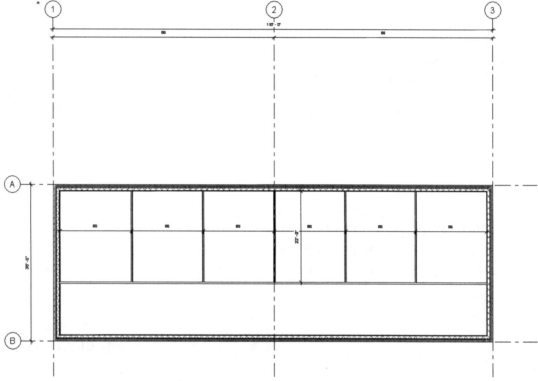

Figure 2-1.21 Adjusting dimensions

59. Click the **Undo** icon on the toolbar to restore the 68' dimension.

Your building should now be 110'-0" x 68'-0".

60. **Save** your project (*Small Office.rvt*).

TIP: You can use the **Tape Measure** tool to list the distance between two points. This is helpful when you want to quickly verify the clear dimension between walls. Simply click the icon and snap to two points and Revit will temporarily display the distance. You can also click "chain" on the *Options Bar* and have Revit add up the total length of several picks.

Exercise 2-2:
Doors

In this exercise you will add doors to your small office building.

1. Open **Small Office.rvt** created in Exercise 2-1.

Placing doors:

2. Click on the **Door** tool under the *Basics* tab in the *Design Bar* (Figure 2-2.1).

Notice that the *Options Bar* has changed to show options related to Doors. Next you will modify those settings.

The *Type Selector* indicates the door style, width and height. Clicking the down arrow to the right lists all the doors pre-loaded into the current project.

Figure 2-2.1 Door tool

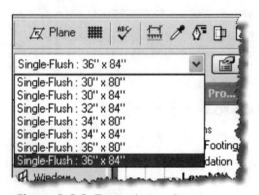

Figure 2-2.2 Type selector: Doors

The default template project that you started from has several sizes for a single flush door. Notice, in Figure 2-2.2, that there are two standard heights in the list. The 80" (6'-8") doors are the standard residential height and the 84" (7'-0") doors are the standard commercial door height.

3. Change the type selector to **Single-Flush: 36" x 84"**.

4. Move your cursor over a wall and position the door as shown in **Figure 2-2.3**. (Do <u>not</u> click yet.) *Notice that the swing of the door changes depending on what side of the wall your cursor is favoring.*

Notice Revit displays temporary dimensions to help you place the door in the correct location.

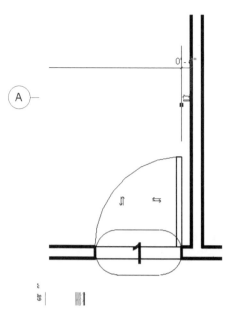

5. Click to place the door. Revit automatically trims the wall and adds a door tag.

   TIP: Press the spacebar before clicking to flip the door swing if needed.

6. While the door is still selected, click on the *change swing (control arrows)* symbol to make the door swing against the wall if it is not already (Figure 2-2.4).

Figure 2-2.3 Adding door

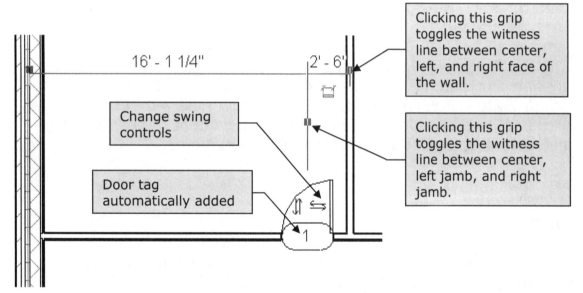

Clicking this grip toggles the witness line between center, left, and right face of the wall.

Change swing controls

Clicking this grip toggles the witness line between center, left jamb, and right jamb.

Door tag automatically added

Figure 2-2.4 Door just placed

Next you will reposition the door relative to the adjacent wall.

7. Click **Modify** to cancel the *Door* tool.

8. Click the door (not the door tag) you just placed to select it.

9. Click the **witness line grips** so the temporary dimension references the right door jamb and the wall face as shown in Figure 2-2.5.

TIP: You can also click and drag the witness line grip to another wall or line if the default location was not what you are concerned with.

10. Click on the dimension text, type **4"** and press *Enter*. Make sure you add the inch symbol or you will get feet rather than inches (Figure 2-2.5).

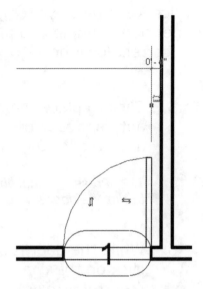

Figure 2-2.5 Edit door location

Unfortunately, the door *Families* loaded in the commercial template do not have frames. So the 4" dimension just entered provides for a 2" fame and 2" of wall. The library installed on your hard drive, along with the Revit "web library", do provide some doors with frames. It is possible to create just about any door/frame combination via the *Family Editor.* The *Family Editor* is a special mode within Revit Architecture that allows custom parametric content to be created, including doors with sidelights, transoms and more!

Mirroring doors:

The *Mirror* command will now be used to create another door opposite the adjacent perpendicular wall.

11. With the door selected, click the **Mirror** icon on the toolbar.

12. On the *Options Bar*, click **Copy**. If copy was not selected, then the door would be relocated rather than copied.

13. With the door selected and the *Mirror* command active: hover the cursor over the adjacent wall until the dashed cyan reference line appears centered on the wall (keep moving the mouse until you see this) and then click (Figure 2-2.6).

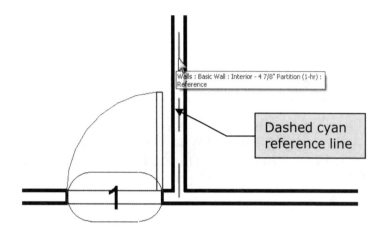

Figure 2-2.6 Mirroring a door

As you can see in Figure 2-2.7, the door has been Mirrored into the correct location.

Revit does not automatically add door tags to mirrored or copied doors. These will be added later.

TIP: The size of the door tag is controlled by the view's scale.

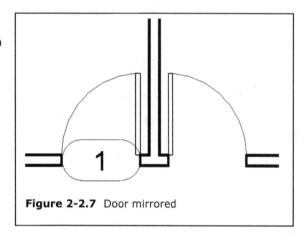

Figure 2-2.7 Door mirrored

Copying doors:

Now you will copy the two doors so the other rooms have doors.

14. Click to select the first door (not the door tag) and then press and hold the **Ctrl** key. *While holding the Ctrl key,* click to add the second door to the selection.

15. With the two doors selected, click the **Copy** icon.

16. On the *Options Bar*, select **Multiple**.

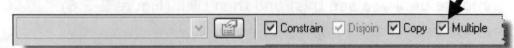

At this point you need to pick two points: a "copy from here" point to a "copy to there" point. The first point does not have to be directly on the object(s) to be copied. The next step will demonstrate this; you will pick the midpoint of the wall adjacent to the two doors (first pick) and then you will pick the midpoint of the wall you want a set of doors at (second pick). With "multiple" checked, you can continue picking "second points" until you are finished making copies (pressing *Esc* or *Modify* to end the command).

17. Pick three points:

    a. *First pick:* midpoint/centerline of wall (see Figure 2-2.8);

    b. *Second pick:* midpoint/ centerline of wall shown in Figure 2-2.9;

    c. *Third pick:* midpoint/centerline of wall shown in Figure 2-2.9.

18. Pick **Modify** to end *Copy*.

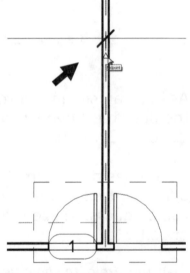

The doors are now copied.

Figure 2-2.8 Copy – first point with midpoint symbol visible

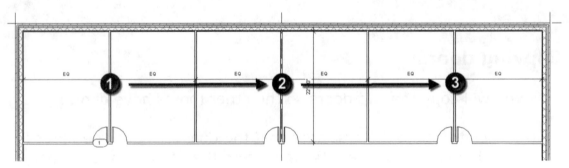

Figure 2-2.9 Numbers indicate pick-points listed in step #17

You will now add two exterior doors using the same door type.

19. Using the **Door** tool, add two exterior doors approximately located per Figure 2-2.10. Match the swing and hand shown.

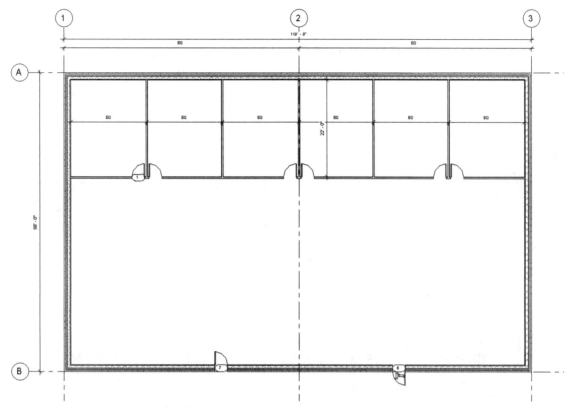

Figure 2-2.10 Adding exterior doors

Tag All Not Tagged:

Revit provides a command to quickly add a tag (e.g., a door tag) to any door that does not currently have one in the current view. The tag might have to be moved and/or rotated once placed, but this still saves time and the possibility of missing a door tag.

20. Under the *Drafting* tab (on the *Design Bar*) click **Tag all not tagged**.

21. In the *Tag All Not Tagged* dialog box, select **Door Tags** under *Category* and set *Orientation* to **Vertical**. Click **OK**.

All the doors should now be tagged in your floor plan.

FYI: Door tags can be deleted at any time and added again later at any time. Tags simply display information in the object being tagged – thus, no information about the object is being deleted (the building information integrity remains intact).

Deleting doors:

Next you will learn how to delete a door when needed. This process will work for most objects (i.e., walls, windows, text, etc.) in Revit.

22. Click **Modify**.

23. Click on door number 7 (the door on the left, not the door tag) and press the **Delete key** on your keyboard.

As you can see, the door is deleted and the wall is automatically filled back in. Also, a door tag can only exist by being attached to a door, therefore the door tag was also deleted.

One last thing to observe: Revit numbers the doors in the order in which they have been placed (regardless of level). Doors are not automatically renumbered when one is deleted. Also, doors can be renumbered to just about anything you want.

24. **Save** your project *(Small Office.rvt)*.

Exercise 2-3:
Windows

In this exercise you will add windows to your small office building.

1. Open **Small Office.rvt** created in Exercise 2-2.

Placing Windows:

2. Click on the **Window** tool under the *Basics* tab on the **Design Bar** (Figure 2-3.1).

Notice that the *Options Bar* has changed to show options related to Windows. Next you will modify those settings.

The *Type Selector* indicates the Window style, width and height. Clicking the down arrow to the right lists all the windows loaded in the current project.

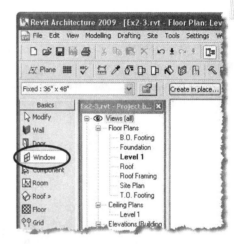

Figure 2-3.1 Window tool

3. Change the type selector to **Fixed: 36" x 48"** and **uncheck** *Tag on Placement*.

4. Move your cursor over a wall and place **two windows** as shown in **Figure 2-3.2**. *Notice that the position of the window changes depending on what side of the wall your cursor favors.*

FYI: *The window sill height is controlled by a Properties dialog that you will study later in this book. For now, the default dimension was used.*

5. Adjust the **temporary dimensions** per the following:
   a. Dimensions per Figure 2-3.2.
   b. Use the witness line grip to adjust the witness line position.
   c. **REMEMBER:** *The selected item moves when temporary dimensions are adjusted. Pick the left window to set the 6'-0" dimension and the right for the 8'-0" dimension.*

6. Using the **Copy** command, in a way similar to copying the doors in the previous exercise, copy the two windows into each office as shown in Figure 2-3.3. (Do not worry about exact dimensions.)

7. **Save** your project *(Small Office.rvt)*.

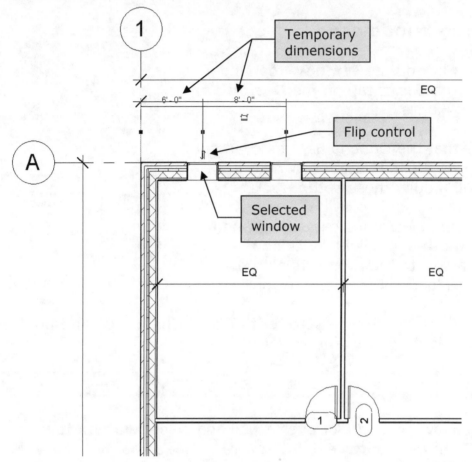

Figure 2-3.2 Adding windows – temporary dimensions still active

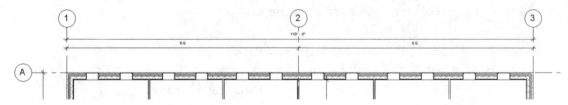

Figure 2-3.3 Windows added to north wall

The windows will not adjust with the grid lines and interior walls; it is possible to add dimensions and get this to work. If you tried to change the overall dimension from 110' to 40' again, Revit would let you know it needed to delete some windows before the change could be made. Like doors, windows need their host to exist.

The windows can all be adjusted via the temporary dimensions. The window selected is the largest width available in the project (based on the template file the project was started from), but it is not a masonry dimension. However, additional window sizes can be added on the fly at any time. Additionally, you can create your own template file that has the doors, windows, walls, etc. that you typically need for the kind of design work you do.

In addition to the preloaded windows, several window styles are available via the family library loaded on your hard drive and the *Autodesk Web Library* (e.g., dbl-hung, casement, etc.). It is also possible to create just about any window design in the *Family Editor*.

Object Snap Symbols:

By now you should be well aware of the snaps that Revit suggests as you move your cursor about the drawing window.

If you hold your cursor still for a moment while a snap symbol is displayed, a tooltip will appear on the screen. However, when you become familiar with the snap symbols you can pick sooner (Figure 2-3.4).

The TAB key cycles through the available snaps near your cursor.

The keyboard shortcut turns off the other snaps for one pick. For example, if you type SE on the keyboard while in the Wall command, Revit will only look for an endpoint for the next pick.

Finally, typing SO (snaps off) turns all snaps off for one pick.

Symbol	Position	Keyboard Shortcut
✕	Intersection	SI
☐	Endpoint	SE
△	Midpoint	SM
○	Center	SC
✕	Nearest	SN
⌐	Perpendicular	SP
Ω	Tangent	ST

Figure 2-3.4 Snap Reference Chart

Exercise 2-4:
Roof

You will now add a simple roof to your building.

1. Open **Small Office.rvt** created in Exercise 2-3.

The first thing you will do is take a quick look at a 3D view of your building and notice an adjustment that needs to be made to the exterior walls.

2. Click the **3D icon** on the toolbar.

The 3D icon switches you to the default 3D view in the current project. Your view should look similar to Figure 2-4.1. Notice the exterior walls are not high enough, which is due to a previous decision to set the wall height to 9'-0". Next you will change this which can be done in plan view or the current 3D view.

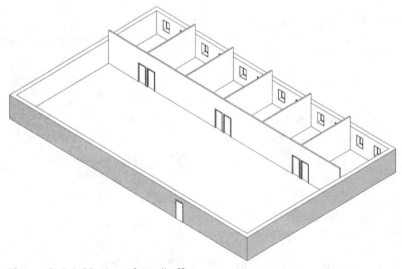

Figure 2-4.1 3D view of small office

3. In the 3D view, hover your cursor over one of the exterior walls to pre-highlight it, then (before clicking) press the **Tab** key to pre-highlight a "chain of walls" (i.e., all the exterior walls), and then click to select them.

Next you will access the properties of the selected walls so you can adjust the wall height. In Revit, most any design decisions that are made can be adjusted at any time.

4. Click the **Properties** button on the *Options Bar*.

5. In the *Element Properties* dialog box, change the following:
    a) Top Constraint: **Up to level: Roof**
    b) Top Offset: **2'-0"**
    c) Click **OK** (Figure 2-4.2B).

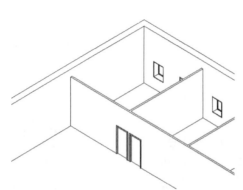

Figure 2-4.2A Exterior wall heights adjusted

Setting the top of wall to be associated with a *Level* establishes a parametric relationship that causes the wall height to automatically adjust if the Level Datum is adjusted (e.g., from 12'-0" to 14'-0").

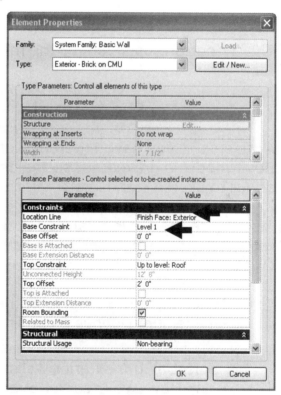

Figure 2-4.2B Selected wall properties

Plus, the *Top Offset* at 2'-0" creates a 2'-0" parapet, which will always be 2'-0" high no matter what the roof elevation is set to. There are instances when you would want the height to be fixed.

All of the settings on the *Option Bar*, while you originally drew the wall, plus many other settings related to the wall show up here.

Sketching a roof:

Now that the exterior walls are the correct height, you will now add the roof. This building will have a flat roof located at the roof level.

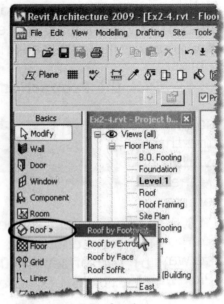

6. Double-click **Level 1** in the *Project Browser* to switch back that view.

7. Click on the **Roof** tool under the *Basics* tab in the *Design Bar*; a fly-out menu will appear (Figure 2-4.3).

Figure 2-4.3 Roof tool

The fly-out prompts you for the method you want to use to create the roof.

8. Click **Roof by footprint**.

At this point you have entered *Sketch Mode* where the Revit model is grayed out so the perimeter you are about to sketch stands out.

Also notice the *Design Bar* has temporarily been replaced with Sketch options relative to the roof (Figure 2-4.4), as with the *Options Bar* (Figure 2-4.5).

9. Click **Extend to Core** on the *Options Bar*; also, make sure *Defines Slope* is not checked.

Figure 2-4.4
Roof sketch tools

10. Select all the exterior walls:
    a) Hover your cursor over one of the exterior walls to **pre-highlight the wall**.
    b) Press **Tab** to select a "Chain of Walls" (i.e., all the exterior walls).
    c) **Click** to select the exterior walls.

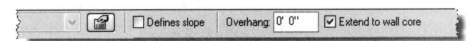

Figure 2-4.5 Roof sketch options

At this point you should have four magenta lines, one on each wall, which represent the perimeter of the roof you are creating. When sketching a roof footprint, you need to make sure that lines do not overlap and corners are cleaned up with the *Trim* command if required. Your sketch lines require no additional edits because of the way you added them. (Pick walls and Tab select.)

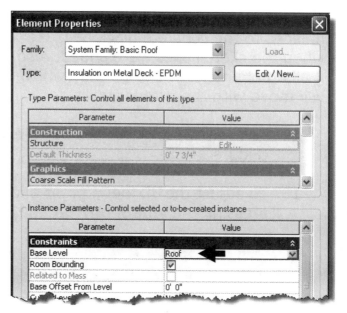

Figure 2-4.6 Roof element properties

Before you finish the roof sketch you need to adjust the level the roof will be created on. By default, the top surface of the roof object will be parametrically aligned with the current level (i.e., Level 1 in this case). You will change this to the roof level.

11. Click **Roof Properties** on the *Design Bar* (Figure 2-4.4).

Notice at the top of the *Element Properties* dialog box, Figure 2-4.6, that the roof type to be created is set to *Insulation on Metal Deck – EPDM*. You can change this now, or later, by selecting the roof and picking from the *Type Selector* on the *Options Bar*.

12. Set *Base Level* to **Roof** and then Click **OK** to close the properties dialog box (Figure 2-4.6).

Now you are ready to finish the roof and exit sketch mode.

13. Click **Finish Roof** on the *Design Bar* (Figure 2-4.4).

14. Click **Yes** to the following prompt (Figure 2-4.7).

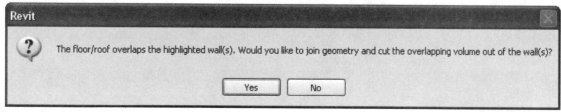

Figure 2-4.7 Join geometry prompt

The roof is now created and, in section, will extend through the finishes to the concrete block because "extend to core" was selected when the sketch lines were added. Also, because you used the "Pick Walls" option on the *Design Bar* (which was the default), the roof edge will move with the exterior walls.

15. To see the roof, click the **3D View** icon (Figure 2-4.8).

16. To adjust the 3D view: press and hold the **Shift** key while pressing the **wheel button** and dragging the mouse around.

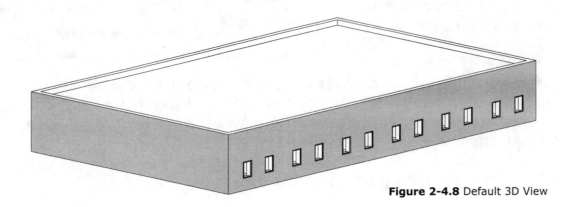

Figure 2-4.8 Default 3D View

17. Click the **X** in the upper right corner of the *Drawing Window* to close the current view (3D). This will close the 3D view but not the project or the Level 1 view.

18. **Save** your project.

Exercise 2-5:
Annotation, Room Tags & Schedules

Adding text is very simple in Revit. In this exercise you will add a label below the floor plan. We will also place room tags.

Placing Text:

1. Open **Small Office.rvt** created in Exercise 2-4.

2. Make sure your current view is **Level 1**. The word "Level 1" will be bold under the heading *Floor Plans* in your *Project Browser*. If Level 1 is not current, simply double-click on the Level 1 text in the *Project Browser*.

3. Select the **Text** tool under the *Basics* tab in the *Design Bar*.

Once again, notice the *Options Bar* has changed to display some text options (Figure 2-5.1).

Figure 2-5.1 Options Bar for Text tool

The *Type Selector* indicates the text style (which determines the font style, height and more); users can create additional text styles. From this *Options Bar* your alignment (i.e., Left justified, Centered or Right justified) can also be set.

4. Set the *Options Bar* settings to match those shown above, **Click** below the floor plan to place the text (Figure 2-5.2).

5. Type **OFFICE BUILDING – Option A**, then click somewhere in the plan view to finish the text (do not press *Enter*).

The text height, in the *Type Selector*, refers to the size of the text on a printed piece of paper. For example, if you print your plan you should be able to place a ruler on the text and read ¼" when the text is set to ¼" in the *Type Selector*.

Text size can be a complicated process in other CAD programs; Revit makes it very simple. All you need to do is change the **view scale** for **Level 1** and Revit automatically adjusts the text and annotation to match that scale – so it always print ¼" tall on the paper.

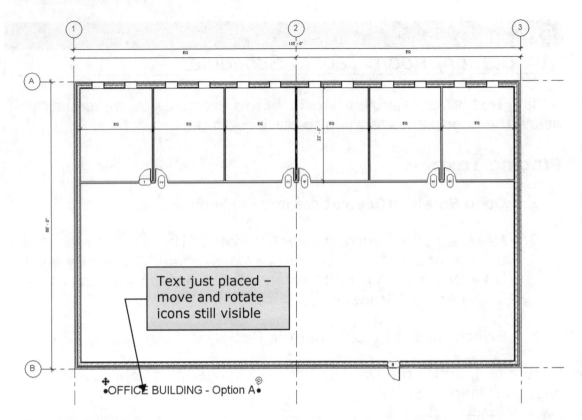

Text just placed – move and rotate icons still visible

•OFFICE BUILDING - Option A•

Figure 2-5.2 Placing text

You will not change the scale now, but it can be done via the *View Control Bar* (Figure 2-5.3). If you want to try changing it, just make sure it is set back to ⅛" = 1'-0" when done.

You should now notice that your text and even your door and window symbols are half the size they used to be when changing from ⅛" to ¼".

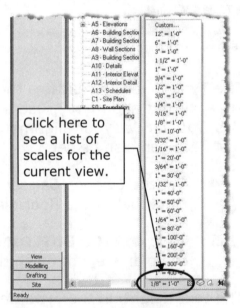

Click here to see a list of scales for the current view.

Figure 2-5.3 Set View Scale

You should understand that this scale adjustment would only affect the current view (i.e., Level 1). If you switched to Level 2 (if you had one) you would notice it is still set to ⅛"=1'-0". This is nice because you may, on occasion, want one plan at a larger scale to show more detail.

Placing Room Tags:

Placing *Room Tags* must be preceded by placing a *Room*. A Room object is used to define a space and hold information about a space (e.g., floor finish, area, department, etc.). Like a *Door Tag*, a *Room Tag* simply lists information contained within the object being tagged.

The Room tool searches for areas enclosed by walls; a valid area is pre-highlighted before you click to create a space.

By default, Revit will automatically place a *Room Tag* at the cursor location when you click to add the *Room* object.

6. Select the **Room** tool under the *Basics* tab on the *Design* Bar.

7. Set the *Type Selector* to **Room Tag: Room Tag With Area** and make sure **Tag on placement** is selected on the *Options Bar*.

8. Click within each room in the order shown in Figure 2-5.4; watch for the dashed green reference line to align the tags.

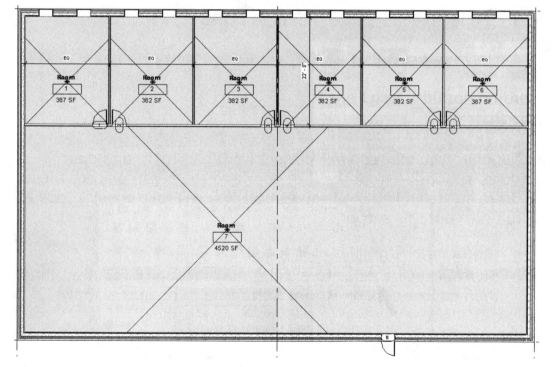

Figure 2-5.4 Placing rooms and room tags

While the *Room* tool is active, the placed rooms in the model are shaded light blue so you can see which spaces already have rooms placed. The large "X" is also part of the room. When the *Room* tool is not active, you can hover the cursor over the approximate location of the "X" until it pre-highlights, then you can click to select the room. With the *Room* object selected you can go to *Properties* to add information or delete it.

9. Click **Modify** to end the current tool.

Notice the rooms are not visible and the "X" is gone. Also notice, the *Room Tag* selected shows the following information stored within the *Room* object: Name, Number and Area. *FYI: The area updates automatically when the walls move.* Next you will change the room names.

10. Click on the *Room Tag* for **room number 1** to select it.

When a *Room Tag* is selected the "blue" text is editable and the "red" text is not.

11. Click on the room name text, type **OFFICE**, and then press **Enter** on the keyboard.

12. Change rooms 2-4 to also be named **OFFICE**.

13. Change the large room name to **LOBBY**.

14. Leave two rooms (5 and 6) as "Room" for now.

Schedules:

The template you started your project from had room and door schedules set up. So from the first door and room you placed, these schedules started filling themselves out! You will take a quick look at this to finish out this section.

15. In the *Project Browser*, click the "**+**" symbol next to *Schedules/Quantities* to expand that section (if required) and then double-click on **Room Schedule** to open that view.

The room schedule is a tabular view of the Revit model. This information is "live" and can be changed (Figure 2-5.5).

Figure 2-5.5 Room Schedule

Next you will change the two rooms named "room", and see that the floor plan is automatically updated!

16. Click in the *Room Name* column for room number 5 and change the text to read **MEN'S TOILET RM.**

17. Click in the *Room Name* column for room number 6 and change the text to read **WOMEN'S TOILET RM.**

18. Click the lower "X" in the upper right of the drawing window to close the room schedule view.

19. Switch to *Level 1* (if required) and **zoom in** on rooms 5 and 6 (Figure 2-5.6).

Notice that the room names have been updated because the two views (floor plan and schedule) are listing information from the same "parameter value" in the project database.

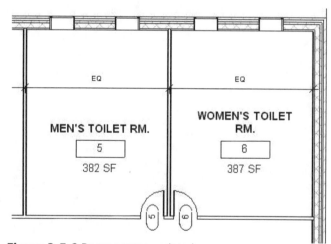

Figure 2-5.6 Room names updated

20. Open and Close the door schedule to view the current status of that schedule.

21. **Save** your project.

Exercise 2-6:
Printing

The last thing you need to know to round off your basic knowledge of Revit is how to print the current view.

Printing the current view:

1. In *Level 1* view, right-click anywhere and select **Zoom to Fit**.

2. Select **File → Print** from the *Menu Bar*.

3. Adjust your settings to match those shown in **Figure 2-6.1**.

    - Select a printer from the list that you have access to.
    - Set *Print Range* to: **Visible portion of current window**.

Figure 2-6.1 Print dialog

4. Click on the **Setup** button to adjust additional print settings.

5. Adjust your settings to match those shown in **Figure 2-6.2**.

    - Set Zoom to: **Fit to page**

Figure 2-6.2 Print Setup dialog

6. Click **OK** to close the *Print Setup* dialog and return to *Print*.

7. Click the **Preview** button in the lower left corner. This will save paper and time by verifying the drawing will be correctly positioned on the page (Figure 2-6.3).

8. Click the **Print** button at the top of the preview window.

9. Click **OK** to print to the selected printer.

FYI: Notice you do not have the option to set the scale (i.e., ⅛" = 1'-0"). If you recall from our previous exercise, the scale is set in the properties for each view.

If you want a quick half-scale print you can change the zoom factor to 50%. You could also select "Fit to page" to get the largest image possible but not to scale.

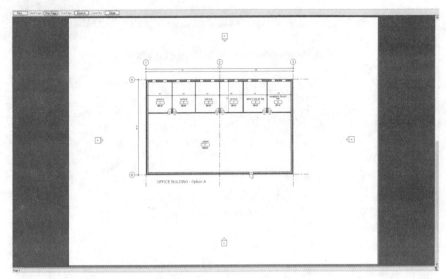

Figure 2-6.3 Print Preview

Printer versus a Plotter?

Revit can print to any printer/plotter installed on your computer.

A <u>Printer</u> is an output device that uses smaller paper (e.g., 8½"x11" or 11"x17"). A <u>Plotter</u> is an output device that uses larger paper; plotters typically have one or more rolls or paper ranging in size from 18" wide to 36" wide. A roll feed plotter has a built-in cutter that can – for example – cut paper from a 36" wide roll to make a 24"x36" sheet.

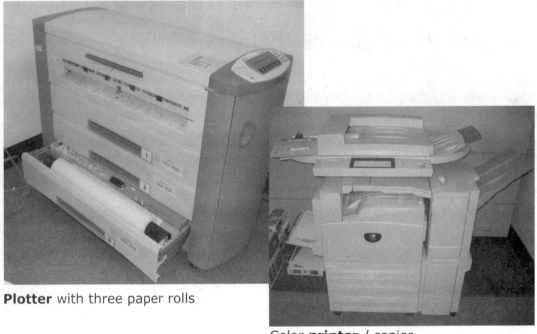

Plotter with three paper rolls

Color **printer** / copier

Self-Exam:

The following questions can be used as a way to check your knowledge of this lesson. The answers can be found at the bottom of this page.

1. The Tape Measure tool is used to dimension drawings. (T/F) *False*

2. Revit will automatically trim the wall lines when you place a door. (T/F) *True*

3. Snap will help you to draw faster and more accurately. (T/F) *True*

4. A 6'-8" door is a standard door height in _____ construction. *Residential*

5. While using the wall tool, the height can be quickly adjusted in the _____ Bar. *Options*

Review Questions:

The following questions may be assigned by your instructor as a way to assess your knowledge of this section. Your instructor has the answers to the review questions.

1. The **view scale** for a drawing/view is set by clicking the scale listed on the View Control *Bar*. (T/F) *True*

2. Dimensions are placed with only two clicks of the mouse. (T/F) *False (3)*

3. The relative size of text in a drawing is controlled by the view scale. (T/F) *True*

4. You can quickly switch to a different view by double-clicking on that views *True* label in the Project Browser. (T/F)

5. You cannot select which side of the wall a window is offset to. (T/F) *False*

6. The _____ key cycles through the available snaps near your cursor. *Tab*

7. The _____ tool can be used to list the distance between two walls without drawing a dimension. *Tape measure*

8. While in the Door tool you can change the door style and size via the _____ _____ within the *Options Bar*. *Type selector*

Notes:

Lesson 3
Office Building: FLOOR PLAN (First Floor)::

In this lesson you will draw the first floor plan of an office building. The office building will be further developed in subsequent chapters. It is recommended that you spend adequate time on this lesson as later lessons build on this one.

Exercise 3-1:
Project Overview

A program statement is created in the pre-design phase of a project. Working with the client (or user group), the architect gathers as much information as possible about the project before starting to design.

The information gathered includes:
- Rooms: What rooms are required?
- Size: How big the rooms need to be? (E.g., toilets for a convention center are much bigger than for a dentist's office.)
- Adjacencies: This room needs to be next to that room. (E.g., the public toilets need to be accessible from the public lobby.)

With the project statement in hand, the architect can begin the design process. Although modifications may (and will) need to be made to the program statement, it is used as a goal to meet the client's needs.

You will not have a program statement, per se, with this project. However, the same information will be provided via step-by-step instructions in this book.

Project overview:

You will model a three-story office building located in a rural setting. Just to the north of the building site is a medium-sized lake. For the sake of simplicity, the property is virtually flat.

The main entry and parking is from the south side of the building. You enter the building into a three-story atrium. Levels 2 and 3 have guard railings that look down into Level 1 in the atrium. The atrium is enclosed on three sides by full height curtain wall (glass walls). See the image on the front cover.

This building is not meant to meet any particular building code. It is strictly a tool to learn how to use Revit. Having said that, however, there are several general comments as to how codes may impact a particular part of the design.

The floor plans are mostly open office areas with a few smaller rooms for toilets, private offices, work and break rooms, etc. These areas have several "punched" window openings on the exterior walls (punched as opposed to ribbon windows).

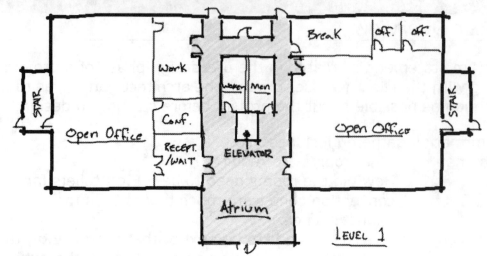

Figure 3-1.1 Level 1 floor plan sketch

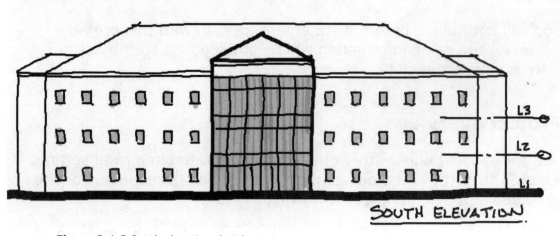

Figure 3-1.2 South elevation sketch

Exercise 3-2:
Exterior Walls

You will begin the first floor plan by drawing the exterior walls. Like many projects, early on you might not be certain what the exterior walls are going to be. So, we will start out using the generic wall styles. Then we will change them to a custom wall style (that you will create) once we have decided what the wall construction is.

Adjust wall settings:

1. Start a new project using the **Default template**, and then select **Wall** from the *Design Bar*.

2. Make the following changes to the wall options in the *Options Bar* (Figure 3-2.1):
   - Wall style: **Basic Wall: Generic – 12"**
   - Height: **Unconnected**
   - Height: **36' 0"**
   - Loc Line: **Finish Face; Exterior**

Figure 3-2.1 Option bar: Walls

Draw the exterior walls:

3. Draw the walls shown in Figure 3-2.2. Make sure your dimensions are correct. Use the *Tape Measure* tool if you need additional lengths listed.
   NOTE: *If you draw in a clockwise fashion, your walls will have the exterior side of the wall correctly positioned. You can also use the spacebar to toggle which side the exterior face is on.*

TIP:
In the Options Bar, while you are in the Wall tool, you can click Chain to continuously draw walls. When Chain is not selected you have to pick the same point twice: once where the line ends and again where the next line begins.

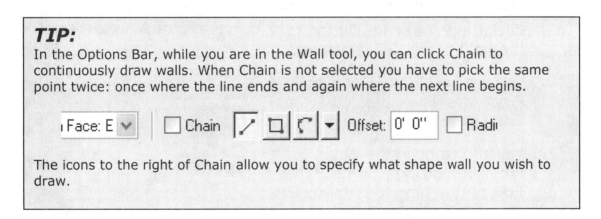

The icons to the right of Chain allow you to specify what shape wall you wish to draw.

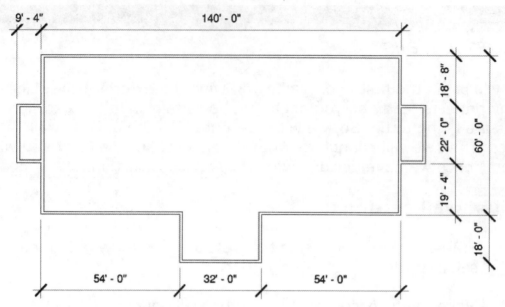

Figure 3-2.2 Exterior walls

Create a custom wall style:

Revit provides several predefined wall styles, from metal studs with gypsum board to concrete block and brick cavity walls. However, you will occasionally need a wall style that has not yet been predefined by Revit. You will study this feature next.

First, you will take a quick look at a more complex wall type that Revit provides so you can see how they are set up.

4. With the *Wall* tool selected, pick the wall type: **Basic Wall: Exterior – Brick on CMU**, from the *Type Selector* drop-down list. (See image to the right.)

5. Click the **Properties** button to the right of the *Type Selector*.

6. You are now in the *Element Properties* dialog box. Click the **Edit/New** button (Figure 3-2.3).

7. You should be in the *Type Properties* dialog box. Click the **Edit** button next to the *Structure* parameter (Figure 3-2.4).

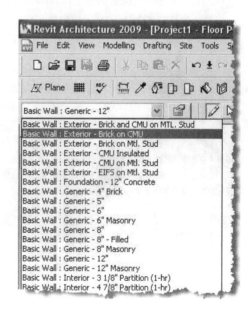

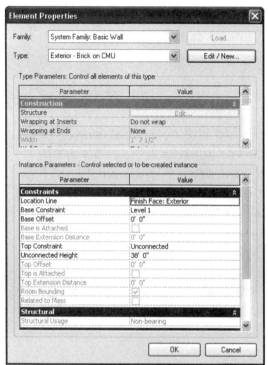

Figure 3-2.3 Element Properties

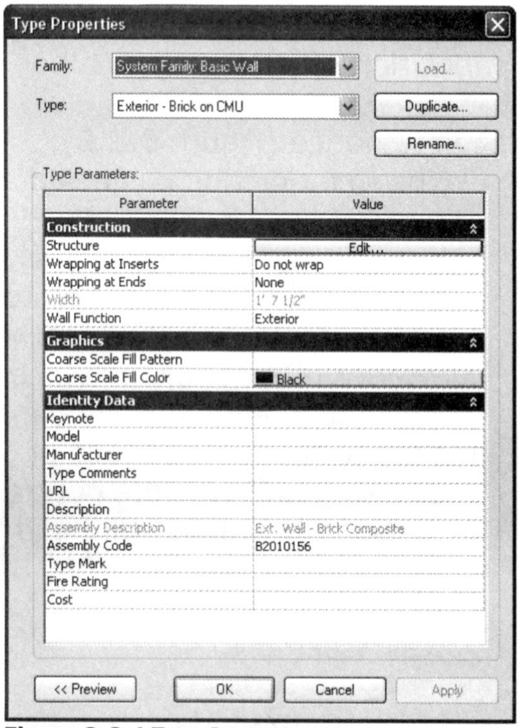

Figure 3-2.4 Type Properties

8.   Finally, you are in the *Edit Assembly* dialog box. This is where you can modify existing wall types or create new ones. Click **<<Preview** to display a preview of the selected wall type. (Figure 3-2.5)

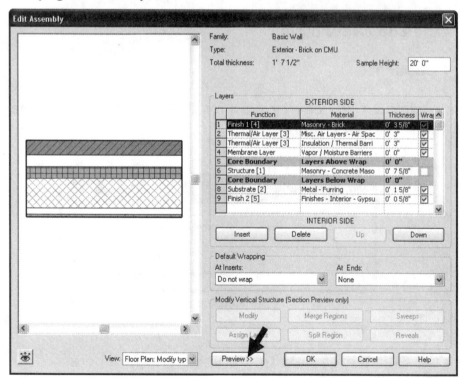

Figure 3-2.5 Edit Structure

Here, the *Edit Assembly* dialog box allows you to change the composition of an existing wall or (similar) to create a new wall.

Things to notice (Figure 3-2.5):
- The exterior side is labeled at the top and interior side at the bottom.
- You will see horizontal lines identifying the core material. The core material can be used to place walls and dimension walls. For example: the *Wall* tool will let you draw a wall with the interior or exterior core face as the reference line. On an interior wall you would typically dimension to the face of CMU rather than to the finished face of gypsum board. This is to work out coursing and give the contractor the information needed for the part of the wall he will build first.
- Each row is called a layer. By clicking on a layer and picking the **Up** or **Down** buttons, you can reposition materials within the wall assembly.

9. Click **Cancel** in each open dialog box to close them.

10. Set the Wall Style back to **Basic Wall: Generic – 12"** in the type selector.

11. Click the **Properties** button next to the type selector.

12. Click the **Edit/New** button.

13. Click **Duplicate**.

14. Enter **Brick & CMU cavity wall** for the new wall type name, and then click **OK** (Figure 3-2.6).

Figure 3-2.6 New wall type name

15. Click the **Edit** button next to the *Structure* parameter.

Using the **Insert** button and the **Up** and **Down** buttons, add the *layers* to your new wall style as shown below in **Figure 3-2.7**.

Function	Material	Thickness
Finish 1 [4]	Masonry -Brick	4"
Thermal/Air Layer	Misc. Air Layers – Air Space	2"
Thermal/Air Layer	Insulation / Thermal Barriers – Rigid Insulation	2"
Core Boundary	*Layers above wrap*	*0"*
Structure [1]	Masonry – Concrete Masonry Units	8"
Core Boundary	*Layers below wrap*	*0"*
Finish 1 [4]	Metal – Stud Layer	2½"
Finish 2 [5]	Finishes – Interior – Gypsum Wall Board	⅝"

Figure 3-2.7 New wall layers

Masonry is typically drawn nominally in plans and smaller scaled details. This helps to figure out coursing for both drawing and dimensioning. For example, 8" concrete block is actually 7⅝".

Also, notice that the CMU, Rigid Insulation, Air Space and Brick add up to 16" in thickness. This portion of the wall would sit on a 16″ concrete block (CMU) foundation wall directly below.

16. Your dialog should look like **Figure 3-2.8**. Click **OK** to close all dialog boxes.

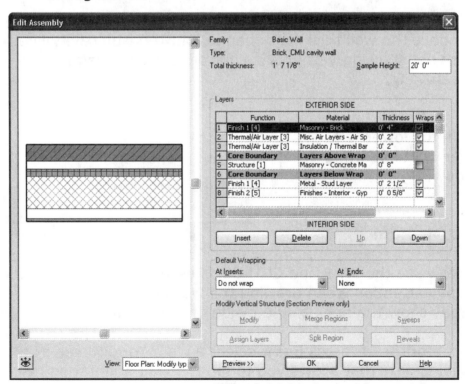

Figure 3-2.8 Edit Structure for new wall type

The next step is to change the wall type for the walls previously drawn.

17. Select the **Modify** button from the *Design Bar*; this allows you to select objects in your drawing.

18. **Zoom out** so you can see the entire plan. Dragging your mouse from one corner to the other, make a window over the plan to select all the walls.

19. With the walls selected, pick **Basic Wall: Brick & CMU cavity wall** from the *Type Selector* drop down.

TIP:

If, after selecting all the walls, the *Type Selector* is not active and does not show any wall types, you probably have some other object selected like text or dimensions. Try to find those objects and delete them (except the elevation tags).

You can also click on the *Filter* button (located on the *Options Bar* when objects are selected) and uncheck the types of objects to exclude from the current selection.

You should notice the wall thickness change, but the wall cavity lines and hatch are not showing yet. This is controlled by the *Detail Level* option for each view.

20. Click on **Detail Level** icon in the lower-left corner of the Drawing Window.

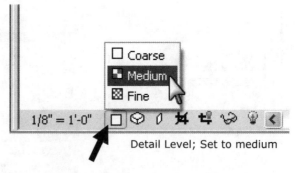

Detail Level; Set to medium

21. Select **Medium**.

You should now see the brick and CMU thicknesses with hatching. If you did not pay attention when drawing the walls originally, some of your walls may show the brick to the inside of the building.

22. Select **Modify** (or press **Esc**); select a wall. You will see a symbol appear that allows you to flip the wall orientation by clicking on that symbol (Figure 3-2.9).

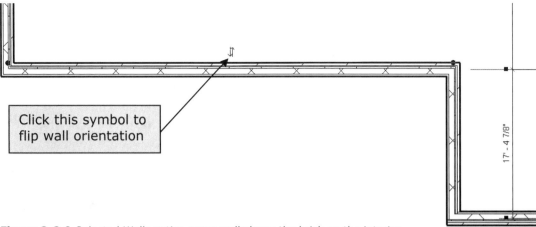

Click this symbol to flip wall orientation

Figure 3-2.9 Selected Wall; notice some walls have the brick on the interior

23. Whether you need to adjust walls or not, click on the flip symbol to experiment with its operation.
    TIP: *The Flip symbol is always on the exterior side (or what Revit thinks is the exterior side) of the wall.*

24. If some walls do need to be adjusted so the brick is to the exterior, do it now. You will probably have to select the wall(s) and use the *Move* tool to reposition the walls to match the required dimensions.

25. **Save** your Project as ex3-2.rvt.

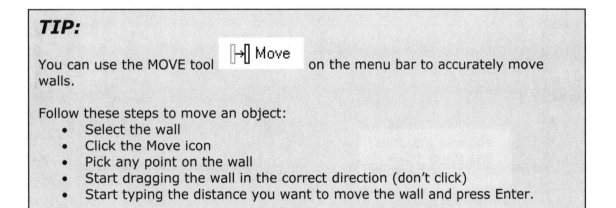

TIP:

You can use the MOVE tool [⊢] Move on the menu bar to accurately move walls.

Follow these steps to move an object:
  • Select the wall
  • Click the Move icon
  • Pick any point on the wall
  • Start dragging the wall in the correct direction (don't click)
  • Start typing the distance you want to move the wall and press Enter.

Finally, you will change the three walls at the atrium to be curtain wall (full glass). This will let lots of light into the atrium and better identify the main entry of the building.

26. Drag a window to select the three walls around the atrium.

27. With the walls highlighted, select **Curtain Wall: Curtain Wall 1** from the *Type Selector* drop-down.

Your atrium is now surrounded by curtain wall (Figure 3-2.10). In a later lesson we will add horizontal and vertical mullions to the curtain wall.

You can see your progress nicely with a 3D view. Click the **Default 3D View** button. Notice that Revit shows the curtain wall as transparent because it knows the curtain wall is glass. The other walls are shaded on the exterior side to make the image read better. You will add mullions to the curtain wall in a later lesson.

28. Save your project as **ex3-2.rvt**.

Revit automatically sets the hatch intensity and line weights.

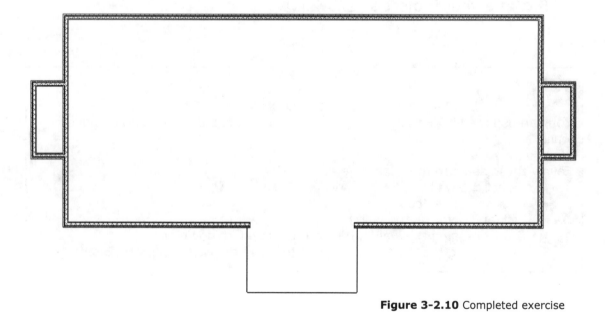

Figure 3-2.10 Completed exercise

Exercise 3-3:
Interior walls

In this lesson you will draw the interior walls for the first floor.

Adjust wall settings:

1. Select **Wall** from the *Design Bar*.

2. Make the following changes to the wall options in the *Options Bar* (Figure 3-2.1):
    *   Wall style: **Basic Wall: Interior – 4 7/8" partition (1-hr)**
    *   Height: **Level 2**
    *   Loc Line: **Wall Centerline**

Draw the interior walls:

3. Draw a vertical wall approximately as shown in Figure 3-3.1. We will adjust its exact position in the step #4.

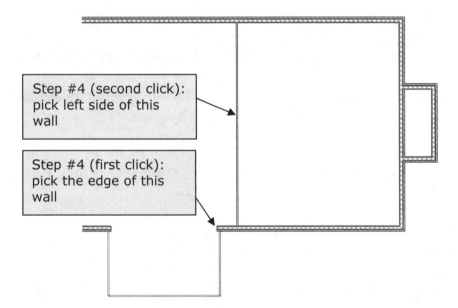

Step #4 (second click): pick left side of this wall

Step #4 (first click): pick the edge of this wall

Figure 3-3.1 First interior wall

4. Select the interior wall you just drew and use the **Align** tool to align it with the edge of the exterior wall in the atrium (Figure 3-3.1). When you are done, the wall should look like Figure 3-3.2.

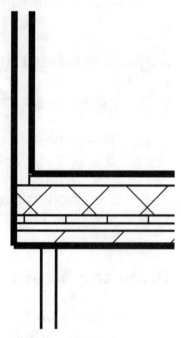

5. Create the same wall for the west side of the atrium repeating the above steps.

Modify an existing wall type:

Next you will add some additional interior walls. You will be drawing 8" CMU walls. Revit does have an 8" Masonry wall type available in the default template file that you started your project from. However, the thickness for this wall type is 7⅝", which is the actual size of a block. Floor plans are usually drawn nominally (i.e., 8") not actual (7⅝"). This is done so you can figure out coursing so minimal cutting is required. Therefore, rather than creating a new wall type you can simply modify the existing wall type.

Figure 3-3.2 First interior wall

6. Select the wall style: **Basic Wall: Generic – 8" Masonry**.

7. Click on the **Properties** button, and then select the **Edit/New** button. Finally click **Edit** next to the *Structure* parameter.

8. Change the masonry thickness from 7⅝" to **8"** in the edit structure dialog box, and then select **OK** to close each dialog.

Occasionally Revit will not list dimensions, relative to the walls you want to draw new walls from, while in the create wall mode. One way to deal with this is to draw temporary walls to use as a reference. After using the temporary wall as a reference you can delete it.

9. With the '**Basic Wall: Generic – 8" Masonry**' wall as the current wall, set the location line (Loc. Line) to **Core Centerline**.

10. Draw the vertical wall shown in Figure 3-3.3; be sure to snap to the *Midpoint* of the atrium wall as your first point.

Next you will draw an elevator shaft, centered on the atrium and 35'-0" back (thus the temp. wall).

The inside dimensions of the elevator are: **7'-4" x 6'-10"**. Because you know the inside dimension you will want to adjust the location line to match the known info.

11. Set the *Loc. Line* to: **Finish Face: Interior**.

12. Draw the elevator shaft. Make sure the location line is to the inside so your shaft is the correct dimension. Draw the shaft anywhere in the drawing; you will adjust the exact position next.

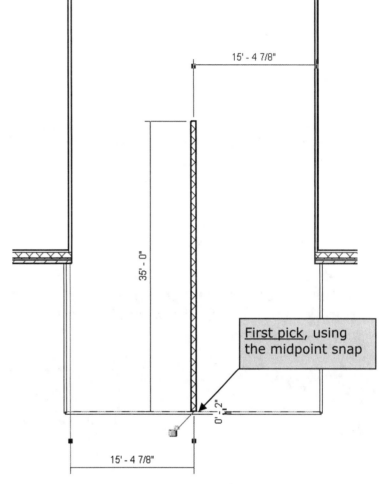

Figure 3-3.3 Temp. wall

13. Select the 4 walls that represent the elevator shaft, and then pick the **Move** tool.

TIP:

Concrete blocks come in various widths, and most are 16" long and 8" high. When drawing plans there is a simple rule to keep in mind to make sure you are designing wall to coursing. This applies to wall lengths and openings within CMU walls.

Dimension rules for CMU coursing in floor plans:
- *e*'-0" or *e*'-8"   where *e* is any even number (e.g., 6'-0" or 24'-8")
- *o*'-4"   where *o* is any odd number (e.g., 5'-4")

14. Snap to the *Midpoint* of the shaft as your first point, and then snap to the *Middle Endpoint* of your temporary wall (Figure 3-3.4). You should zoom in to verify your snaps.

The elevator shaft is now perfectly centered in the atrium and exactly 35'-0" back from the south curtain wall.

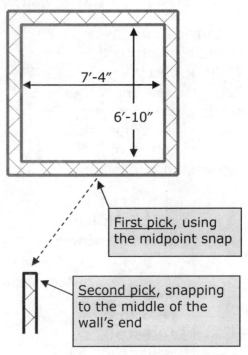

15. At this point you can **delete** the temporary wall. Select the wall and then right-click and select delete (or press the Delete key on the keyboard).

A temporary wall can be useful for other tasks as well. One example is the *Mirror* tool requires (by default) a vertical line centered on the atrium to perfectly mirror objects from the east side to the west side of the building.

First pick, using the midpoint snap

Second pick, snapping to the middle of the wall's end

Figure 3-3.4 Move tool

FYI:
When a wall is selected, you can click the Properties button on the Options Bar to see that wall's properties. Click on of the elevator shaft walls and verify that they are 36'-0" tall.

Modify an existing wall:

Next we want to change the portion of wall between the building and the east and west stair shafts. To do this you will need to split the current wall, trim the corners and then draw an 8" masonry wall.

16. **Zoom** in on the west stair shaft and select the **Split** tool.

17. Pick somewhere in the middle of the wall (Figure 3-3.5).

18. Use the **Trim** tool to trim the corners so the exterior wall only occurs at exterior conditions (Figure 3-3.6).
    TIP: Select the portion of wall you wish to retain.

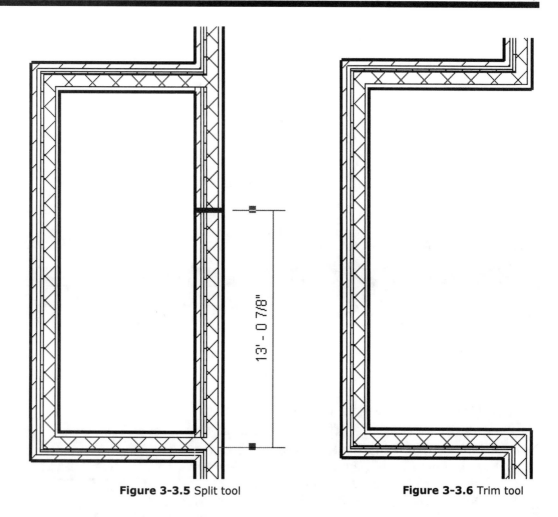

Figure 3-3.5 Split tool   **Figure 3-3.6** Trim tool

Additional custom wall types:

We decide that the stair shafts are mostly utilitarian and do not require gypsum board on the walls. In the next steps you will create a new exterior wall type just like the one previously created less the gypsum board and metal studs. Also, you will create a custom wall type to close the open side we created in the previous steps. This wall type will have gypsum board and metal studs on one side.

19. Using wall type: *Basic Wall: Brick & CMU cavity wall* as a starting point, create a new wall type named **Brick & CMU cavity wall (no GWB)**. Remove the gypsum board and metal studs and save the new wall type. *(Remember to click Duplicate.)*

20. Change the three exterior walls around the west stair shaft to the new wall type created in the previous step.

21. Using wall type: *Basic Wall: Brick & CMU cavity wall* as a starting point, create a new wall type named **8" Masonry with GWB 1S.** Remove the brick, air space and rigid insulation and save the new wall type (Figure 3-3.7).
    FYI: *It will be useful to come up with a standard naming system for your custom wall types. If the names get to long they are hard to read. The example above has:*
    - *GWB = Gypsum Wall Board (and would imply studs)*
    - *1S = finish only occurs on one side of the wall.*

Function	Material	Thickness
n/a	*n/a*	*n/a*
Core Boundary	*Layers above wrap*	*0"*
Structure [1]	Masonry – Concrete Masonry Units	8"
Core Boundary	*Layers below wrap*	*0"*
Finish 1 [4]	Metal – Stud Layer	2½"
Finish 2 [5]	Finishes – Interior – Gypsum Wall Board	⅝"

Figure 3-3.7 New wall layers

22. Draw a wall so the gypsum finish continues on the office side, using the *Align* tool if necessary (Figure 3-3.8).
    Use the Measure tool to make sure the stair shaft is the correct size; don't draw the dimensions.

Next you will use the *Mirror* tool to update the east stair.

23. Erase the four walls of the east stair shaft; this will include the main east wall of the office building (Figure 3-3.9)

24. Select the six walls at the west stair (Figure 3-3.9).

    TIP: Make sure the count is correct on the *Status Bar*.

25. Select the **Mirror** tool and then select the atrium wall identified in Figure 3-3.9.

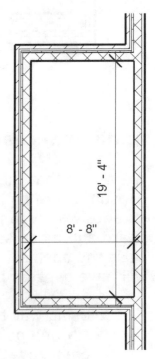

Figure 3-3.8 Revised west stair

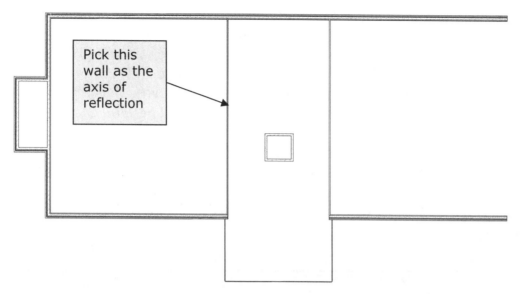

Figure 3-3.9 Mirror west stair – step 1

26. Use the **Move** tool to reposition the mirrored walls; they should be selected by default (Figure 3-3.10).

27. Use the **Measure** tool to verify the overall length of the building is 140'-0". Adjust as necessary.

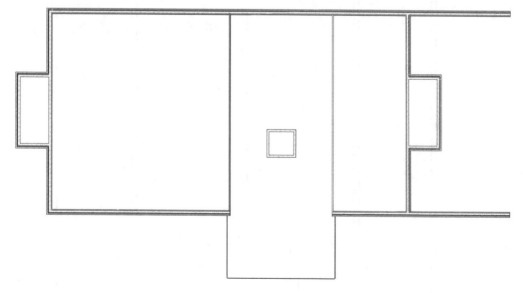

Figure 3-3.10 Mirror west stair – step 2

Finally, you will draw a few more interior walls to compete the first floor plan.

28. Set the Wall style to:
    Basic Wall: Interior – 4 7/8" partition (1-hr)

29. Draw the additional walls shown in Figure 3-3.11. Make sure to position the walls per the dimensions shown. Use the *Measure* tool to verify accuracy. Also, modify the *Loc Line* as required.

Drawing Tips: Copy the existing atrium wall 6'-4⅞" over (6'-0" plus one wall thickness), draw a wall from the midpoint of the elevator shaft with centerline reference (Loc Line), and use *Trim* and *Mirror* tools.   Do not draw the dimensions. **SAVE YOUR PROJECT as ex3-3.rvt.**

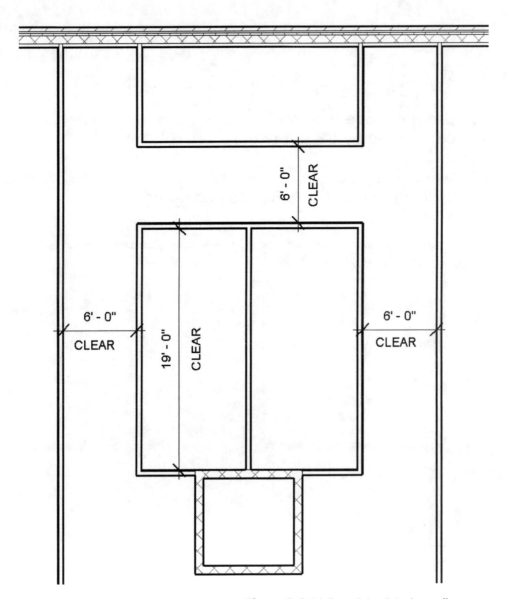

Figure 3-3.11 Remaining interior walls

Exercise 3-4:
Elevator

This lesson will show you how to insert an elevator into your elevator shaft.

Insert elevator:

Revit provides many *Families*, which are packages of predefined objects ready to insert into your project. However, many objects are not readily available, like elevators for example. Revit is continually adding content with each new release and to its online library. The online library is where you will acquire an elevator family for use in your project.

1. Open project ex3-3.rvt and **Save As ex3-4.rvt**.

2. Switch to the *Recent Files* view; if you closed this you will have to shut down Revit and reopen it.

You will have to download the elevator from the web. *Of course you will need to be connected to the Internet.*

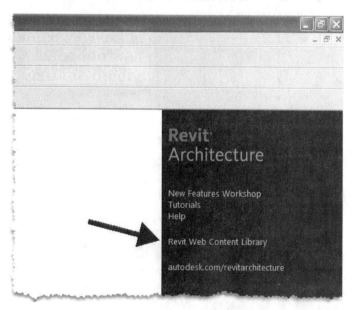

Figure 3-4.1 Recent Files

3. Click the **Revit Web Content Library** button in the upper right of the *Recent Files* list (Figure 3-4.1).

Revit will open your web browser, and then you will be looking at the contents of Revit's Content Distribution Center (Figure 3-4.2).

4. Click on "**Revit Architecture 2009 Library**".

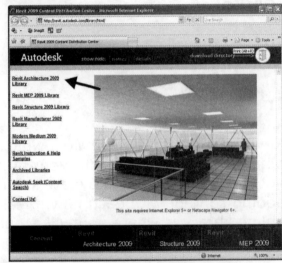

Figure 3-4.2 Web content via browser

Revit Architecture 2009 Library

- ⊞ FRA Library
- ⊞ UK Library
- ⊟ US Library
  - ⊟ Families
    - ⊞ Annotations
    - Balusters
    - ⊞ Casework
    - Columns
    - Curtain Wall Panels
    - ⊞ Detail Components
    - Doors
    - ⊞ Electrical Fixtures
    - Entourage
    - Furniture
    - Furniture System
    - ⊞ Lighting Fixtures
    - Mass
    - Mechanical Equipment
    - Misc. Architectural
    - Planting
    - Plumbing Fixtures
    - ⊞ Profiles
    - ⊞ Site
    - ⊟ Specialty Equipment
      - Church
      - Classroom-Library
      - Domestic
      - Exercise Equipment
    - ⊞ Fire Protection
    - Food Service
    - Lab
    - Ladders

Figure 3-4.3
Web content categories

5. Click the plus next to **US Library**, **Families, Specialty Equipment**, and then select **Conveying Systems**. (Figure 3-4.3)

Within the web browser you should see a graphical representation of each family available for download (Figure 3-4.4).

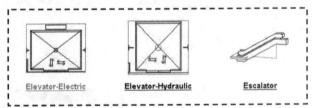

Figure 3-4.4 Web content visuals

6. Click "**Elevator-Electric**" to download that family.

7. Select **Save** (Figure 3-4.5a).

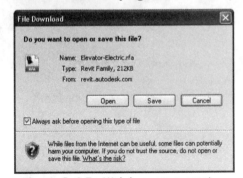

Figure 3-4.5a Web browser prompt

8. Save the file to the *Desktop* using the default name provided.

Now that you have saved the elevator family file to the hard drive, you need to load it into your current project.

9. Select **File** → **Load from Library** → **Load Family...** from the *Menu Bar*.

10. Browse to the *Desktop* and select the **Elevator-Electric.RFA**, and then click **Open**.

11. In the *Project Browser*, click the plus next to Families to expand the list (Figure 3-4.5b).

12. Expand the **Specialty Equipment** list, and then **Elevator-Electric**. (Figure 3-4.5b)

As you can see, four elevator types were loaded into your project. Similar to wall types, you can add one of these types as-is, or you can modify or create a new type. Next, you will add information in the *Type Properties* dialog to better document the elevator specified.

13. Right-click on the elevator type: **2000 lbs**, and then select **Properties** from the pop-up menu.

You will now see a listing of the properties for the selected elevator type.

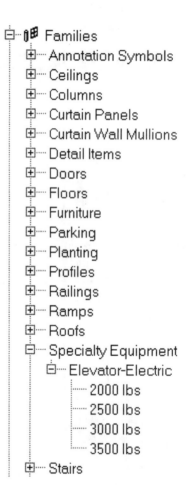

Figure 3-4.5b Elevator library: Project Browser

14. Click the **Preview** button (if necessary) to see the graphical review of the elevator type. Set the *View* to 3D View: View 1.

15. Add the following information (Figure 3-4.6):

- Model: **MadeUp 8864**
- Manufacturer: **ThyssenKrupp Elevator**
- URL: **www.thyssenelevator.com**

The three entries in step 15 are optional (although not for this exercise), but this is a great way to better document the project.

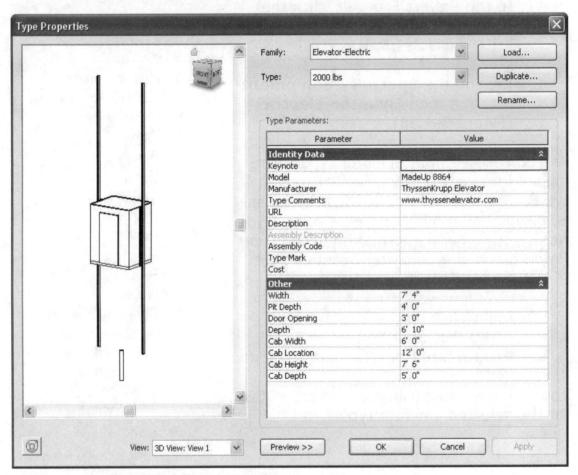

Figure 3-4.6 Elevator properties

16. Click **OK** to close the open dialog box.

17. Drag the **2000 lbs** elevator type from the project browser into the first floor plan.

The elevator type will be attached to you cursor, ready for insertion.

18. Move your cursor within the elevator shaft and adjust it until the elevator "snaps" in place; then click.

19. Press **Esc** twice to tell Revit you are finished placing elevators.

Now you have to add an elevator door in the shaft walls; this is similar to a regular door in a wall. Like the elevator, the elevator door has to be downloaded from the internet. You will do that next.

20. Similar to the steps previously covered, load the **Elevator Door – Center** family from the *Web Library* (Figure 3-4.7).

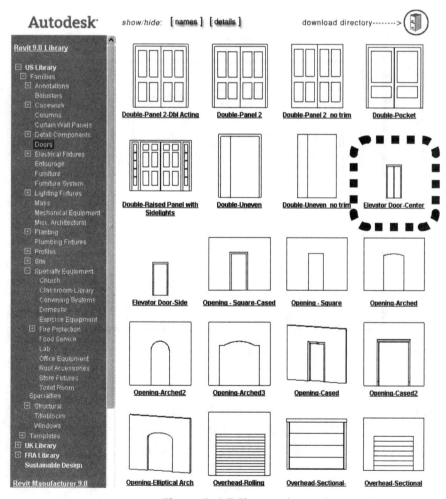

Figure 3-4.7 Elevator door in Revit Web Library

21. Drag the **36" x 84"** elevator door type from the project browser into the first floor plan (Figure 3-4.8a).

22. Place the elevator door at the center of the wall, aligned with the elevator door on the cab (Figure 3-4.8b).

   TIP: If the door is inserted on the wrong side of the wall, select the wall and click the Control Arrows to flip it within the wall.

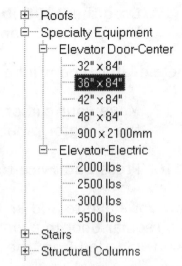

Figure 3-4.8a Elevator doors in Project Browser

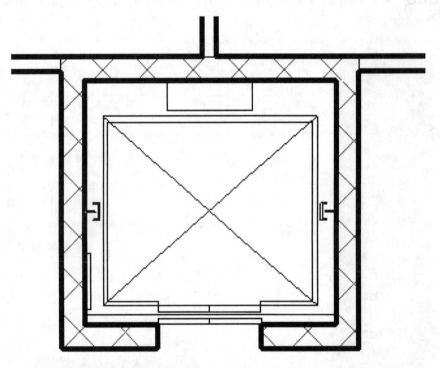

Figure 3-4.8b Elevator door added to plan

Notice when the elevator is selected, the Flip icon (control arrow) is displayed. Similar to the doors and walls, you can click this icon to flip the orientation of the elevator within the shaft.

23. Save your project as **ex3-4.rvt**.

Exercise 3-5:
Doors and Windows

This lesson will take a closer look at inserting doors and windows.

Insert doors:

Revit has done an excellent job providing several different door libraries. This makes sense seeing as doors are an important part of an architectural project. Some of the provided libraries include bi-fold, double, pocket, sectional (garage), and vertical rolling, to name a few. In addition to the library groups found on your local hard drive, many more are available via the Web Library feature.

The default template you started with only provides the **Sgl Flush** (Single Flush) group in the Doors family. If you want to insert other styles you will need to load them from the library. The reason for this step is that, when you load a library, Revit actually copies the data into your project file. If every possible group was loaded into your project at the beginning, not only would it be hard to find what you want in a large list of doors, but also the files would be several megabytes in size before you even drew the first wall.

You will begin this section by loading a few additional groups into your project.

1. Open project ex3-4.rvt and **Save-As ex3-5.rvt**.

2. With the *Door* tool selected, select the **Load...** button on the *Options Bar* (Figure 3-5.1).

3. Browse through the **Imperial Library** folder for a moment.

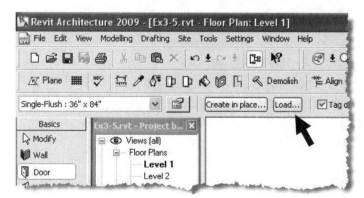

Figure 3-5.1 Load from Library

Each file represents a Family; next you will load four door Families into your project (Figure 3-5.2).

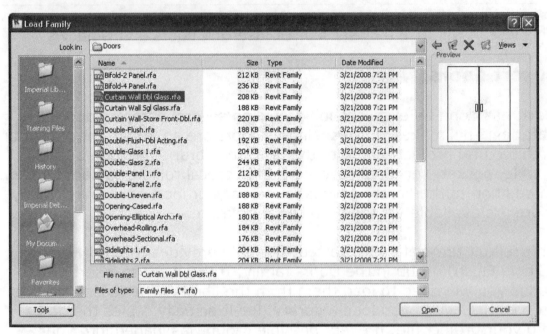

Figure 3-5.2 Door groups on hard drive

4. Select **Curtain Wall Dbl Glass.rfa**, and then click Open. (Figure 3-5.2)

5. Repeat steps 2 – 4 to load the following door groups:
   a. **Double-Glass 1**
   b. **Sidelights 1**
   c. **Single-Glass 1**

6. In the *Project Browser*, expand *Families* and *Doors* to see the loaded door groups (Figure 3-5.3).

If you expand the door group itself in the *Project Browser* you see the predefined door sizes associated with that group. Right-clicking on a door size allows you to rename, delete or duplicate it. To add a door size you duplicate and then modify properties for the new item.

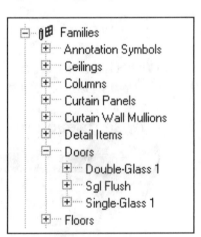

Figure 3-5.3 Loaded door groups

Next you will insert the doors into the stair shafts.

7. With the *Door* tool selected, pick **Sgl Flush: 36" x 84"** from the *type selector* on the *Options Bar*.

8. Insert two doors in the west stair shaft as shown in Figure 3-5.4. Remember you are inserting a door into a masonry wall so your door position and size need to work with coursing. Thus the 8" dimension.

9. Repeat the previous step to insert doors into the east stair shaft.

10. Finish inserting doors for the first floor (Figure 3-5.5). Use the following guidelines:

    a. All doors should be 36" wide and 7'-0" tall.
    b. You will not insert doors into the curtain wall for now. You will do that in a later lesson when you design the curtain wall.
    c. Use the style and approximate location shown in Figure 3-5.5.
    d. Doors across from each other in the two atrium walls should align with each other. **TIP:** *While inserting the second set of doors, watch/wait for the reference line to show up, indicating alignment.*
    e. Place doors approximately as shown, exact location not given.

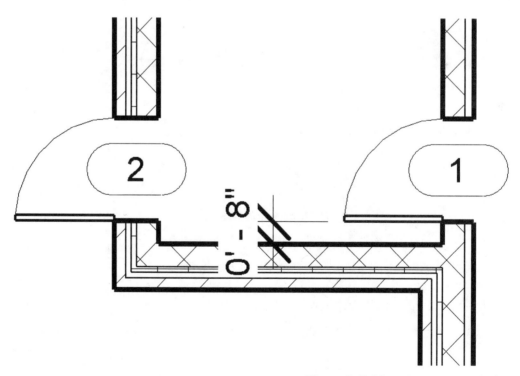

Figure 3-5.4 Door in west stair shaft

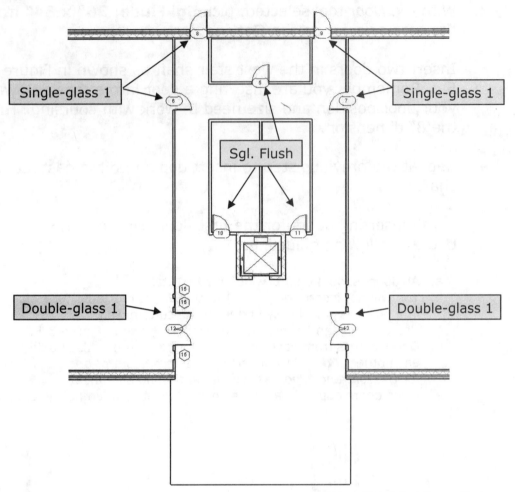

Figure 3-5.5 First floor with doors

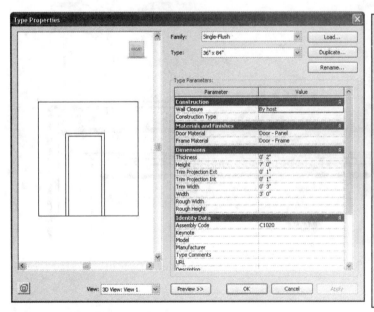

Figure 3-5.6 Door properties

Door Properties:

If you select Properties while the Door tool is active (selected), you can modify various properties related to the door.

You can easily add another standard door size to the Group as required. Click "Duplicate," type a name (Figure 3-5.6).

Standard doors sizes (and Groups) can be added to your template file, so you don't re-load it again.

Insert windows:

Adding windows to your project is very similar to adding doors. Like the doors, the template file you started from has one group preloaded into your project, the FIXED group. Looking at the Type Selector drop-down you will see the various sizes available for insertion. At this point you should also see the SIDELIGHT group that you loaded in the previous exercise. First, you will add a few interior borrowed lights using the sidelight group.

Interior windows (borrowed lights):

11. With the *Window* tool selected, pick: **Sidelights 1 : 18" x 84"** from the *type selector*.

12. On the west side of the atrium, insert the borrowed lights as shown in Figure 3-5.7; do not draw the dimensions.

Make sure the borrowed light frames are flush with the atrium side of the wall. You can control that option by moving your cursor to the side of the wall you want the frame flush with before clicking to insert. After drawing the window, you can select the frame and use the flip icon (similar to doors and walls).

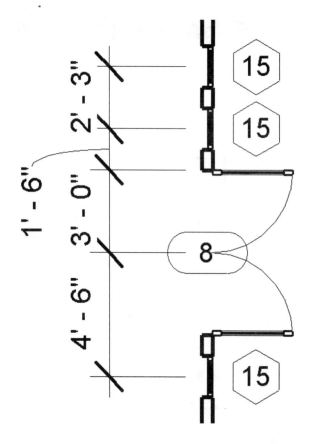

Figure 3-5.7 Sidelights added

13. Repeat the previous steps to insert the borrowed lights on the east side of the atrium.

Exterior windows:

14. Using the methods previously covered in this book, create a new window size in the *FIXED* family. Create: **Fixed: 32" x 48"**. You are creating this new size to fit coursing in plan view. The largest window (preloaded) that fits coursing in plan view is 24". That is not wide enough for this design.

15. Adjust the sill height for your new window size to fit within coursing as well. Set the sill height for **Fixed: 32" x 48"** to be **3'-4"** (Figure 3-5.8).

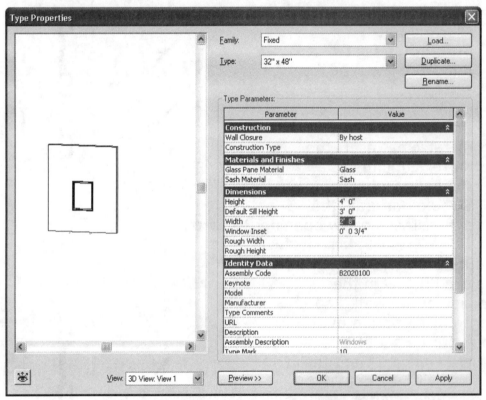

Figure 3-5.8 Added window size

16. Insert the window as shown in **Figure 3-5.9**. The window should be inserted in masonry coursing.

   NOTE: *The dimensions displayed while inserting the window will not work as displayed for coursing because Revit is measuring from the center of the adjacent exterior wall. Thus, you will have to insert the window as close as possible and adjust its location, verifying with the Measure tool.*

Array window:

The *Array* tool allows you to quickly copy several objects that have the same distance between them. You will use *Array* to copy the windows:

17. Click the *Modify* tool and then select your window.

18. With the window selected, pick the **Array** tool from the *edit toolbar*.

19. In the *Options Bar*, type **6** for the *Number* field (Figure 3-5.10).

20. Click the left mouse button at the midpoint of the window and move your mouse to the east until the dimension displayed is 8'-6".

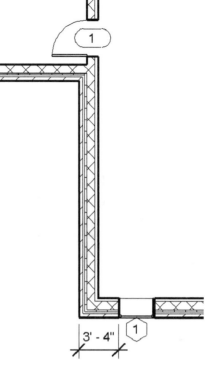

Figure 3-5.9 Exterior window

21. You should now see the windows arrayed in the wall. 8'-6" is not coursing, so select the **Activate Dimensions** button on the *Options Bar* and then enter 8'-8" in the displayed dimension to adjust the window openings. This allows you to more accurately adjust the dimensions.

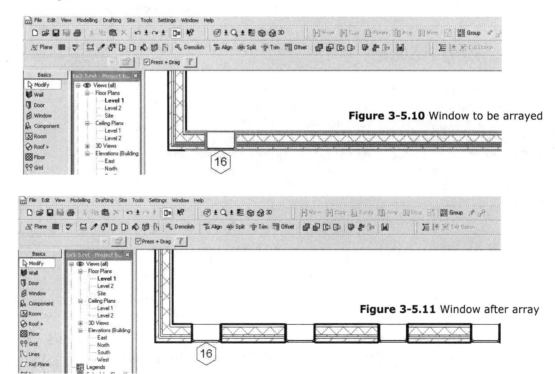

Figure 3-5.10 Window to be arrayed

Figure 3-5.11 Window after array

22. Set the windows up on the three remaining walls of the first floor (Figure 3-5.12). Consider the following:
    a. This would be a good use for the *Mirror* tool.
    b. If you need to create a temporary wall for a mirror reflection axis, make sure the temporary wall is set to centerline. ***TIP:*** *Try the pencil icon while in sketch mode.*
    c. If drawn accurately, you should be able the use the wall between the two toilet rooms (center, north of elevator shaft) to mirror the windows in the east west direction.
    d. Use the *Tape Measure* tool to verify accuracy.
    e. Use the Ctrl key to select multiple windows.

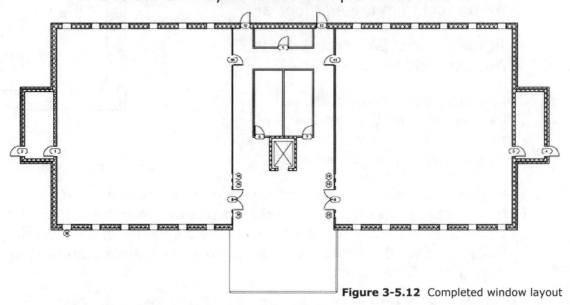

Figure 3-5.12 Completed window layout

Cleaning house:

As previously mentioned, you can view the various Families and groups loaded into your project. The more Families and Types you have loaded the larger your file is, whether or not you are using them in your project. Therefore, it is a good idea to get rid of any door, window, etc., that you know you will not need in the current project.

```
☐ Windows
  ☐ Fixed
      16" x 24"
      16" x 48"
      16" x 72"
      24" x 24"
      24" x 48"
      24" x 72"
      32" x 48"
      36" x 24"
      36" x 48"
      36" x 72"
  ☐ Sidelights 1
```

Figure 3-5.13 Project Browser

23. In the *Project Browser*, navigate to Families → Windows → Fixed. Right click on **36" x 48"** and select **Delete**.

Self-Exam:

The following questions can be used as a way to check your knowledge of this lesson. The answers can be found at the bottom of this page.

1. The *Option Bar* allows you to select which level your wall will be drawn on. (T/F)
   T

2. It is not possible to draw a wall with the interior or exterior face of the core as the reference point. (T/F)
   F

3. Objects cannot be move accurately with the **Move** tool. (T/F)
   F

4. The _____ tool, in the *Design Bar*, has to be selected in order to select an object in your project. *modify*

5. A wall has to be _____ to see its flip icons.
   selected

Review Questions:

The following questions may be assigned by your instructor as a way to assess your knowledge of this section. Your instructor has the answers to the review questions.

1. Revit comes with many predefined doors and windows. (T/F)
   T

2. The length 3'-8" is a masonry dimension. (T/F)
   F

3. You can delete unused families and types in the Project Browser. (T/F)
   T

4. It is not possible to load families and types from the Internet. (T/F)
   T

5. It is not possible to select which side of the wall a window should be on while you are inserting the window. (T/F)
   F

6. What tool will break a wall into two smaller pieces? _____
   split

7. The _____ tool allows you to match the surface of two adjacent walls. *align*

8. Occasionally you have to draw _____ lines to use as a reference point for another object or as a reflection mirror.
   temporary line

9. You can use the _____ tool to copy an object multiple times in one step. *array*

10. The _____ file has a few doors, windows and walls preloaded in it.
    template

Self-Exam Answers:
1 – T, **2** – F, **3** – F, **4** – Modify, **5** – Selected

Notes:

Lesson 4
Office Building: FLOOR PLAN (2ⁿᵈ and 3ʳᵈ Floors)::

In this lesson you will setup the upper two floors. This will mostly involve copying objects from the first floor with some modifications along the way. You will also adjust the floor-to-floor height and insert stairs into the stair shafts.

Exercise 4-1:
Copy common walls from first floor

Setting up the second (and third) floor view:

The first thing you need to do is make a few adjustments to the second (and third) floor settings. The default template you started your project from already has a second floor view setup in the project. The third floor has not been set up, so you will do that.

1. Open Exercise ex3-5.rvt and Save-As **ex4-1.rvt**.

2. In the *Project Browser*, double-click on the **Level 2** view under Floor Plans (Figure 4-1.1).

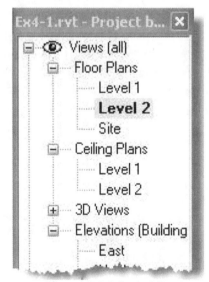

Figure 4-1.1 Project Browser; Level 2 view

You should now see the second floor plan. Notice that the dark wall lines, shown in this view, exist at this level. The light gray lines are walls for the floor below. (Figure 4-1.2)

You will turn off the view of the lower level and set the Detail Level to show more detail in the walls.

3. Right-click on the label **Level 2** (under *Floor Plans*) in the *Project Browser*, and then select Properties.

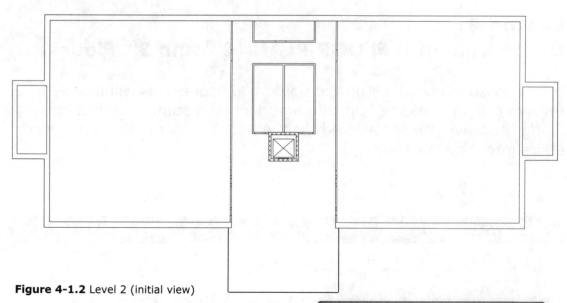

Figure 4-1.2 Level 2 (initial view)

4. Make the following adjustments (*Element Properties* dialog):
   a. Detail Level: **Medium**
   b. Underlay: **None**
   c. See image to right.

5. Click **OK**. Your Level 2 floor plan should look like the plan shown below (Figure 4-1.3).

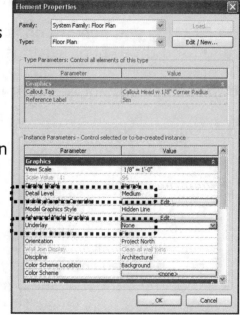

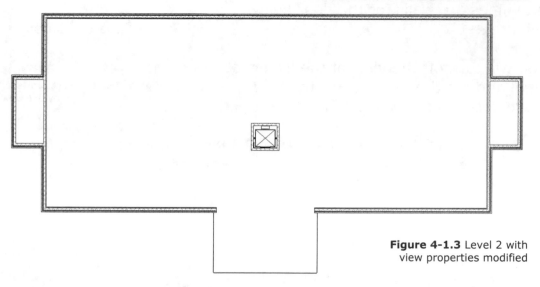

Figure 4-1.3 Level 2 with view properties modified

Because the walls and doors you will copy from the first floor are set up to extend to the floor above, you need to setup the third floor before you copy the walls from first to second (so the second floor walls have a floor to extend to).

Adding another floor is surprisingly simple. You switch to an elevation view and draw in a Level datum. By doing that Revit automatically sets up a Level 3 view in the project browser.

6. Double-click on one of the four elevation views listed under *Elevations* in the *Project Brows*er. If you do not see your drawing in elevation, try another view and/or see the tip below.

7. With an elevation on the computer screen, select *Modify* from the *Design Bar* and then select the **Level** tool.

8. As you move your cursor near the Level 2 symbol you will see a dimension displayed, indicating the distance between Level 2 floor and Level 3 floor you are about to insert. For now, **set Level 3 to be 10'-0" above Level 2** (Figure 4-1.4).

   a. Pick two points (left to right) to draw the *Level* datum.

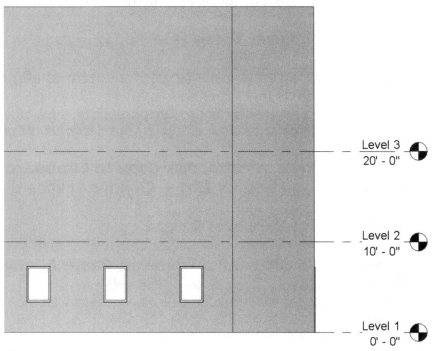

Figure 4-1.4 (Partial) South elevation

Notice that the Level 3 floor plan view was automatically added to the project browser. (See image to the right.)

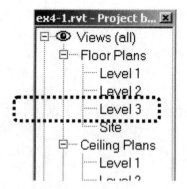

TIP:

You have probably figured out on your own what the symbol at the right is for. If not, here it is:

The default template has four Elevation symbols shown in plan view. These symbols represent what the four pre-setup views (under elevation) will see. Therefore, you should start drawing your plan in the approximate center of the four symbols. The symbols can be moved by dragging them with your mouse. This is covered more thoroughly in Lesson 7.

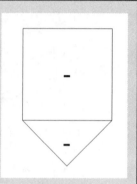

Next you will copy walls and doors from the first floor.

9. Switch to the **Level 1** view (see step 2).

10. Select all the interior walls (except elevator shaft), doors and interior windows.
    TIP: You will need to hold the Ctrl key to select multiple objects with multiple picks. You can drag a window(s) to select multiple objects at once.

11. With the objects selected, pick **Copy to Clipboard** from the *Edit* pull-down menu, or **Ctrl + C** on the keyboard.

12. Switch back to the **Level 2** view.

13. From the *Edit* pull-down menu select **Paste Aligned →
    Current View**.
    FYI: Paste aligned will make the new objects align with the copied objects below.

Notice the walls, doors and interior windows are now copied to Level 2 (Figure 4-1.5). We still need to copy the exterior windows and the elevator door.

Also, notice that the new doors have different numbers while the interior windows have the same number. Why is this? It relates to industry standards for architectural drafting. Each interior window that is the same size and configuration has the same type number throughout the project. Each door has a unique number because doors have so many variables (i.e., locks, hinges, closer, panics, material, and fire rating). To make doors easier to find, many architectural firms will make the door number the same as the room number the door opens into. You can change the door number by selecting the symbol and then clicking on the text. The door schedule will be updated automatically.

14. Using the same techniques described in the previous steps, copy the exterior windows and elevator door to Level 2. **TIP:** *You will need to ungroup your windows (grouped with array) before copying them. Select one of the windows and pick the ungroup button on* the Options Bar.

Why not draw these walls 36'-0" high like the exterior walls and elevator shaft?

Simulating real-world construction is ideal for several reasons. Mostly, you can be sure shafts align from floor to floor when the shaft is one continuous wall. Although the toilet and atrium walls align, they do not necessarily have to because they are separated by floor construction, this allows one floor to be later modified easily.

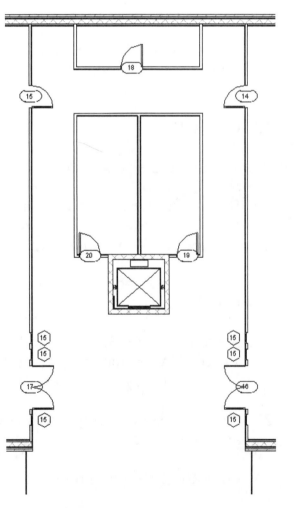

Figure 4-1.5 (Partial) Level 2 – walls added

Finally, you will copy the walls and such to Level 3. But first you need to change the height setting for the walls (on Level 2) before you paste them to Level 3 because there is nothing above (yet) to extend the walls to (e.g., roof or floor).

15. In the Level 2 view, select all the interior walls, doors and windows (except the elevator shaft).

You need to narrow your selection down to just the walls.

16. Select the **Filter** button on the *Options Bar*.

17. **Uncheck** all the items listed except *Walls* (Figure 4-1.6).

The list varies depending on what objects are in the selection set. (Figure 4-1.6)

18. Click **OK**.

Figure 4-1.6 Filter dialog

Now only the walls are selected.

19. Select the **Properties** button on the *Options Bar*.

20. Change the *Top Constraint* to **Unconnected**, then **OK**.

21. Select the objects again; you can copy the selected objects to the *Clipboard*.

22. Switch to Level 3, right-click on Level 3 and select **View Properties...** and then make the changes listed in step 4 above (e.g., Underlay and Detail Level).

23. Paste the Level 2 objects to Level 3, including Exterior windows and elevator door.

24. Copy the exterior windows to Level 3 per previous steps.

25. **Save your project**.

Exercise 4-2:
Additional interior walls

This short exercise will help reinforce the commands you have already learned. You will add walls and openings to your project.

Adding walls:

1. Add the interior walls and doors to **Level 1** as shown in Figure 4-2.1. Use the stud wall you used previously. Use the *Align* tool to align the walls, which are not dimensioned, with the adjacent walls previously drawn. ***FYI:*** *Doors not labeled to be single flush.*

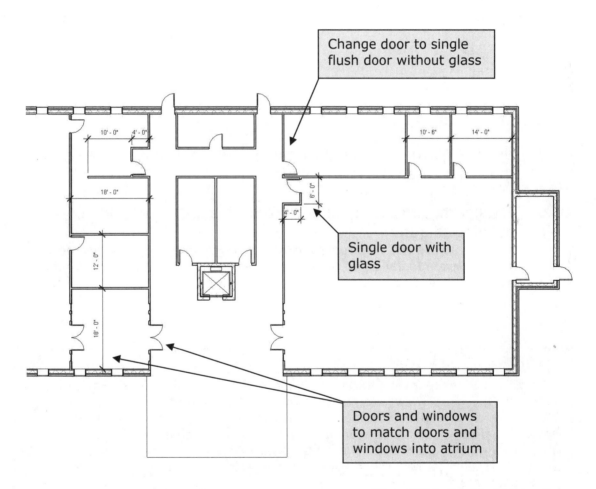

Figure 4-2.1 Level 1 Added walls

2. Similar to step 1, add the walls and doors shown in Figure 4-2.2 to **Level 3**.

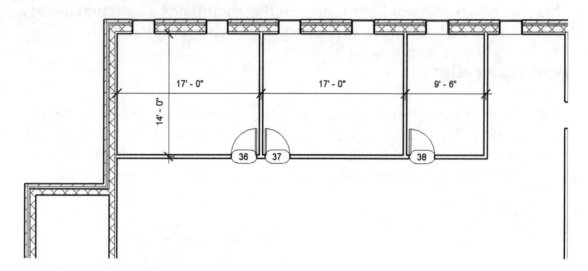

Figure 4-2.2 Level 3 Added walls

3. Use the *Mirror* command to mirror the walls in Figure 4-2.2 to the other three corners of Level 3.

4. Finally, modify the small office on the south, each side of building (Figure 4-2.3).
    TIP: *If you use the Trim tool (per the TIP in Figure 4-2.3), you will need to select "Delete Instance" to tell Revit to delete the door from the portion of wall that is being deleted.*

FYI:
Your modifications to level 3 included adding a few executive offices to the top floor with the "good" views. You deleted the small office on the south side to make room for a reception desk at the main doors from the atrium. Ideally you would add windows to the interior walls of the executive offices to let borrowed light into the open office area. The center area will be open office area for executive assistants. You will add doors to the stair shaft in Exercise 4-4, when you add the stairs.

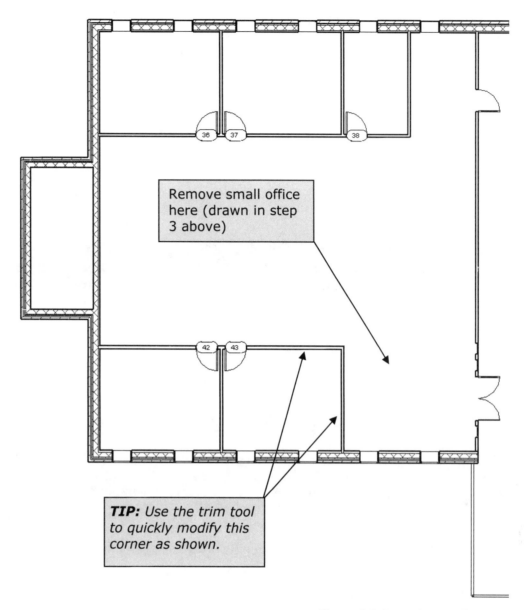

Remove small office here (drawn in step 3 above)

TIP: *Use the trim tool to quickly modify this corner as shown.*

Figure 4-2.3 Level 3 Modify walls

5. Save your project as **ex4-2.rvt**.

Exercise 4-3:
Setting the floor-to-floor height

You will modify the building's floor-to-floor height in this lesson. The reasons for doing this vary. Some examples might be to make the building shorter or taller to accommodate ductwork in the ceilings or the depth of the floor structure (the longer the span the deeper the structure). The default floor-to-floor height in the template file you started from is 10'-0", which is not typically feasibly for commercial construction.

Don't forget to keep a backup of your files on a separate disk (i.e., Flash Drive, CD or DVD). Your project file should be about 3 MB when starting this exercise. Remember, your Revit project is one large file (not many small files). You do not want anything to happen to it!

Modify the buildings floor-to-floor height:

1. Open ex4-2.rvt, Save As **ex4-3.rvt**.

2. Open the **South** exterior elevation from the *Project Browser*.

Change the floor-to–floor height to be 12'-0" for each level.

3. Select the floor elevation symbol, and then select the text displaying the elevation. You should now be able to type in a new number. Press Enter to see the changes. Notice the windows move because the sill height has not been changed. (Figure 4-3.1)

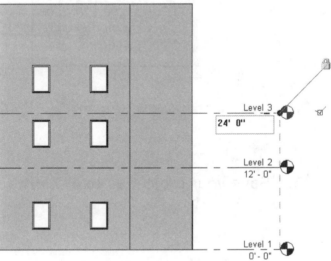

4. **Save** your project.

Figure 4-3.1 Exterior elevation: modifying Level 3 elevation

Exercise 4-4:
Stairs

Next you will add stairs to your stair shafts. Revit provides a powerful *Stairs* tool that allows you to design stairs quickly with various constraints previously specified (i.e., 7″ maximum riser).

Pre-defining parameters:

Before you draw the stair it will be helpful to review the options available in the stair family.

1. Open ex4-3.rvt and Save As **ex4-4.rvt**.

2. From the *Project Browser*, expand the Families → Stairs → Stair (i.e., click the plus sign next to these labels).

3. Right-click on the stair type: **7" max riser 11" tread**, and select the **properties** option from the pop-up menu.

You should now see the options shown in Figure 4-4.1.

Take a couple minutes to see what options are available. You will quickly review a few below.

- Tread: depth of tread in plan view.

- Nosing Length (Depth?): Treads are typically 12″ deep (usually code min.) and 1″ of that depth overlaps the next tread. This overlap is called the nosing.

- Riser: This provides Revit with the maximum dimension allowed (by code, or if you want it, less). The actual dimension will depend on the floor-to-floor height.

- Stringer dimensions: These dimensions usually vary per stair depending on the stair width, run and materials, to name a few. A structural engineer would provide this information after designing the stair.

- Cost: Estimating placeholder.

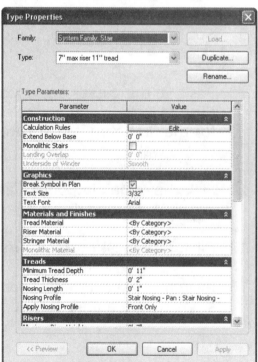

Figure 4-4.1 Stair type properties

Drawing the stairs in plan:

You will be drawing a standard switch-back stair. At first, when using Revit to draw stairs, it may be helpful to figure out the number of risers and landings. That information will be helpful when drawing the stair. As you become more familiar with the *Stairs* tool you will not need to do those calculations to draw a stair. Dividing the floor-to-floor height of 12'-0" by 7" we get 20.57. Obviously you cannot have a fraction of a riser so you need to round up to 21 (rounding down would make the riser higher than 7"). Therefore, 12'-0" divided by 21 equals 6.86". Thus you have 21 risers that are 6.86" high. Additionally, most codes would require a landing in a stair rising 12'-0".

4. Make sure you are in the **Level 1** floor plan view.

5. **Zoom in** to the west stair shaft.

6. Click on the **Modeling** tab in the *Design Bar*.

7. Select the **Stairs** tool (on the modeling tab).

8. Click on the **Stairs Properties** button that appeared in the *Design Bar*. (Figure 4-4.2)

9. Set the Width to **3'-6"**, and then select **OK**. (Figure 4-4.3)

10. Position the cursor approximately as shown in **Figure 4-4.4**; you are selecting the start point for the first step. Make sure you are snapping to the wall with *nearest*.

11. Pick the remaining points as shown in Figures 4-4.5, 4-4.6 and 4-4.7.

12. Click **Finish Sketch** (Figure 4-4.2).

13. Switch to Level 2 and repeat the previous steps to add a stair from Level 2 to Level 3.

Figure 4-4.2

Notice as you draw the stairs, Revit will display the number of risers drawn and the number of risers remaining to be drawn to reach the next level. If you click Finish Sketch before drawing all the required risers, Revit will display an error message. You can leave the problem to be resolved later.

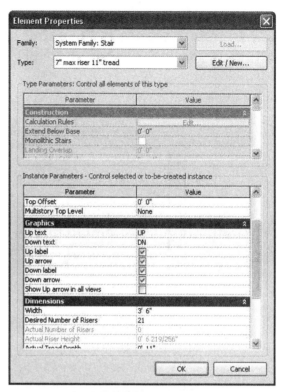

Figure 4-4.3 Stair properties

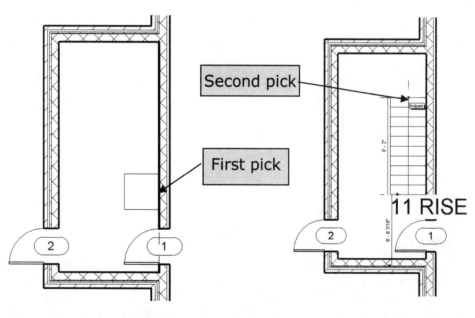

Figure 4-4.4 1st pick

Figure 4-4.5 2nd pick

Notice the **Multistory Top Level** parameter in Figure 4-4.3. If the floor to floor distance is the same for each floor you can use this feature to have Revit automatically repeat the stair all the way up the stair shaft!

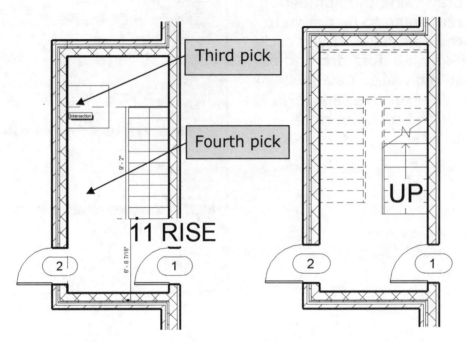

Figure 4-4.6 3rd and 4th picks   **Figure 4-4.7** Finished (Level 1)

14. Repeat these steps for the east stair shaft.

15. **Add doors** to the <u>second</u> and <u>third floors</u> for both the east and west stair shafts.

16. **Save** your project.

FYI:
Revit has drawn the intermediate landings between levels. However, the landings at the main floor levels have not been created. Many projects extend the primary floor structure into the stair shaft to act as the landing for that level and also support the stair. In a later lesson you will draw a floor system that extends into the stair shaft.

Stair sample file from Revit's web site:

Be sure to check out the sample stair project file on Revit's online content library (revit.autodesk.com/library/html). You can download this file and see examples of several different stair types side-by-side (see image below). You can select one and view its properties to see how it is done. You can also Copy/Paste one into your project, select your stair, and then select the newly imported type(s) from the Type Selector. The partial view of the sample file, shown below, has open riser, single stringer, no stringer, spiral, etc.

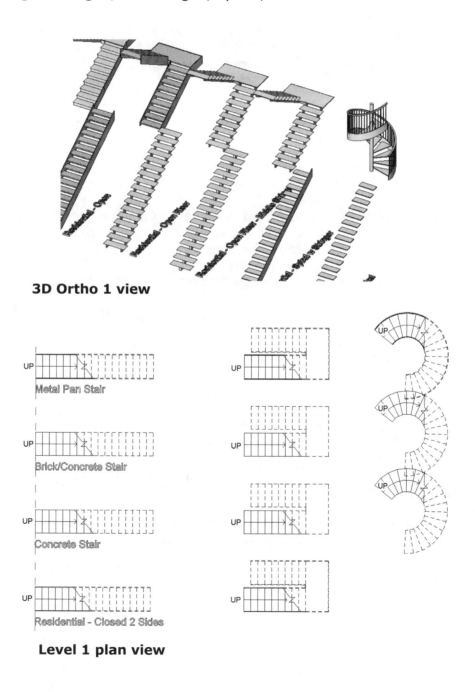

3D Ortho 1 view

Level 1 plan view

Self-Exam:

The following questions can be used as a way to check your knowledge of this lesson. The answers can be found at the bottom of this page.

1.   The default settings for the floor plan view shows the walls for the floor below. (T/F)
     T

2.   It is not possible to add a new floor level while in an elevation view. (T/F)
     F

3.   You should start drawing your floor plan generally centered on the default elevation tags in a new project. (T/F)
     T

4.   You can use the Align tool to align one wall with another across a hallway from the other line. (T/F)
     T

5.   Where do you change the maximum riser height? _____
     Properties

Review Questions:

The following questions may be assigned by your instructor as a way to assess your knowledge of this section. Your instructor has the answers to the review questions.

1.   It is not possible to copy/paste objects from one floor to another and have them line-up (with the original objects). (T/F)
     F

2.   If a shaft wall is to be built from the lowest level to the roof, and not interrupted at each floor level, the wall should be drawn with that height (not separate walls on each floor level). (T/F)
     T

3.   Each Revit view is saved as a separate file on your hard drive. (T/F)
     F

4.   You select the part of the wall to be deleted when using the Trim tool. (T/F)
     F

5.   You can change the floor-to-floor height by changing the level label (e.g., 24'-0" to 22'-0") in elevation. (T/F)
     T

6.   What parameter should be set to none, in the view properties dialog, if you do not want to see the walls from the floor below?

     _____
     underlay

7.   You use the _____ tool to create a new floor plan level when in an elevation view.
     level

8.   You can use the _____ tool to quickly select a certain type of object from a large group of selected objects.
     Filter

9.   The number of _____ remaining is displayed while sketching a stair.
     risers

Lesson 5
Office Building: ROOF::

This lesson will look at some of the various options and tools for designing a roof for your building. You will also add skylights.

Exercise 5-1:
Hip roof

The first step is to create a floor plan view at the roof level (top of your exterior masonry wall). This will create a working plane for the Roof tool.

Add elevation symbol:

1. Open ex4-4.rvt and **Save As ex5-1.rvt**.

2. Open the **South** elevation view.

3. Click on the **Level** tool from the *Design Bar's Basic* tab. Level

4. Draw a Level symbol at the top of the exterior wall, at elevation 36'-0" – see the wall properties. Draw the symbol so both ends align with the other symbols below it.

Next, you will rename the Level.

5. Press **Esc** or select **Modify** from the *Design Bar*.

6. Now select the level symbol you just drew.

7. With the level symbol selected, click on the text to rename the level label.

8. Change the label to **T.O. Masonry** (Figure 5-1.1).
   FYI: *T.O. means "Top Of".*

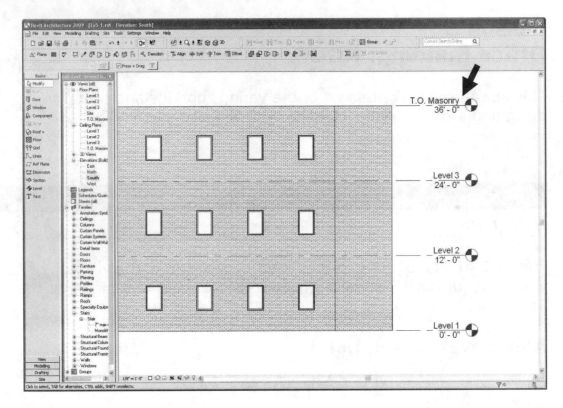

Figure 5-1.1 Renamed level symbol

9. Click **Yes** when prompted to rename corresponding views. (Figure 5-1.2)

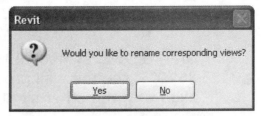

Figure 5-1.2 Rename prompt

These steps are the same you used to add the third floor. Notice the "T.O. Masonry" label is now listed in the *Floor Plans* section of the *Project Browser*.

Add a sloped roof:

10. Open the newly created **T. O. Masonry** Floor Plan view.

11. Select the **Roof** tool from the *Design Bar*.

12. Select "**Roof by footprint**" from the pop-up menu.

Before you start the roof you will change the slope (pitch) of the roof.

13. Click the **Properties** button on the *Options Bar*.

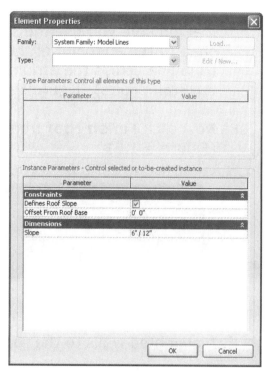

Figure 5-1.3 Properties

14. Change the **Slope** to **6"/12"**. Click **OK**.

This will make the roof pitch 6/12, which means; for every 12" horizontally the roof will *rise* 6" vertically.

15. You are now prompted to select exterior walls to define the footprint. Select ONLY the wall segments that define the 120'-0" x 60'-0" portion of the building. (Figure 5-1.4) Pick the exterior side of the walls.

You will notice in Figure 5-1.4 that there are three sections along the perimeter of the rectangle that are open because no wall is available to pick. You will need to draw three lines to close the "footprint."

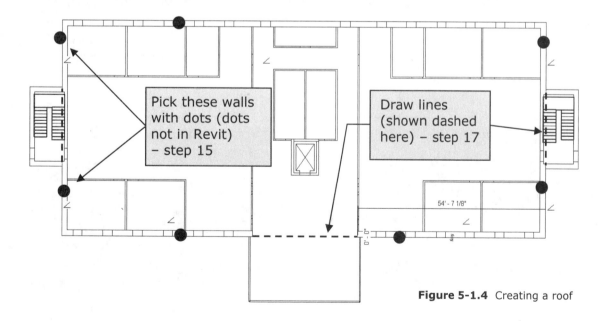

Pick these walls with dots (dots not in Revit) – step 15

Draw lines (shown dashed here) – step 17

54' - 7 1/8"

Figure 5-1.4 Creating a roof

16. Select the **Lines** tool from the *Design Bar* (Figure 5-1.5).

17. Draw three lines to create a complete rectangle, making sure you use the snaps to accurately snap to the endpoint of the lines already present (one line across the atrium and the other two at the stair shafts) (Figure 5-1.4).

18. Now click **Finish roof** from the *Design Bar*. (Figure 5-1.5)

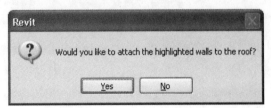

Figure 5-1.6 Prompt

Figure 5-1.5
Roof sub-tools

19. Click **NO** when prompted to attach the highlighted walls to the roof (Figure 5-1.6).

You will now see a portion of the roof in your plan view. The cutting plane is 4'-0" above the floor level, so you are seeing the roof thickness in section at 4'-0" above the T.O. Masonry level.

- Switch to an elevation view to see the roof, south elevation, shown in Figure 5-1.7.

- You can also switch to the default 3D view to see the roof in isometric view.

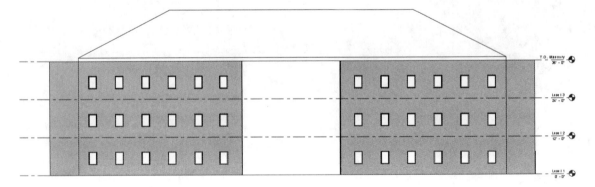

Figure 5-1.7 South elevation

After looking at the roof you have created, switch back to the plan view: **T.O. Masonry**. You will now add a roof over the east stair shaft.

20. **Zoom in** on the east stair shaft.

21. Select the **Roof** tool; and click *"Roof by Footprint."*

22. With **Defines Slope** checked in the *Options Bar*, pick the three exterior walls at the stair shaft.

23. Uncheck **Defines Slope**, and then select the **Line** tool and draw a line as shown in Figure 5-1.8 to close the footprint. Be sure to use snaps to accurately draw the enclosed area.

24. Pick the **Modify** button and then select the line you just drew.

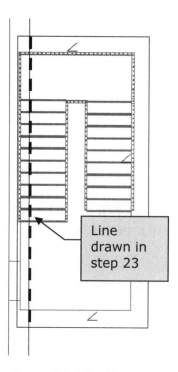

Line drawn in step 23

Figure 5-1.8 Roof footprint; East stair

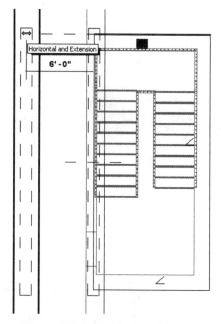

Horizontal and Extension

6'-0"

Figure 5-1.9 Modified roof footprint; East stair

25. Use the **Move** command to move the line **6'-0"** to the west. (Figure 5-1.9)

26. Select **Finish Roof** from the *Design Bar* (Figure 5-1.5).

27. Click **NO** when prompted to attach the highlighted walls to the roof (Figure 5-1.6).

28. Switch to the **south** elevation view. (Figure 5-1.10)

29. Switch back to the **T.O. Masonry** view.

30. Select the roof object over the east stair shaft.

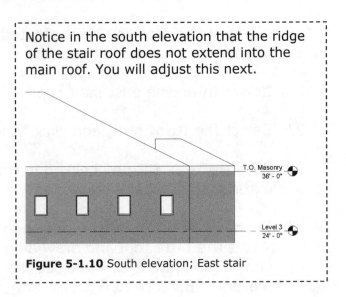

Notice in the south elevation that the ridge of the stair roof does not extend into the main roof. You will adjust this next.

T.O. Masonry
36' - 0"

Level 3
24' - 0"

Figure 5-1.10 South elevation; East stair

31. Switch to the **Default 3D View** and Adjust your view to look similar to **Figure 5-1.11**.

32. Select **Join/Unjoin Roof** from the *Tools* pull-down menu.

You will now select the two edges of the roofs that you want to come together.

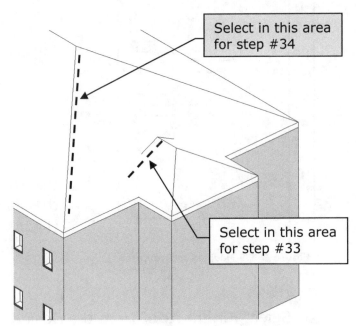

Select in this area for step #34

Select in this area for step #33

Figure 5-1.11 Default 3D View

33. Select the edge of the smaller roof; see Figure 5-1.11.

34. Select the edge of the larger roof; see Figure 5-1.11.

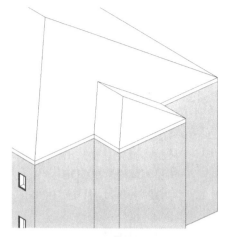

Your roof should now look similar to Figure 5-1.12. Take another look at the south elevation to see the revision.

35. Repeat the previous steps to create a roof over the west stair shaft.

Figure 5-1.12 Joined roof

Atrium roof:

Next you will create a roof over the atrium area. We want a 4'-0" high aluminum panel above the curtain wall, thus pushing the atrium roof up higher. You will need to create a new wall type for the aluminum panels.

36. Switch to the **T.O. Masonry** view.

37. Select the **Wall** tool and then select the **Basic Wall – Generic – 5"** type.

38. Click **Properties**, click **Edit /New**, click **Duplicate**.

39. Type **exterior wall – aluminum** for the name.

40. Add an **exterior finish** (via edit wall structure) with the material set to **Metal – Aluminum** and edit structure thickness (Figure 5-1.13).

41. Draw three walls, so their exterior faces align with the exterior face of the curtain wall below. Be sure to use snaps and set the wall height to **4'-0"** (Figure 5-1.14).

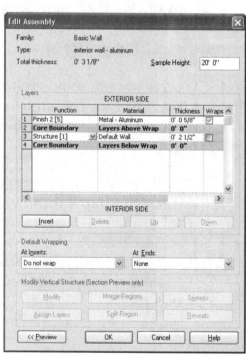

Figure 5-1.13 New wall structure

The walls running north-south need to extend far enough back into the main roof to avoid any holes.

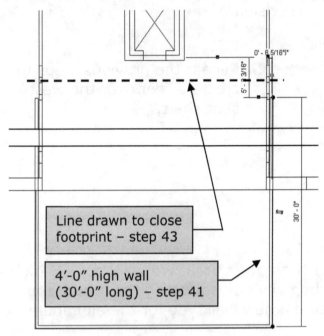

Line drawn to close footprint – step 43

4'-0" high wall (30'-0" long) – step 41

Figure 5-1.14 4'-0" high wall above curtain wall in atrium

42. Use the **Roof** tool to select the three walls just drawn, using the footprint option; "Defines slope" checked.

43. Use the **Lines** tool to draw a line to close the open side (Figure 5-1.14). This will create a closed rectangle to complete the roof; "Defines slope" unchecked.

44. Before finishing the roof, select **Roof Properties** and set the **Base offset from level** to **4'-0"**. This will place the roof on top of the 4'-0" high wall you just drew.

45. Select **Finish Roof**.

Your 3D view should look similar to **Figure 5-1.15**. Like the stair roof, the atrium roof needs to be joined to the main roof.

46. **Click NO** when prompted to attach the highlighted walls to the roof (Figure 5-1.6).

47. Use the **Join/Unjoin Roof** tool to join the atrium roof to the main roof.

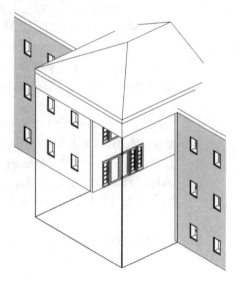

Figure 5-1.15 3D view

Look at the side elevations. If the roof does not extend all the way to the main roof, select the roof and pick Edit (on the *Options Bar*) to move the line further into the building. When finished it should look like Figure 5-1.16.

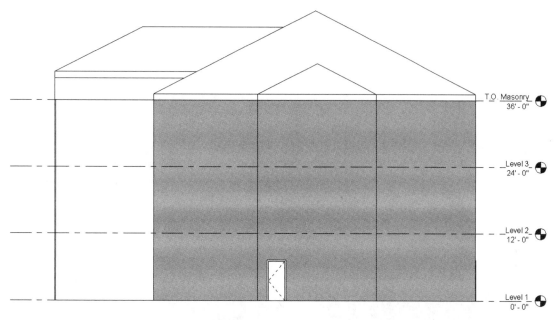

Figure 5-1.16 Atrium roof

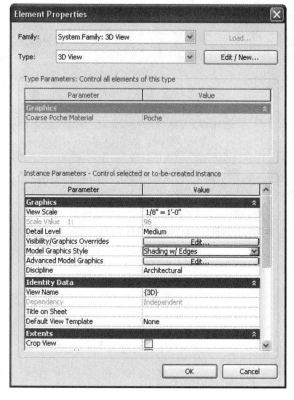

Figure 5-1.17 Setting model graphics style

Next you will take a quick look at the project, thus far, in an isometric view.

48. Click the 3D icon.

The 3D view can be improved by shading the surfaces.

49. Right-click on the **3D** view under *3D Views* in the *Project Browser* and pick **Properties**.

50. Set the **Model Graphics Style** to **Shaded w/ Edges** and then click **OK**. (Figure 5-1.17)

TIP: *The previous setting can also be controlled via the View Control Bar at the lower left of your screen (see image to right).*

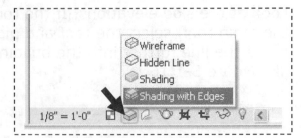

TIP: *You can also turn on the real-time shadows from the View Control Bar (see image to right).*

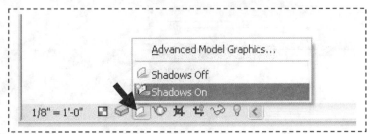

The 3D Model should now be shaded (Figure 5-1.18).

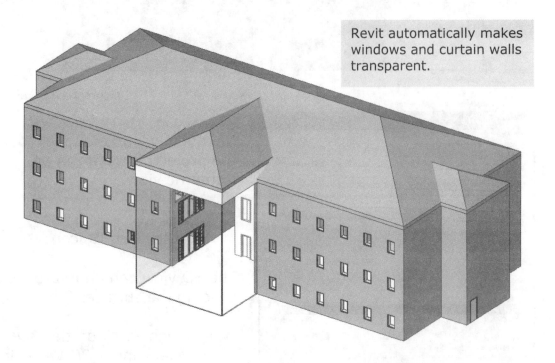

Revit automatically makes windows and curtain walls transparent.

Figure 5-1.18 Shaded model

51. **Save** your project.

Try adjusting the view; click and drag on the ViewCube.

Exercise 5-2:
Skylights

This short exercise covers inserting skylights in your roof. The process is much like inserting windows. In fact, Revit lists the skylight types with the window types, so you use the *Window* tool to insert skylights into your project.

Inserting skylights:

You will place the skylights in an elevation view.

1. Load project file **ex5-1.rvt**.

2. Switch to the **South** elevation view.

3. Select the **Window** tool and load the *skylight* group (skylight.rfa) into the project (via the *Load* button on the *Options Bar*).

4. Select **Skylight: 24" x 27"** from the type selector.

You are now ready to place skylights in the roof. Revit will only look for roof objects when placing skylights, so you don't have to worry about a skylight ending up in a wall.

5. Roughly place four skylights as shown in Figure 5-2.1.

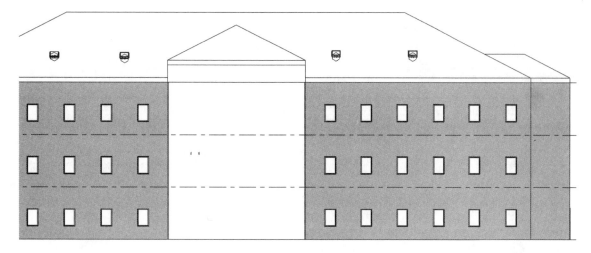

Figure 5-2.1 South elevation, skylights added

6. Press **Esc** or click the **Modify** tool to cancel in *Window* tool.

Next, you will want to align the skylights with each other.

7. Switch to the **West** elevation view.

8. Select one of the visible skylights.

You should now have the skylight selected and see the reference dimensions that allow you to adjust the exact location of the object. Occasionally, the dimension does not go to the point on the drawing that you are interested in referencing from. Revit allows you to adjust where those temporary dimensions point to.

9. Click and drag the grip shown in Figure 5-2.2 to (wait until it snaps) to the ridge of the main roof (Figure 5-2.3).

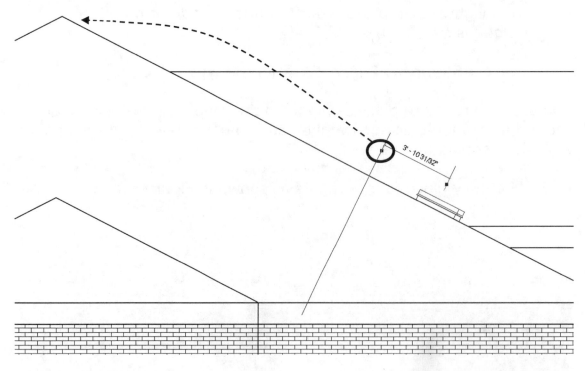

Figure 5-2.2 West elevation: default dimension shown when selecting skylight.

10. Click on the dimension text and change the text to **22'-8"**. **NOTE:** *This would adjust the position of the skylight relative to the roof.*

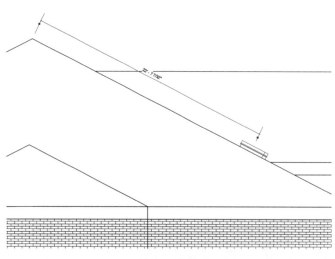

11. Select the other skylight on the west elevation and adjust it to match the one you just revised.

Figure 5-2.3 West elevation: default dimension shown when selecting skylight.

12. Switch to the East elevation and repeat the above steps to adjust.

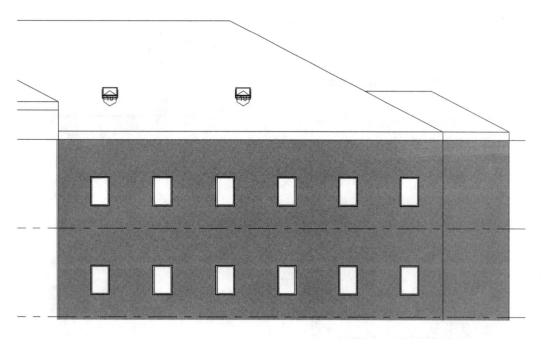

Figure 5-2.4 South elevation: with skylights added

Your drawing should look similar to the one above. Notice that the skylight tag is right on top of the skylight. You will adjust that next.

13. **Zoom in** on one of the skylights and **click** on the skylight tag (south view).

14. You should see a symbol appear near the bottom of the symbol, Drag on this symbol to move the tag down (Figure 5-2.5).

15. Position the skylight tag so the tag does not overlap the skylight. (Figure 5-2.6)

16. Adjust the other skylights tags; as you reposition these tags you may see a reference line appear indicating the symbol will automatically align with an adjacent symbol.

Take a minute to look at your shaded 3D view and try changing the view so you can see through the skylight glass into the spaces below (Figure 5-2.7).

17. **Save** as **ex5-2.rvt**.

Figure 5-2.5 Enlarged skylight detail

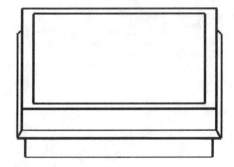

Figure 5-2.7 Shaded skylight view

Figure 5-2.6 Enlarged skylight detail — revised

Exercise 5-3:
Roof Design options (Style, Pitch and Overhang)

In this lesson you will look at the various ways to use the **Roof** tool to draw the more common roof forms used in architecture today.

Start a new Revit Project:

You will start a new project for this lesson so you can quickly compare the results of using the **Roof** tool.

1. Start a new project using the **default.rte** template.

2. Switch to the **North** elevation view and rename the Level named *Level 2* to **T.O. Masonry**. This will be the reference point for your roof. Click **Yes** to rename corresponding views automatically.

    TIP: *Just select the Level datum and click on the Level tag's text to rename.*

    T.O. Masonry
    10' - 0"

3. Switch to the **Level 1** floor plan view.

Draw walls to setup for using the Roof tool:

4. Set the Level 1 "*Detail Level*" to **medium,** so the material hatching is visible within the walls.

    TIP: *Right-click on Level 1 in project browser and select Properties or use the View Control Bar at the bottom.*

5. Using the **Wall** tool and wall type set to "**Exterior - Brick on Mtl. Stud**," draw a **40'-0" x 20'-0"** building (Figure 5-3.1).

    FYI: *The default Wall height is okay. (It should be 20'-0".)*

Be sure to draw the
building within the
elevation tags.

*TIP: You can draw the
building in one step if you
use the rectangle option on
the Options Bar (while using
the Wall tool).*

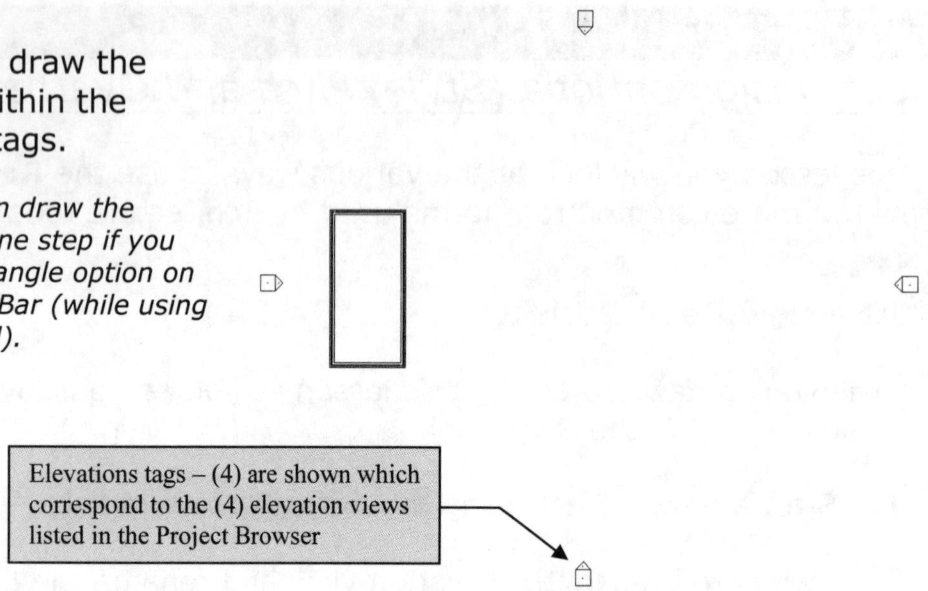

Elevations tags – (4) are shown which
correspond to the (4) elevation views
listed in the Project Browser

Figure 5-3.1 Bldg. and Elev. tags

You will copy the building so that you have a total of four. You will
draw a different type of roof on each one.

6. Drag a window around the walls to select them. Then use the
   Array command to setup four buildings **35'-0" O.C.**
   (Figure 5-3.2); see *ARRAY TIP* below.

*TIP: Zoom in and make
sure the brick is on the
exterior side of the wall, if
not you can select each
wall and click its flip icon.*

*ARRAY TIP: Select the
first building, select Array,
and then, just like the
Copy command, define a
copy 35' to the right, and
then enter the number of
copies.*

Figure 5-3.2 Four buildings

7. Select all of the buildings and click **Ungroup** from the *Options
   Bar*.

Hip roof:

The various roof forms are largely defined by the "Defines Slope" setting. This is displayed in the *Options Bar* while the **Roof** tool is active. When a wall is selected, while the "Defines slope" option is selected, the roof above that portion of wall slopes. You will see this more clearly in the examples below.

8. Switch to the **T.O. Masonry** view.

9. Select the **Roof** tool, and then **Roof by Footprint** from the pop-up menu that appears after selecting the **Roof** tool.

10. Set the overhang to **2'-0"** and make sure **Defines slope** is selected (checked) in the *Options Bar*.

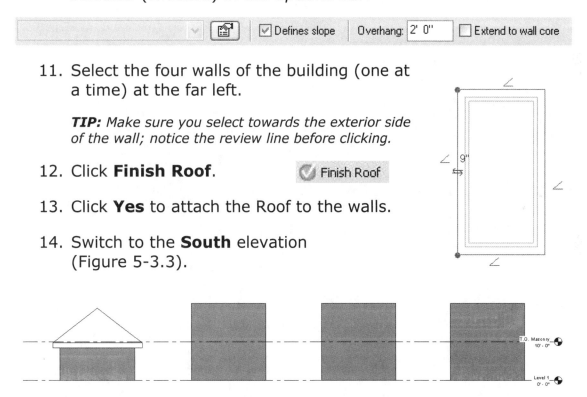

11. Select the four walls of the building (one at a time) at the far left.

    TIP: Make sure you select towards the exterior side of the wall; notice the review line before clicking.

12. Click **Finish Roof**.

13. Click **Yes** to attach the Roof to the walls.

14. Switch to the **South** elevation (Figure 5-3.3).

Figure 5-3.3 South elevation – hip roof

You will notice that the default wall height is much higher than what we ultimately want. However, when the roof is drawn at the correct elevation and you attach the walls to the roof, the walls automatically adjust to stop under the roof object. Additionally, if the roof is raised or lowered later, the walls will follow; you can try this in the South elevation view by simply using the *Move* tool. **REMEMBER:** *You can make revisions in any view.*

15. Switch to the **3D** view using the icon on the *View* toolbar (Figure 5-3.4).

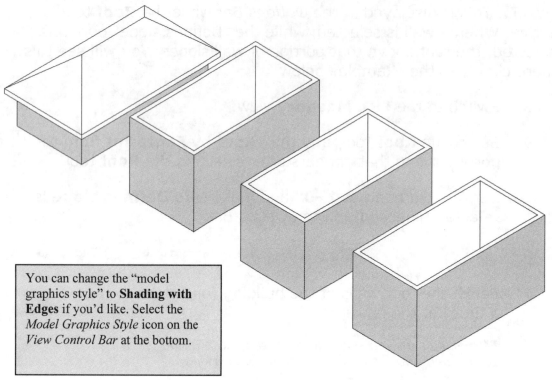

You can change the "model graphics style" to **Shading with Edges** if you'd like. Select the *Model Graphics Style* icon on the *View Control Bar* at the bottom.

Figure 5-3.4 3D view – hip roof

Gable roof:

16. Switch back to the **T.O. Masonry** view.

17. Select the **Roof** tool, and then **Roof by Footprint**.

18. Set the overhang to **2'-0"** and make sure **Defines slope** is selected (checked) in the *Options Bar*.

19. Only select the two long (40'-0") walls.

20. **Uncheck** the **Defines slope** option.

21. Select the remaining two walls (Figure 5-3.5).

22. Pick **Finish Roof**. ✅ Finish Roof

23. Select **Yes** to attach the walls to the roof.

24. Switch to the **South** elevation view (Figure 5-3.6).

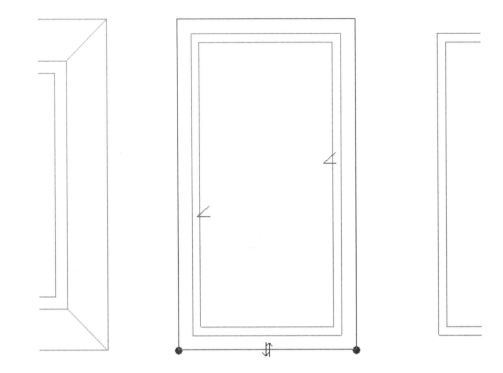

Figure 5-3.5 Gable – plan view

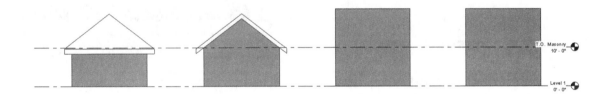

Figure 5-3.6 South elevation – gable roof

25. Switch to the **3D** view (Figure 5-3.7).

Notice the wall extends up to conform to the underside of the roof on the gable ends.

FYI:

You may be wondering why the roofs look odd in the floor plan view. If you remember, each view has its own cut plane. The "cut plane" happens to be lower than the highest part of the roof – thus, the roof is shown cut at the "cut plane". If you go to *View Properties → View Range* and then adjust the "cut plane" to be higher than the highest point of the roof, then you will see the ridge line.

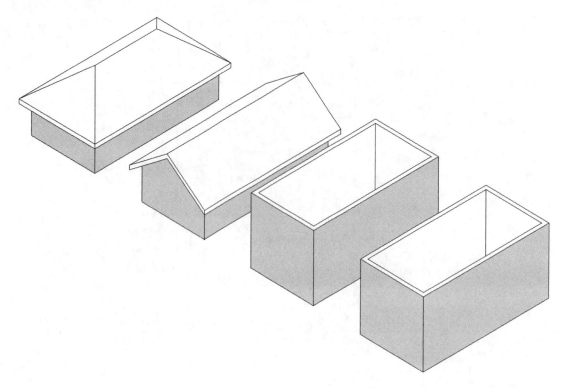

Figure 5-3.7 3D view – gable roof

Shed roof:

26. Switch back to the **T.O. Masonry** view.

27. Select the **Roof** tool, and then **Roof by Footprint**.

28. Check **Defines slope**.

29. Click on the **Properties** button on the *Options Bar*.

30. Set the roof pitch to 3/12 (Figure 5-3.8); click **OK**.

    FYI: The "Defines slope" option must be selected to change the pitch.

31. Set the overhang to **2'-0"** and make sure **Defines slope** is selected (checked) on the *Options Bar*.

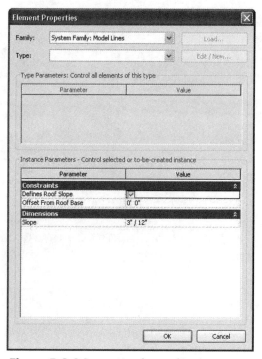

Figure 5-3.8 Properties for roof tool

32. Select the east wall (40'-0" wall, right).

33. **Uncheck Defines slope** in the *Options Bar*.

34. Select the remaining three walls. (Figure 5-3.9)

35. Pick **Finish Roof**.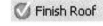

36. Select **Yes** to attach the walls to the roof.

FYI: *You can also change the pitch of the roof by changing the Pitch Control text (see Figure 5-3.9); just select the text and type a new number.*

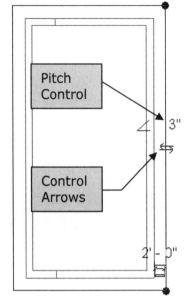

Figure 5-3.9 Selected walls

TIP:

You can use the **Control Arrows** (while the roof line is still selected) to flip the orientation of the roof overhang if you accidentally selected the wrong side of the wall (and the overhang is on the inside of the building).

---

37. Switch to the **South** elevation view (Figure 5-3.10).

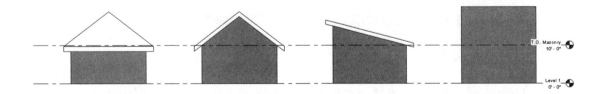

Figure 5-3.10 South elevation – shed roof

38. Switch to the **3D** view (Figure 5-3.11).

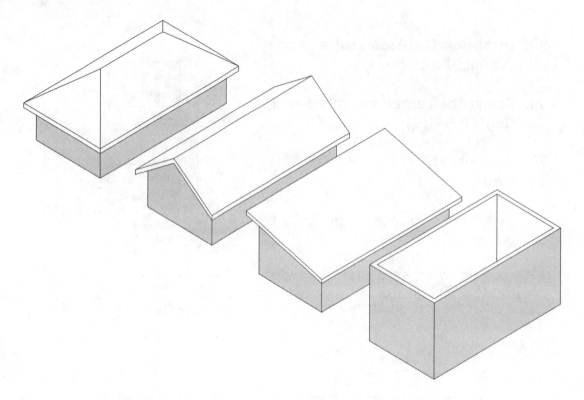

Figure 5-3.11 Default 3D view – shed roof

Once the roof is drawn, you can easily change the roof's overhang. You will try this on the shed roof. You will also make the roof slope in the opposite direction.

39. In **T.O. Masonry** view, select **Modify** from the *Design Bar*, and then select the *Shed* roof.

40. Click **Edit** from the *Options Bar*.   Edit

41. Click on the east (right) roof sketch-line to select it.

42. **Uncheck Defines slope** from the *Options Bar*.

43. Now select the west roofline and check **Defines slope**.

If you were to select Finish Roof now, the shed roof would be sloping in the opposite direction. But, before you do that, you will adjust the roof overhang at the high side.

44. Click on the east roofline again, to select it.

45. Change the overhang to **6'-0"** in the *Options Bar*.

Changing the overhang only affects the selected roofline.

46. Select **Finish Roof**.

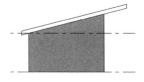

47. Switch to the South view to see the change (Figure 5-3.12).

That concludes the shed roof example.

Figure 5-3.12 South elevation – shed roof (revised)

Flat roof:

48. Switch back to the **T.O. Masonry** view.

49. Select the **Roof** tool and then **Roof by Footprint**.

50. Set the overhang to **2'-0"** and make sure **Defines slope** is not selected (i.e., un-checked) in the *Options Bar*.

51. Select all four walls.

52. Pick **Finish Roof**.

53. Select **Yes** to attach the walls to the roof.

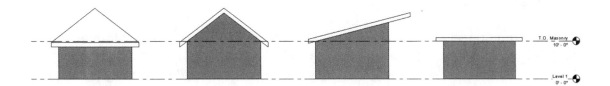

Figure 5-3.13 South elevation – flat roof

54. Switch to the **South** elevation view (Figure 5-3.13).

55. Also, take a look the **3D** view (Figure 5-3.14).

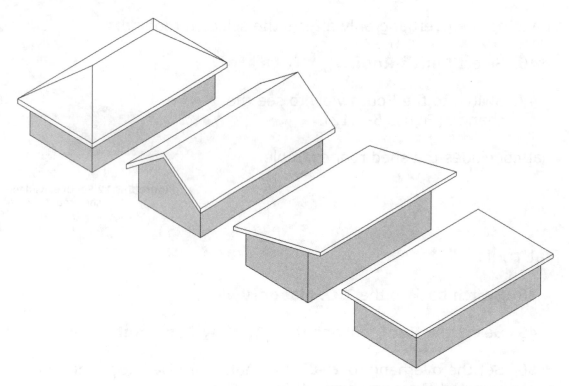

Figure 5-3.14 Default 3D view – flat roof

56. Save your project as **ex5-3.rvt**.

Want more?

Revit has additional tools and techniques available for creating more complex roof forms. However, that is beyond the scope of this book. If you want to learn more about roofs, or anything else, take a look at one of the following resources:

- Revit **Tutorials** from the *Help* pull-down menu
- Revit **Web Site** (www.autodesk.com)
- Revit **Newsgroup** (potential answers to specific questions)
  (www.augi.com; www.revitcity.com; www.autodesk.com)

Self-Exam:

The following questions can be used as a way to check your knowledge of this lesson. The answers can be found at the bottom of this page.

1. You don't have to click *Finish Roof* when you are done defining a roof. (T/F)
   F

2. The wall below the roof automatically conforms to the underside of the roof when you join the walls to the roof. (T/F)
   T

3. The roof overhang setting is available from the *Options Bar*. (T/F)
   T

4. To create a gable roof on a building with 4 walls, two of the walls should not have the _____ option checked.
   defines slop

5. Is it possible to change the reference point for a temporary dimension that is displayed while an object is selected? (Y/N)
   Yes

Review Questions:

The following questions may be assigned by your instructor as a way to assess your knowledge of this section. Your instructor has the answers to the review questions.

1. When creating a roof using the "*create roof by specifying footprint*" option, you need to create a closed perimeter. (T/F)
   T

2. Can the "*Defines Slope*" setting be changed after the roof is "finished?" (Y/N)
   YES

3. Skylights need to be rotated to align with the plane (pitch) of the roof. (T/F)
   F

4. Skylights automatically make the glass transparent in shaded views. (T/F)
   T

5. While using the **Roof** tool, you can use the _____ tool from the *Design Bar* to fill in the missing segments to close the perimeter.
   Line

6. You use the _____ parameter to adjust the vertical position of the roof relative to the current working plane (view).
   offset from roof base

7. While using the **Roof** tool, you need to select the _____ tool from the *Design Bar* before you can select a roofline for modification.
   modify arrow

8. You need to use the _____ _____ to flip the roofline when you pick the wrong side of the wall and the overhang is shown on the inside.
   Control arrows

Self-Exam Answers:
1 - F, **2** – T, **3** – T, **4** – defines slope, **5** – Y

Notes:

Lesson 6
Office Building: FLOOR SYSTEMS AND REFLECTED CEILING PLANS::

In this lesson you will learn to create floor structures and reflected ceiling plans.

Even though you currently have floor levels defined, you do not have an object that represents the mass of the floor systems. You will add floor systems with holes for stairs, elevators, and the atrium.

Ceiling systems allow you to specify the ceiling material by room and the height above the floor. Once the ceiling has been added it will show up in section views (sections are created later in this book).

Exercise 6-1:
Floor Systems

Similar to other Revit objects, you can select from a few pre-defined object types. You can also create new types. In your office building you will use a pre-defined floor system for the two upper levels and create a new type for the first level.

Level 1, Slab on Grade:

Sketching floors is a lot like sketching roofs (Lesson 5); you can select walls to define the perimeter and draw lines to fill in the blanks and add holes (cut-outs) in the floor object.

1. Open ex5-2.rvt and **Save As ex6-1.rvt**.

2. Switch to the **Level 1** floor plan view.

3. From the *Basic* tab on the *Design Bar*, select **Floor**.

4. Click the **Floor Properties** command on the *Design Bar.*

5. Click **Edit/New**.

6. Click **Duplicate**.

7. Type **6" Slab on Grade**, then **OK**.

8. Click the **Edit** button next to the *Structure* Parameter.

9. Change the material for the structure layer shown to **Concrete: cast-in-place concrete**, and change the thickness to **6"**.

10. Next you will add carpet on top of the slab.

11. Add another layer:
    a. *Function*: **Finish 1 [4]**
    b. *Material*: **Carpet (1)**
    c. *Thickness:* **1/4"**.
    (Figure 6-1.1)

12. Click **OK** to close the open dialog boxes.

13. Select all the exterior walls on **Level 1**; this should include the curtain wall at the atrium and the stair shafts (Figure 6-1.3).

    TIP: *Select the interior side of the wall; you can use the control arrows if needed.*

14. Click **Finish Sketch**.

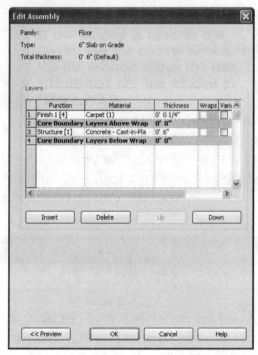

Figure 6-1.1 New Floor System

You will most likely get an error message. This is because the main exterior walls extend into the atrium (past the curtain wall). Because this is not a perfect corner (and it does not need to be), you can trim the "edge of slab" lines while in sketch mode to create a true corner, i.e., a closed line (Figure 6-1.2).

15. *(If you did not get an error skip ahead to step 18.)* Click **Continue**.

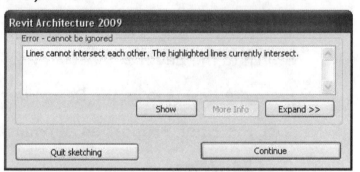

Figure 6-1.2 Floor error message

16. Use the **Trim** tool; select the two lines leading to the corner that needs to be trimmed. Do this for both sides of the atrium (Figure 6-1.3).

17. Click **Finish Sketch**.

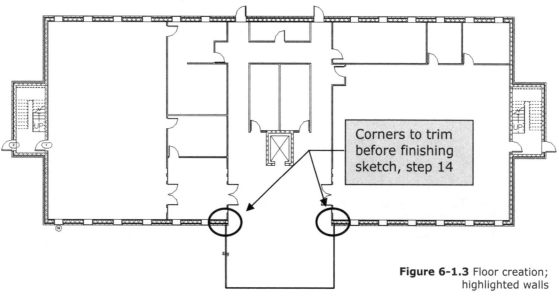

Corners to trim before finishing sketch, step 14

Figure 6-1.3 Floor creation; highlighted walls

You now have a floor at the first level. You should see a stipple pattern representing the floor area. You would most likely want to turn that pattern off for a floor plan. You will do that next.

18. In the *Project Browser*, right-click on the **Floor Plan: Level 1** view.

19. Select **Properties**.

20. Select **Edit**, next to the *Visibility* parameter (Figure 6-1.4).

21. In the *View Visibility/ Graphics window*, click the "cell" at the intersection of *Floors* (row) and *Surface/ Patterns* (column); select **Override** (Figure 6-1.5).

22. Uncheck **Visible**.

23. Click **OK** to close the dialogs.

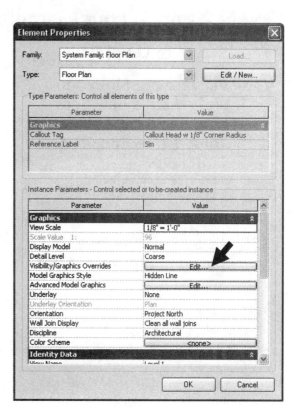

Figure 6-1.4 Level 1 view Properties

The stipple pattern is no longer visible.

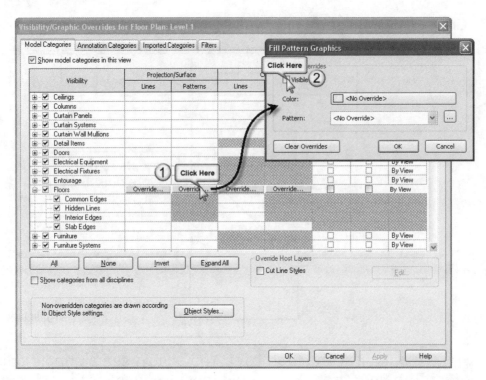

Figure 6-1.5 View Visibility

 ## Levels 2 and 3, conc. + metal deck + bar joists:

24. Switch to **Level 2** view.

25. Activate the **Floor** tool and create a new floor type named: **Steel Bar Joist 14" – Carpet on Concrete.**
    TIP: Use a similar floor type as a starting point (duplicate) when creating new floor types.

26. Adjust/add the layers shown in **Figure 6-1.6.**

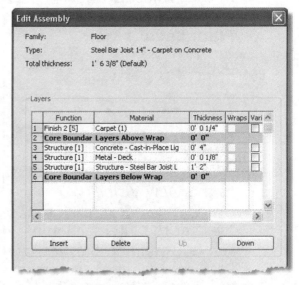

Figure 6-1.6 Floor system – edit structure

FYI:

Notice the Metal Deck thickness is set to ⅛" in Figure 6-1.6. Mtl. Deck is commonly 1½", but occurs within the thickness of the concrete. If both the deck and the concrete had thickness, the floor would be shown thicker than it should be. Of course you need to consult a structural engineer to get the correct joist and slab dimensions.

Creating the second and third floors will be a little more involved than was the first floor. This is because the upper floors require several openings. For example, you need to define the openings for the elevator, the stair shafts and the atrium space. Revit makes the process very simple.

You should still be in the *Floor* tool.

27. In the *Options Bar*, check "**extend into wall (to core)**."

FYI:

The *"extend into wall (to core)"* option will extend the slab to your CMU (CMU is the core in our example), and go under the furring. Depending on the design, the floor may extend to the exterior face of the CMU, allowing the CMU to bear on the floor slab at each level. In this exercise you will select the interior side.

---

28. Select the exterior walls indicated in Figure 6-1.7. *Remember to select the interior side of the wall, use the control arrows if needed.*

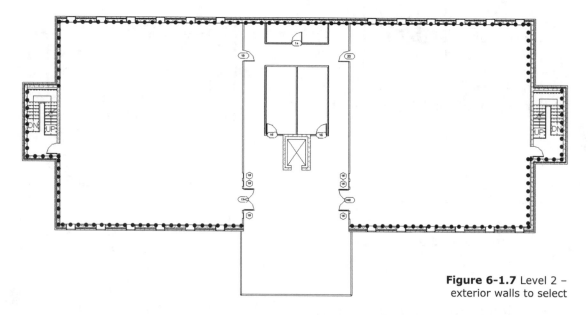

Figure 6-1.7 Level 2 – exterior walls to select

Next you will define the portion of floor that extends into the stair shaft to be the landing at this level. You will need to use the *Lines* tool and the *Trim* tool to define this area.

29. Click on the **Lines** tool from the *Design Bar*.

30. **Zoom In** to the west stair shaft.

31. Draw a <u>horizontal</u> line defining the edge of the landing; use Revit's snaps to accurately pick the top riser as shown in **Figure 6-1.8**.

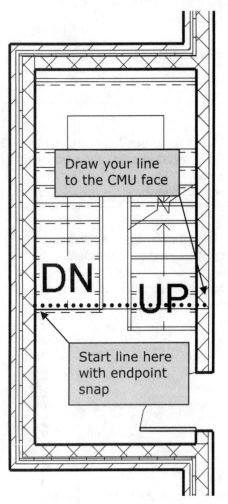

Draw your line to the CMU face

Start line here with endpoint snap

Figure 6-1.8 Level 2 – west stair

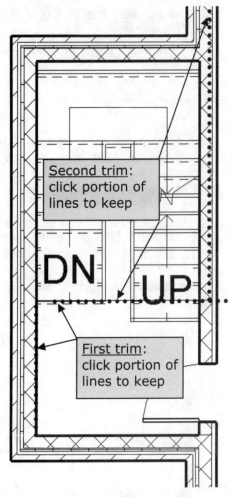

Second trim: click portion of lines to keep

First trim: click portion of lines to keep

Figure 6-1.9 Level 2 – west stair trim lines

32. Select the *Trim* tool and trim the three lines referenced in **Figure 6-1.9**.

33. Repeat these steps for the east stair shaft.

34. Next you will pick the four walls at the elevator shaft, selecting the shaft side of the wall; be sure to use the **Pick Walls** feature from the *Design Bar*.

You are now ready to define the edge of the slab at the atrium.

35. Use the **Lines** tool to draw the edge of slab in the atrium (5 lines) as shown in **Figure 6-1.10**.

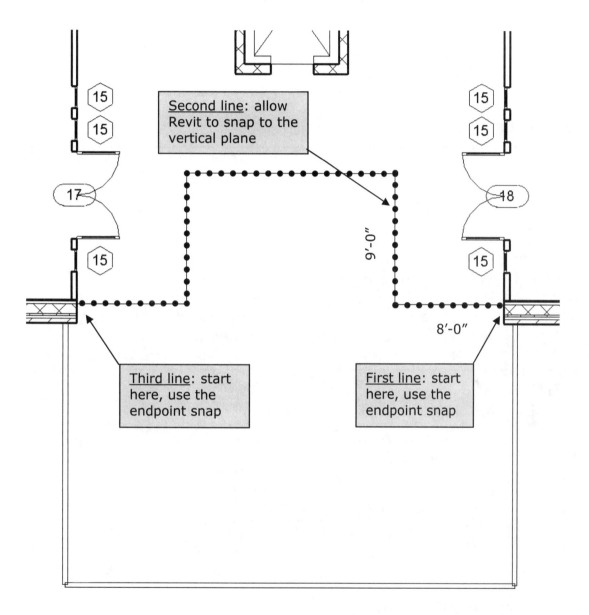

Figure 6-1.10 Atrium slab definition

36. Click **Finish Sketch**.

37. If you get this prompt: Click **Yes** to the prompt *"Would you like the walls that go up to this floor's level to attach to its bottom?"*

38. Click **Yes** for the prompt to join the walls that overlap the floor system (Figure 6-1.11).

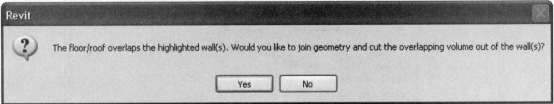

Figure 6-1.11 Join walls to floor prompt

39. Change Level 2's *Visibility* to turn off the floor hatch.

That completes the Level 2 floor system. Next you will copy the floor you just created to Level 3.

40. Select the Level 2 floor you just created and select **Copy to Clipboard** from the *Edit* pull-down menu.

> **TIP:**
> Selecting objects that overlap, like the exterior walls and the edge of slab (floor system), may require the use of the **TAB key**. The only way to select a floor object is by picking its edge. Revit temporarily highlights objects when you move your cursor over them. But, because the floor edge may not have an "exposed" edge to select (e.g., like we have in the atrium area), you will have to toggle through your selection options for your current cursor location. With the cursor positioned over the edge of the floor (probably with an exterior wall highlighted), press the TAB key to toggle through the available options. A tool-tip will display the objects; when you see *floor:floor-name*, click the mouse.

41. Switch to **Level 3**.

42. Pick **Edit → Paste Aligned → Current View**.

43. Change Level 3's *Visibility* to turn off the floor hatch.

44. Explore your work by looking at the model in 3D.
(Figure 6-1.12)
Notice again how Revit automatically applies colors and patterns to surfaces to help you (and your client) better visualize your design with minimal effort.

45. Save your project as **ex6-1.rvt**.

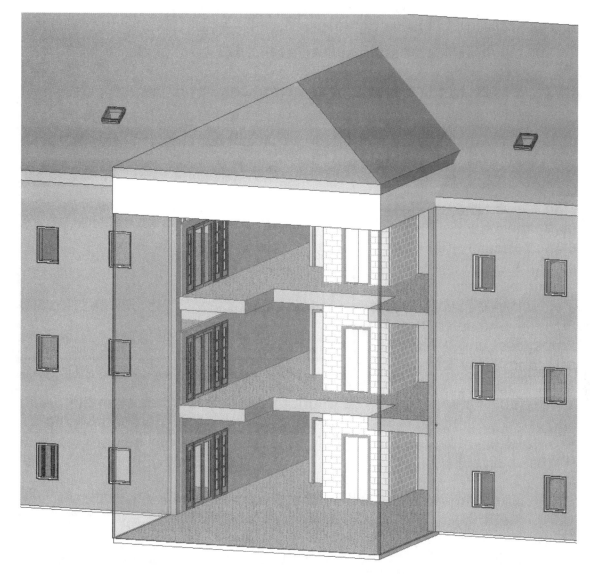

Figure 6-1.12 3D view with floors

Exercise 6-2:
Ceiling Systems (Susp. ACT and Gypsum Board)

This lesson will explore Revit's tools for drawing reflected ceiling plans. This will include drawing different types of ceiling systems.

Suspended Acoustical Ceiling Tile System:

1. Open ex6-1.rvt and Save As **ex6-2.rvt**.

2. Switch to the **Level 1** <u>ceiling plan</u> view, from the *Project Browser.*

Notice the doors and windows are automatically turned off in the ceiling plan views. The ceiling plan views have a cutting plane similar to floor plans. You can see this setting by right-clicking on a view name in the *Project Browser* and selecting *Properties*, and then selecting **View Range**.

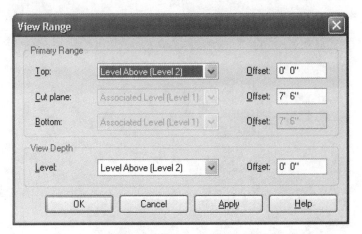

Figure 6-2.1 Properties: View Range settings

The default value is 7'-6". You might increase this if, for example, you had 10'-0' ceilings and 8'-0" high doors. Otherwise, the doors would show because the 7'-6" cutting plane is below the door height. (Figure 6-2.1)

3. From the *Modeling* tab on the *Design Bar*, select **Ceiling**.

You have 4 ceiling types (by default) to select from (Figure 6-2.2).

4. Select **Compound Ceiling: 2'x4' ACT System**.

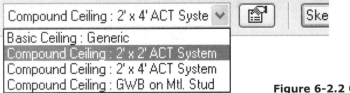

Figure 6-2.2 Ceiling: Options Bar

Next you will change the ceiling height. The default setting is 8'-0" above the current level. You will change the ceiling height to 9'-0" to make the large open office areas feel more spacious. This setting can be changed on a room by room basis.

5. Click the **Properties** button. (Figure 6-2.2)

6. Set the *Height Offset From Level* setting to **9'-0"**. (Figure 6-2.3)

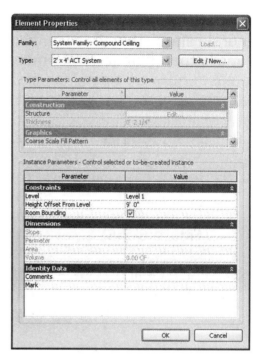

Figure 6-2.3 Ceiling: Properties

You are now ready to place ceiling grids. This process can not get much easier, especially compared to traditional CAD programs.

7. Move your cursor anywhere within the large open office area in the west side of the building. You should see the perimeter of the room highlighted.

8. Pick within the large room; Revit places a grid in the room (Figure 6-2.4).

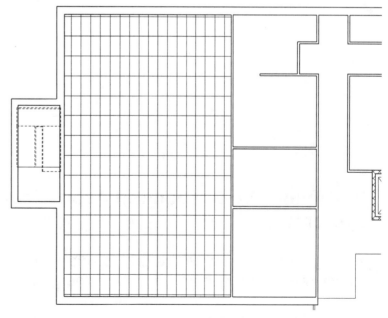

You now have a 2x4 ceiling grid at 9'-0" above the floor (Level 1 in this case).

Figure 6-2.4 Level 1: Ceiling

When you place a ceiling grid, Revit centers the grid in the room. The general rule-of-thumb is you should try to avoid reducing the tile size by more than half at its perimeter. You can see in Figure 6-2.4 that the east and west sides look ok. However, the north and south sides are small slivers. You will adjust this next.

9. Select **Modify** from the *Design Bar*.

10. **Select** the ceiling grid (only one line will be highlighted).

11. Use the **Move** tool to move the grid 24" to the north. (Figure 6-2.5)

12. Place ceiling grids as shown in Figure 6-2.5.
    a. *Be sure to adjust the ceiling heights shown in Figure 6-2.5.*
    b. *Adjust the grids to avoid small tiles at the perimeter.*

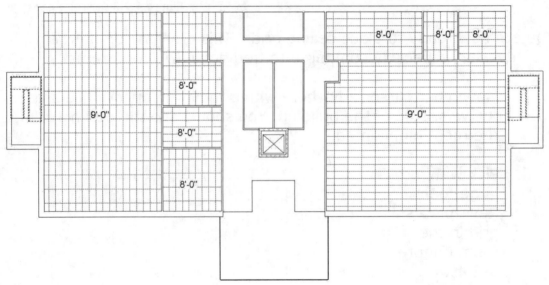

Figure 6-2.5 Level 1: Ceiling Grids

Modifying the Suspended Acoustical Ceiling Tile System:

Making modifications to the grid is relatively easy. Next, you will adjust the ceiling height and rotate the grid.

13. Zoom in to the room in the upper right corner on *Level 1*.

14. Select the grid and then select the **Properties** button from the *Options Bar.*

15. Change the height to **8'-6"**, then click **OK**.

16. With the grid still selected, pick **Compound Ceiling: 2'x2' ACT System** from the *Type Selector* on the *Options Bar.*

17. Again, with the grid still selected, use the *Rotate* tool to rotate the grid 45 degrees.

TIP:

When using the **Rotate** tool | Rotate | you need to pick two points. The first point is your reference line. The second point is the number of degrees off that reference line. In this example, try picking your first point to the right as a horizontal line. Then move the cursor counter-clockwise until 45 degrees is displayed. You can also type the angle instead of picking a second point.

---

18. Your drawing should look similar to **Figure 6-2.6**.

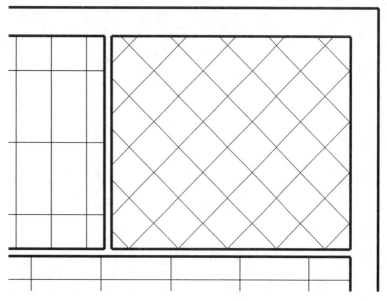

Figure 6-2.6 Level 1: Modified Ceiling

Next, you will look at drawing gypsum board (or drywall) ceiling systems. The process is identical to placing the grid system. Additionally, you will create a ceiling type.

Gypsum Board Ceiling System:

You will create a new ceiling type for a gypsum board ceiling. To better identify the areas that have a gypsum board ceiling, you will set the ceiling type to have a stipple pattern. This will provide a nice graphical representation for the gypsum board ceiling areas.

19. From the *Settings* pull-down menu, select **Materials**.
    This is the list of materials you select from when assigning a material to each layer in a wall system, etc.

20. Select *Gypsum Wall Board,* click **Duplicate** and then enter the name: **Gypsum Ceiling Board**.

21. In the *Surface Pattern* area, pick the down-arrow and select **Gypsum-Plaster** from the list, and then click **OK**. (Figure 6-2.7)

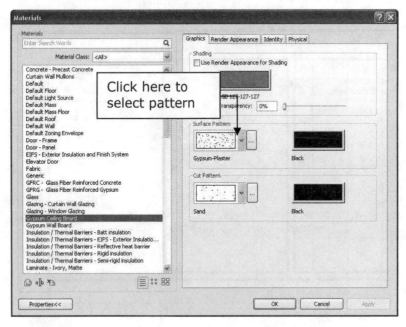

Figure 6-2.7 Material dialog

The *Surface Pattern* setting is what will add the stipple pattern to the gypsum board ceiling areas. With this set to *none*, the ceiling has no pattern (like the basic ceiling type).

Thus, if you wanted Carpet 1 finish to never have the stipple hatch pattern, you could change the surface pattern to none via the Materials dialog and not have to change each views visibility override.

22. From the *Modeling* tab on the *Design Bar*, select **Ceiling**.

23. Click the **Properties** button (Figure 6-2.2).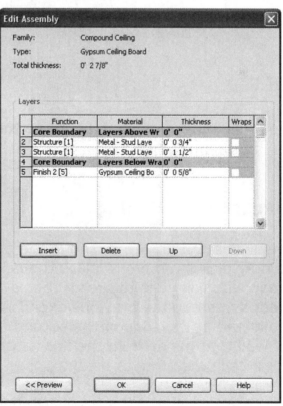

24. Set the Type to **GWB on Mtl. Stud**.
    FYI: *You are selecting this because it is similar to the ceiling you will be creating.*

25. Click the **Edit/New** button.

26. Click *Duplicate* and type **Gypsum Ceiling Board** for the name.

27. Select **Edit** next to the Structure parameter.

28. Set the Values as follows (Figure 6-2.8):
    a. **1½" Mtl. Stud**
    b. **¾" Mtl. Stud**
    c. **Gypsum Ceiling Board**
       (This is the material you created in step 21.)

29. Click **OK** three times.

FYI:

The ceiling assembly you just created represents a typical suspended gypsum board ceiling system. The Metal Studs are perpendicular to each other and suspended by wires, similar to an ACT (acoustical ceiling tile) system.

You are now ready to draw a gypsum board ceiling.

30. Make sure **Gypsum Ceiling Board** is selected in the *Type Selector* on the *Options Bar.*

31. Set the ceiling height to **8'-0"**.

Figure 6-2.8 New ceiling – Edit assembly

32. Pick the two bathrooms: the two rooms north of the elevator (Figure 6-2.9).

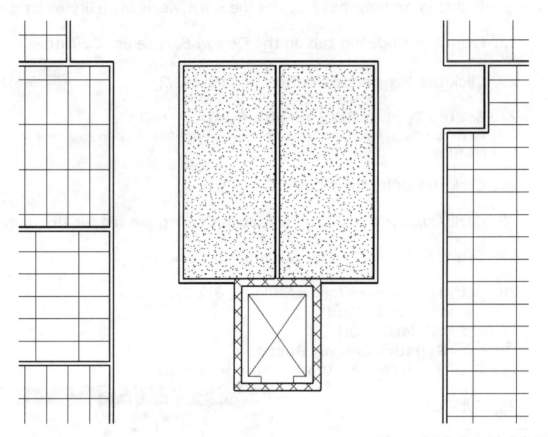

Figure 6-2.9 Gyp. Bd. Ceiling

You now have a gypsum board ceiling at 8'-0" above the finished floor in the toilet rooms.

Sketching a Ceiling:

Next, you will draw a ceiling in the atrium area. However, you cannot simply pick the room to place the ceiling because of the opening in the floor. You will need to sketch the ceiling just like you sketched the floor system in the previous exercise. First, you will need to draw a bulkhead at the edge of the second floor slab. A bulkhead is a portion of wall that hangs from the floor above and creates a closed perimeter for a ceiling system to die into.

33. While still in the Level 1 Reflected Ceiling Plan view, select the **Wall** tool.

34. Click **Properties** from the *Options Bar.*

35. Set the *wall type* to: **Interior - 4 7/8" Partition (1-hr)** and the *Base Offset* to **9'-6"**. *(This will put the bottom of the wall to 9'-6" above the current floor level, Level 1 in this case.)* (Figure 6-2.10)

36. Set the Top Constraint to: **Up to level: Level 2** (Figure 6-2.10).

TIP: *The next time you draw a wall you will have to change the Base Offset back to 0'-0" or your wall will be 9'-6" off the floor.*

37. **Draw the bulkhead**; make sure you snap to the edge of the slab. Also, make sure the wall is under the floor system, not out in the opening. (Do this by drawing the wall either from right to left or left to right depending on how you have the Loc Line set.) (Figure 6-2.11)

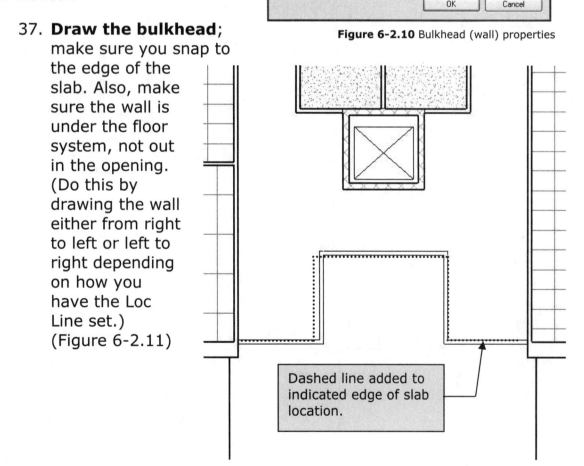

Figure 6-2.10 Bulkhead (wall) properties

Dashed line added to indicated edge of slab location.

Figure 6-2.11 Bulkhead drawn

38. Select the **Ceiling** tool and then click **Sketch** from the *Options Bar*.

39. Select the **Sketch** button from the *Options Bar*, and then use the **Pick Walls**, **Lines**, and **Trim** tools to sketch a line at the perimeter of the ceiling area as shown in **Figure 6-2.12**. You will also need to sketch a line around the toilet/elevator area to define the area within the larger area that will not receive the ceiling pattern: **2'x2' ACT ceiling, with the ceiling height set to 9'-6"**.

40. Click **Finish Sketch** and save Project as **ex6-2.rvt**.

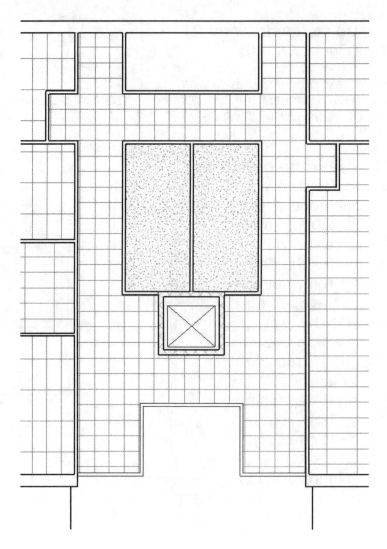

Figure 6-2.12 Atrium Ceiling

Exercise 6-3:
Placing Fixtures (Lights and Diffusers)

In this exercise, you will learn to load and place light and mechanical fixtures in your reflected ceiling plans.

Loading Components:

Before placing fixtures, you need to load them into your project.

1. Select **Component** from the *Modeling* tab on the *Design Bar.*

2. Select **Load** on the *Options Bar.* (Figure 6-3.1)

Figure 6-3.1 Component; Options Bar

3. Double-click the *Lighting Fixtures* folder, and then double-click **Troffer - 2x4 Parabolic.rfa**. (Figure 6-3.2)

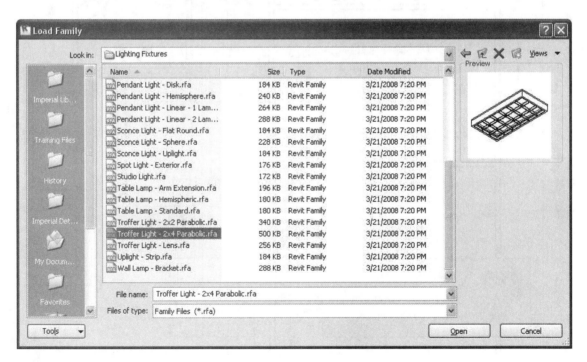

Figure 6-3.2 Load component

Before placing the light fixture you will load the other fixtures first.

4. Select **Load** again, browse to the **Mechanical Equipment** folder.

5. Select **Square Supply Diffuser** and **Square Return Register** (you can select both holding the Ctrl key) and then **Open**.
    TIP: You can hold the Ctrl key to select and load multiple components at once.

Placing instances of components:

You are now ready to place the fixtures in your ceiling plans.

6. With **Component** still selected from the *Design Bar*, pick **Troffer – 2' x 4' Parabolic: 2'x4' (2 Lamp) – 277V** from the type selector drop down on the *Options Bar*.

7. On **Level 1 RCP**, place fixtures as shown in **Figure 6-3.3**.

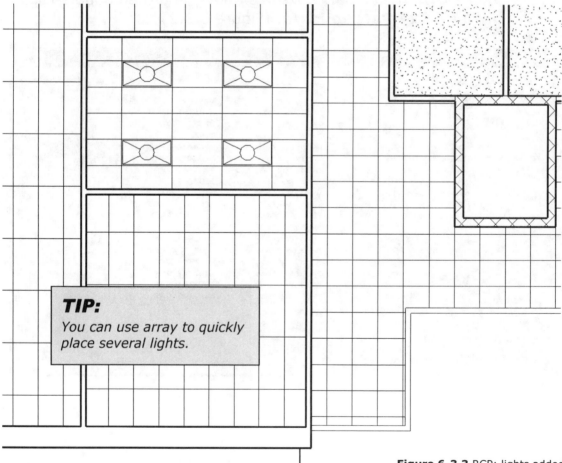

TIP:
You can use array to quickly place several lights.

Figure 6-3.3 RCP; lights added

You may have to use the *Move* command to move the fixture so it fits perfectly in the ACT grid.

8. Now place another **2x4 light fixture** as shown in **Figure 6-3.4**.

Notice the fixture does not automatically orientate itself with the ceiling grid. There may be an occasion when you want this.

Also, notice the light fixture hides a portion of the ceiling grid. This is nice because the grid does not extend through a light fixture.

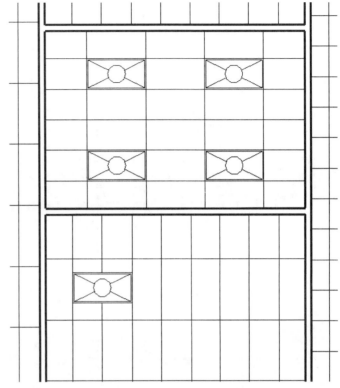

Figure 6-3.4 RCP; lights added

9. Use **Rotate** and **Move** to rotate the fixture to align with the grid (Figure 6-3.5).

10. Once you have one fixture rotated, it is easier to use the *Copy* tool and the snaps to add rotated light fixtures. **Copy** the light fixture to match the layout in **Figure 6-3.5**.

11. Select **Square Supply Diffuser: 24"x24"** from the *Type Selector.*

12. Place the diffusers as shown in Figure 6-3.6.

13. Select **Square Return Register: 24"x24"** from the *Type Selector.*

14. Place the Registers as shown in Figure 6-3.6.

15. Save your project as **ex6-3.rvt**.

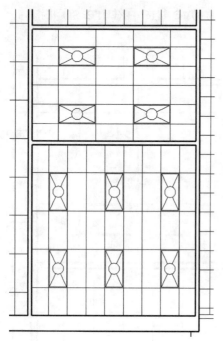

Figure 6-3.5 RCP; rotated lights

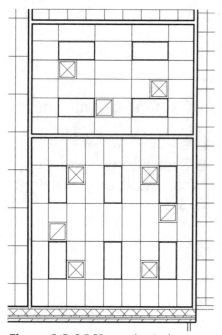

Figure 6-3.6 RCP; mechanical

Reflected Ceiling Plan Symbols:

Revit provides many of the industry standard symbols necessary in drawing reflected ceiling plans (RCP). As shown in Figure 6-3.4, supply air is represented with an X and return air has a diagonal line. It is typical to have a RCP symbol legend showing each symbol and material pattern and list what each one represents.

Component Properties

If you want to adjust the properties of a component, such as a light fixture, you can browse to it in the Project Browser and right click on it *(notice the right click menu also has the option to select all instances of the item in the drawing)* and select Properties. You will see the dialog below for the 2x4 (2 Lamps).

You can also click duplicate and add more sizes (e.g., 4'x4' light fixture).

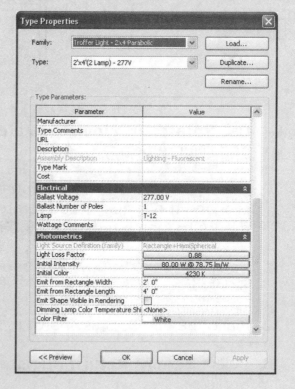

You can also select an inserted component and click the Properties button on the *Options Bar* for additional properties for that particular instance.

Exercise 6-4:
Annotations

This short section will look at adding notes to your RCP.

Adding Annotations:

1. Select the **Text** tool from the *Design Bar.*

2. Pick **3/32" Arial** from the type selector (Figure 6-4.1).

3. Select the **Leader** button circled in **Figure 6-4.1**.

Figure 6-4.1 Text; options bar

Next, you will add a note indicating that the atrium area is open to the floor above (i.e., no floor or ceiling here). First you will draw a leader, and then Revit will allow you to type the text.

4. Add one of the leaders (i.e., arrows) shown in Figure 6-4.2.

5. Add the note "**OPEN TO ABOVE**" shown in **Figure 6-4.2**.
   a. Do the following to add the right-hand arrow:
      i. Click Modify;
      ii. Click the text to select it;
      iii. Click the right-hand arrow icon on the *Options Bar*.

Notice in the image of the *Options Bar* above, with the text selected, the ability to remove leaders is available. The arrows are removed in the order they were added.

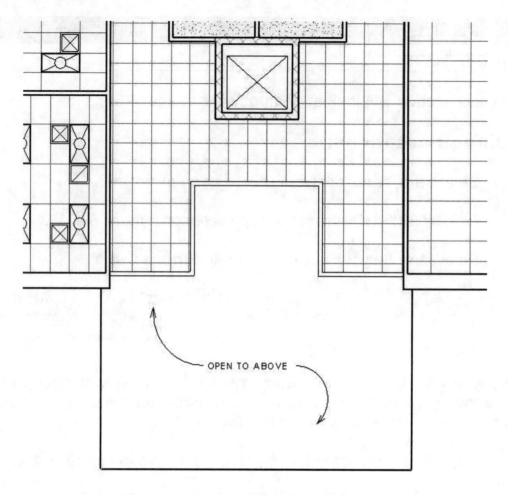

OPEN TO ABOVE

Figure 6-4.2 Text with leaders

Adding text styles to your project:

You can add additional text styles to your project. Some firms prefer a font that has a hand lettering look and others prefer something like the Arial font. These preferences can be saved in the firm's template file so they are consistent and always available. You will add a test style next.

6. Click on the **Text** tool.

7. Select **Properties** on the *Options Bar*.

8. Next, click **Edit/New**.

9. Select **Duplicate** and enter **1/4" outline text**. (Figure 6-4.3)

10. Next, make the following adjustments to the Type Properties (Figure 6-4.4):
    a. Text Font: **Swis721 BdOul BT**
    b. Text Size: **1/4"**

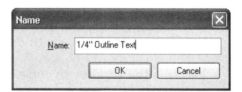

Figure 6-4.3 New text name

NOTE: *You can use any Windows True-Type font. If you do not have this font, select another that best matches (see Figure 6-4.5 below).*

The text size you entered in step 9 is the size of the text when printed. If you change the scale of the drawing, the text size will automatically change, so the text is always the correct size when printing. It is best to set the drawing to the correct scale first. As changing the drawing scale can create a lot of work; repositioning resized text that may be overlapping something or too big for a room.

11. Select **OK** to close the open dialog boxes.

You should now have the new text style available in the *Type Selector* on the *Options Bar*.

12. Use the new text style to create the text shown below (Figure 6-4.5).

13. Erase the sample text (unless your instructor tells you otherwise).

14. Save as **ex6-4.rvt**.

Figure 6-4.4 New text properties

TEST TEXT IN REVIT

Figure 6-4.5 New text style sample

Self-Exam:

The following questions can be used as a way to check your knowledge of this lesson. The answers can be found at the bottom of this page.

1. You must pick Walls to define floor areas. (T/F)
   F

2. Use the Ctrl key to cycle through the selection options. (T/F)
   F

3. When you add a floor object in plan view, the floor does not show up right away in the other views; i.e., 3D, Sections, etc. (T/F)
   F

4. You use the _____ tool; if you need to add a new product, like exterior plaster, so you can add it to wall types and other systems.
   material

5. You have _____ different types of leader options with the *Text* tool.
   4

Review Questions:

The following questions may be assigned by your instructor as a way to assess your knowledge of this section. Your instructor has the answers to the review questions.

✓ 1. It is not possible to create new text styles. (T/F)
   F

2. You can add additional diffuser sizes to the Family as required. (T/F)
   T

✓ 3. The light fixtures automatically turn to align with the ceiling grid. (T/F)
   F

✓ 4. You can adjust the ceiling height room by room. (T/F)
   T

5. Use the _____ button to add additional objects, for insertion, into the current project (e.g., ceiling: linear box group).
   load from library

6. Leaders can only be removed in the order in which they were originally drawn (T/F).
   T

✓ 7. Use the _____ tool if the ceiling grid needs to be at an angle.
   Rotate

✓ 8. Use the _____ tool to adjust the ceiling grid location if a ceiling tile is less than half its normal size.
   move

9. Use the _____ tool to adjust whether an object's surface pattern is displayed (i.e., the stipple for the gypsum board ceiling).
   visibility graphics

10. What is the current size of your project (after completing exercise 6-4)?

   _____ MB.

Lesson 7
Office Building: ELEVATIONS::

This lesson will cover interior and exterior elevations. The default template you started with already has the four main exterior elevations set up for you. You will investigate how Revit generates elevations and the role the elevation tag has in that process.

Exercise 7-1:
Creating and Viewing Parametric Exterior Elevations

Here you will look at setting up an exterior elevation and how to control some of the various options.

Setting up an exterior elevation:

Even though you already have the main exterior elevations set, you will go through the steps necessary to set one up. Many projects have more than four exterior elevations, so all exterior surfaces are elevated.

1.   Open your project, ex6-4.rvt, and **Save As ex7-1.rvt**.

2.   Switch to your **Level 1** *Floor Plan* view.

3.   Select **Elevation** ⬦ Elevation , from the *View* tab on the *Design Bar*.
     TIP: *If you do not see the view tab on the Design Bar, right-click on one of the visible tabs and select View from the pop-up menu (displaying all available Design Bar Tabs).*

4.   Place the temporary elevation tag in plan view as shown in Figure 7-1.1.
     NOTICE: *As you move the cursor around the screen, the elevation tag automatically turns to point at the building.*

You now have an elevation added to the *Project Browser* in the *Elevations* group. This process is similar to adding another floor using the Level tool, as you did in a previous lesson.

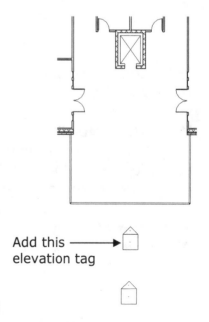

Add this ———▶ elevation tag

Figure 7-1.1 Added elevation tag

After placing an elevation tag, you should rename the elevation label in the project browser.

5. In the *Project Browser*, under *Elevations*, select the elevation label that was just added.

6. Right-click on the view label and select **Rename**.

7. Type: **South Temp**

The name should be fairly descriptive so you can tell where the elevation is just by the label. This will be essential on a large project that has several exterior elevations and even more interior elevations.

8. Double-click on **South Temp** in the *Project Browser*.

The elevation may not look correct right away. You will adjust this in the next step. Notice, though, that an elevation was created simply by placing an elevation tag in plan view.

9. Switch back to **Level 1** view.

Next you will study the options associated with the elevation tag. This, in part, controls what is seen in the elevation.

10. The elevation tag has two parts: the pointing triangle and the square center. Each part will highlight as you move the cursor over it. **Select the square center part**.

You should now see the symbol shown on the right (Figure 7-1.2).

View direction boxes:
The checked box indicates which way the elevation tag is looking. You can check (or uncheck) the other boxes.

Rotation control:
Allows you to look perpendicular to an angled wall in plan, for example.

Figure 7-1.2 Selected elevation tag

Move elevation tag:

While selected, you simply drag the tag to move it.

11. Press the **ESC** key to unselect the elevation tag.

12. Select the "pointing" portion of the elevation tag.

13. In *Properties*, set *Far Clipping* to "Click without line" and then click **OK**.

Your elevation tag should look similar to Figure 7-1.3.

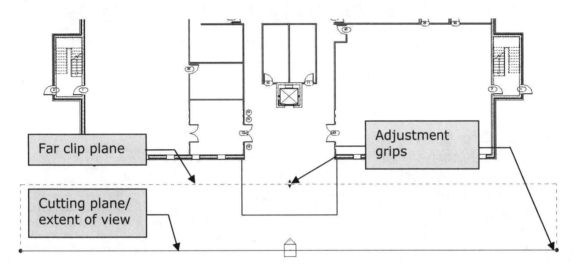

Figure 7-1.3 Selected elevation tag

The elevation tag, as selected in Figure 7-1.3, has several features for controlling how the elevation looks. Here is a quick explanation:

- **Cutting plane/extent of view line:** This controls how much of the 3D model is elevated from left to right (i.e., the width of the elevation).
- **Far clip plane:** This controls how far into the 3D model the elevation can see.
- **Adjustment grips:** You can drag this with the mouse to control the features mention above.

14. Right-click on the view label: **South Temp** in the *Project Browser*, and then select **Properties**.

You have several options in the Properties window (Figure 7-1.4). Notice the three options with check boxes next to them, plus the parameter below them; these control the following:

- **Crop View**: This crops the width and height of the view in elevation. *Adjusting the width of the cropping window in elevation also adjusts the "extent of view" control in plan view.*

- **Crop Region Visible**: This displays a rectangle in the elevation view indicating the extent of the cropping window (described above). *When selected in elevation view, the rectangle can be adjusted with the adjustment grips.*

- **Far Clip Active**: If this is turned "off", Revit will draw everything visible in the 3D model *(within the "extent of view")*.

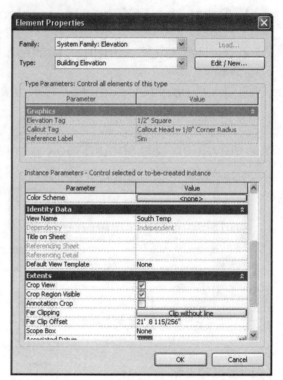

Figure 7-1.4 Elevation view: South Temp - Properties

You will manipulate some of these controls next.

15. With the elevation tag still selected (as in Figure 7-1.3), drag the "cutting plane/extent of view" line up into the atrium as shown in Figure 7-1.5.

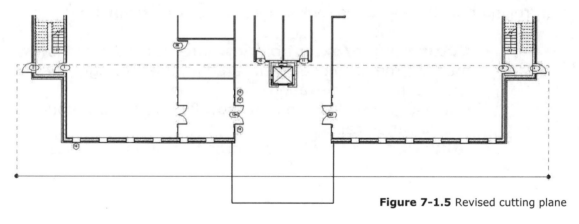

Figure 7-1.5 Revised cutting plane

16. Now switch to the *Elevation view*: **South Temp**.

Your elevation should look similar to Figure 7-1.6. If required, click on the cropping window and resize it to match Figure 7-1.6.

The atrium curtain wall and roof are now displayed in section because of the location of the "cutting plane" line in plan.

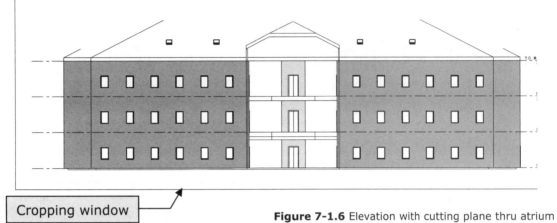

Cropping window

Figure 7-1.6 Elevation with cutting plane thru atrium

Notice that the roof is not fully visible. This is not related to the cropping window shown in Figure 7-1.6. Rather, it is related to the "Far Clip Plane" set in the plan view.

17. Adjust the "Far Clip Plane" in **Level 1** plan view so that the entire roof shows in the **South Temp** view.

Next you will adjust the elevation tag to set up a detail elevation for the atrium curtain wall.

18. In **Level 1** plan view, adjust the elevation tag to show only the atrium curtain wall (Figure 7-1.7).

19. Switch to **South Temp** view to see the "detail" elevation. (Figure 7-1.8)

20. Adjust the South Temp view's **Properties** to turn off the crop window's visibility.

21. **Save** your project as **ex7-1.rvt**.

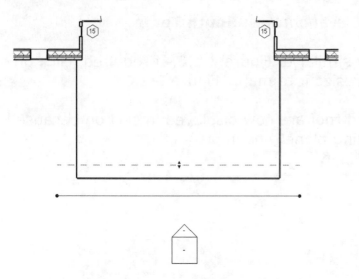

Figure 7-1.7 Atrium curtain wall detail elevation

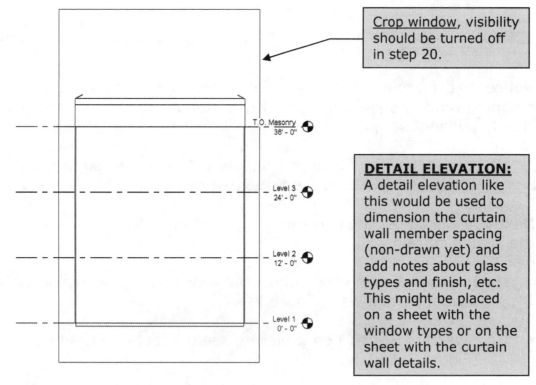

Crop window, visibility should be turned off in step 20.

DETAIL ELEVATION:
A detail elevation like this would be used to dimension the curtain wall member spacing (non-drawn yet) and add notes about glass types and finish, etc. This might be placed on a sheet with the window types or on the sheet with the curtain wall details.

Figure 7-1.8 Atrium curtain wall detail elevation

Exercise 7-2:
Modifying the Project Model: Exterior Elevations

The purpose of this exercise is to demonstrate that changes can be made anywhere and all other drawings are automatically updated.

Modify an exterior elevation:

1. Open ex7-1.rvt and **Save As ex7-2**.

2. Open the **East** exterior elevation view.

3. Use the Window tool and select **Fixed: 32" x 48"**.

You will insert a window in elevation. This will demonstrate, first, that you can actually add a window in elevation not just plan view, and second, that the other views are automatically updated.

Notice, with the window selected for placement, you have the usual dimensions helping you accurately place the window. As you move the window around you should see a dashed horizontal green line indicating the default sill height.

4. Place a window as shown in **Figure 7-2.1**; make sure the bottom of the window "snaps" to the green sill line.

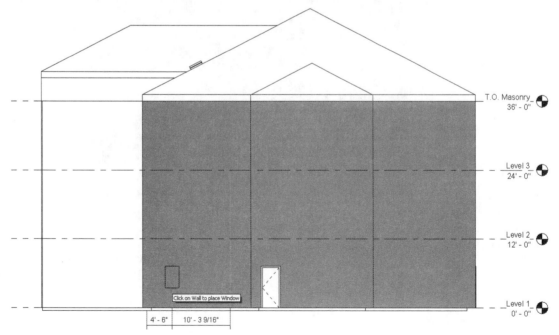

Figure 7-2.1 Placing a window

5. Switch to **Level 1** plan view; notice the window is added. (Figure 7-2.2)

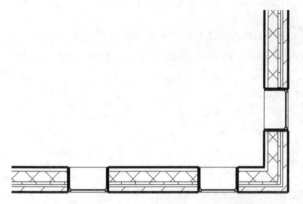

TIP:
If the window is towards the inside, use the control arrows to flip the window within the wall. It should look like the window in Figure 7-2.2.

Figure 7-2.2 Level 1 – south-east corner

6. Switch back to the **East** elevation view.

7. Add windows as shown in Figure 7-2.3.

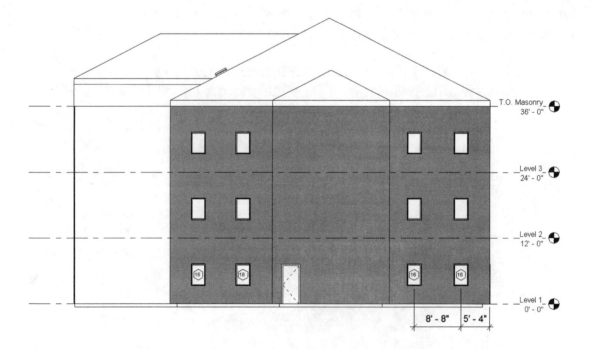

Figure 7-2.3 East elevation –
windows added

If you laid out the interior walls as described in Lesson 3, you should get a warning message when inserting the windows on Level 1, towards the north side of the building. This is because the interior wall for the room in the north-east corner conflicts with the exterior window. Revit is smart enough to see that conflict and bring it to your attention. In this case you probably want the windows to be uniformly spaced, so you will ignore the conflict and move the wall in plan view.

8. Click the red X (in the upper right) to ignore the wall/window conflict warning (Figure 7-2.4).
   If you did not get this warning, skip this step.

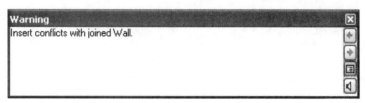

Figure 7-2.4 Conflict warning

9. Switch to **Level 1** plan view and revise the wall as shown in **Figure 7-2.5**.
   TIP: *You will need to use the Split tool to break the wall where it offsets. You can then select the wall (just the wall; the doors will automatically move with the wall) and use the Move tool to move it north.*
   Also notice that the windows on the east wall need to be flipped.

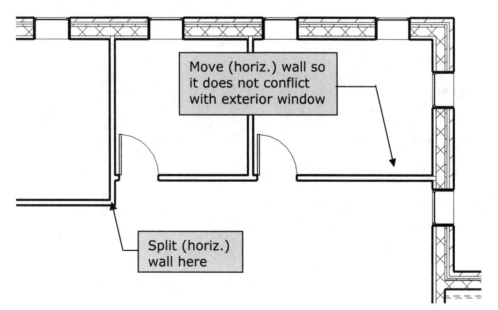

Move (horiz.) wall so it does not conflict with exterior window

Split (horiz.) wall here

Figure 7-2.5 Level 1 – north-east corner

10. Switch to the **Level 1** RCP view. Fix the ceiling.
    NOTICE: *The ceiling grids are likely not aligned with the revised walls. If this is the case, see the explanation below (Figure 7-2.6).*

Most of the time, when you move a wall, Revit will automatically update the ceiling gird to fit the new room. However, occasionally the definition of the room boundary is lost while making modifications. In this case, you will have to delete the grid and reinsert it.

Deleting a ceiling grid:

When selecting a ceiling grid, Revit only selects one line. This does not allow you to delete the ceiling grid. To delete: hover cursor over a ceiling grid line and press the TAB key until you see the ceiling perimeter highlight, then click the mouse. The entire ceiling will be selected. Press Delete.

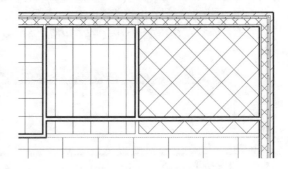

Figure 7-2.6 Level 1 RCP – north-east corner

11. Add the same layout of windows (Figure 7-2.2) to the west elevation. **TIP:** *Mirror the windows in plan view, each floor.*

12. **Save** your Project as **ex7-2.rvt**.

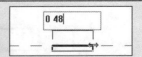

TIP: **ENTERING DIMENSIONS IN REVIT**

As your experience with Revit grows, you will want to learn some of the shortcuts to using the program. One of those shortcuts is how you enter dimensions when drawing. You probably already know, maybe by accident, that if you enter only one number (e.g., 48) and press enter, Revit interprets that number to be feet (e.g., 48'-0"). So, if you want to enter 48", you may be typing 0'-48" or 48". Both work, but having to press the shift key to get the inch symbol takes a little longer.

Here are some options for entering dimensions:

0 48	*Revit reads this as 48" (zero space forty-eight)*
48	*Revit reads this as 48'-0"*
5.5	*Revit reads this as 5'-6"*
0 5.5	*Revit reads this as 5 ½"*
2 0 1/4	*Revit reads this as 2'-0¼" (two space zero space fraction)*

Exercise 7-3:
Creating and Viewing Parametric Interior Elevations

Creating interior elevations is very much like exterior elevations. In fact, you use the same tool. The main difference is that you are placing the elevation tag inside the building, rather than on the exterior.

Adding interior elevation tag:

1. Open project ex7-2.rvt and **Save As ex7-3.rvt**.

2. Switch to **Level 1** floor plan view, if necessary.

3. Select the **Elevation** tool. ⊕ Elevation

4. Select **Elevation: Interior Elevation** from the Type Selector and then place an elevation tag, looking east, in the atrium area (Figure 7-3.1); place as shown in center of room.

Remember, the first thing you should do after adding a new view is to give it an appropriate name in the *Project Browser* list.

5. Change the name of the elevation to **East Atrium**.

6. Switch to the East Atrium view. *Try double-clicking on the elevation tag.*

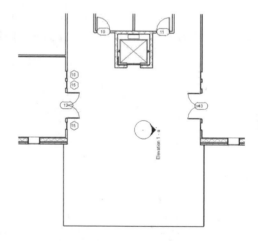

Figure 7-3.1 Level 1 - Atrium

Initially, your elevation should look something like Figure 7-3.2. You will adjust this view next. *Notice how Revit automatically controls the line weights of things in section vs. things in elevations.*

FYI:
The elevation tags are used to reference the sheet and drawing number so the client or contractor can find the desired elevation quickly while looking at the floor plans. This will be covered in a later lesson. It is interesting to know, however, that Revit automatically does this (fills in the elevation tag) when the elevation is placed on a sheet, and will update it if the elevation is moved.

---

7. Switch back to the **Level 1** view.

8. Pick the "pointing" portion of the elevation tag, so you see the view options. (Figure 7-3.3)

You should compare the two drawings on this page (Figures 7-3.2 and 7-3.3) to see how the control lines in the plan view dictate what is generated/visible in the elevation view, for both width and depth.

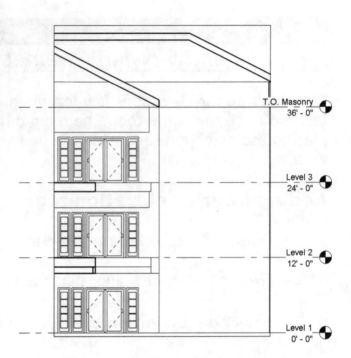

Figure 7-3.2 East Atrium – initial view

The goal is to set up an interior elevation of the entire east atrium wall, with the floor structure and roof shown in section.

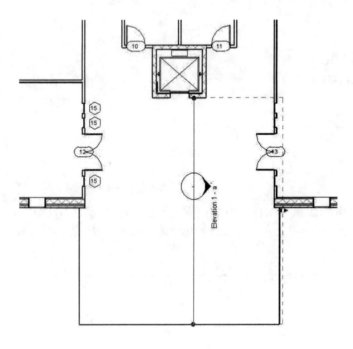

Figure 7-3.3 Elevation tag selected

9. Adjust the control lines for the elevation tag as shown in Figure 7-3.4. Drag the "cutting plane/extent of view" line to the location shown. Make sure the "far clip plane" extends past the door alcove; otherwise it will not show up.

10. Switch back to the **East Atrium** view.

Other than adjusting the height of the view, you have the view ready.

11. Select the cropping window and drag the top middle grip upward, to increase the view size vertically. (Figure 7-3.5)

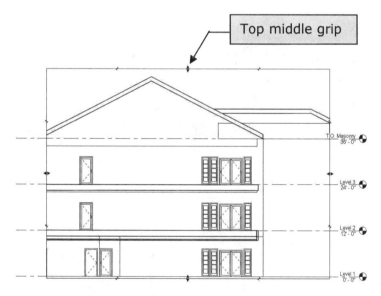

Figure 7-3.5 East Atrium Elevation – crop window selected

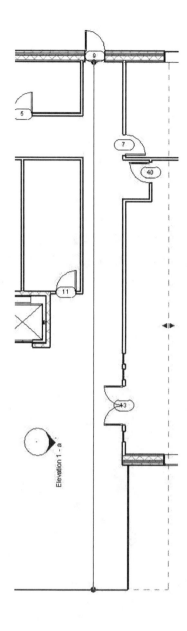

Figure 7-3.4 Elevation tag adjustments

If the ceiling were drawn for the third floor (your instructor may have assigned this), you would probably stretch the crop window down to it. Interior elevations don't normally show walls, roofs and floors in section. An atrium elevation like this could be an exception for the floors.

12. Now stretch the top of the crop window down to approximately 9'-6" above Level 3. (Go to the ceiling if you have drawn one for Level 3).

13. Stretch the bottom of the crop window up to align with the top of the Level 1 floor slab.

14. In the view **Properties**, set the scale to **¼"=1'-0"**.

Your elevation should look like Figure 7-3.6.

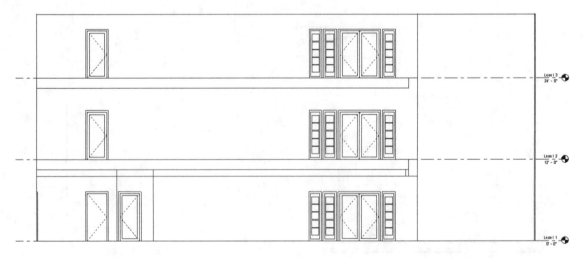

Figure 7-3.6 East Atrium Elevation

You can leave the crop window on to help define the perimeter of the elevation. You can also turn it off. However, some lines that are directly under the crop window might disappear. You could use the Line tool to manually define the perimeter.

Also, notice the Level datum automatically resized to match the new scale. When space permits, most interior elevations are ¼" = 1'-0".

15. Save your project as **ex7-3.rvt**.

Exercise 7-4:
Modifying the Project Model: Interior Elevations

This short exercise, similar to Exercise 7-2, will look at an example of Revit's parametric change engine. All drawings are generated from one 3D model.

Modify the interior elevations:

1. Open ex7-3.rvt and **Save As ex7-4.rvt**.

2. Open the **East Atrium** elevation view.

You will move two doors and add one.

3. Select both of the single doors on Levels 2 and 3; use the Ctrl key to select multiple objects at one time.

4. Use the **Move** tool to move the door 6'-0" to the right (south). (Figure 7-4.1)

5. In the East Atrium elevation view, use the **Door** tool to place a **Sgl Flush: 36" x 84"** door on Level 2 to the far left (north). (Figure 7-4.1)

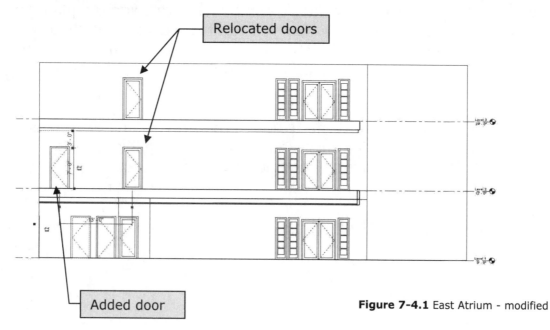

Relocated doors

Added door

Figure 7-4.1 East Atrium - modified

Now it's time to see the effects to the plan views.

6. Switch to **Level 2** floor plan view. (Figure 7-4.2)
    You can also see a similar change on Level 3.

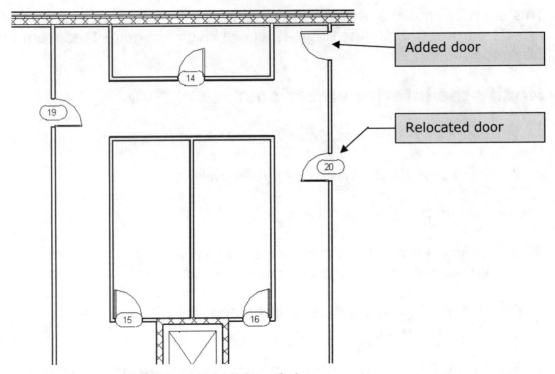

Figure 7-4.2 Level 2 plan with changes

When placing a door in elevation, you may have to switch to plan view to verify the door swing is the way you want it; you cannot control the door swing in elevation (well, actually, you can via a right-click on the door in elevation, but you would first need to know which way it is swinging).

In elevation, you can adjust many things this way. Some examples are: ceiling height, interior and exterior windows, wall locations (perpendicular to the current view), etc.

7. Save your project as **ex7-4**.

Exercise 7-5:
Adding Mullions to a Curtainwall

This exercise will cover the steps involved in designing a curtainwall system (only from an aesthetic viewpoint, not structurally). This is surprisingly simple to do.

Adding Curtain Grid:

First, you draw a grid on your curtainwall. This sets up the location for your mullions, which you will add later.

1. Open ex7-4.rvt and **Save As ex7-5.rvt**.

2. Switch to your **South Temp** view.

3. From the *Modeling* tab on the *Design Bar*, select **Curtain Grid**.

4. Draw the grid as shown in **Figure 7-5.1**.
    Be sure to add horizontal grids at Levels 2 and 3.

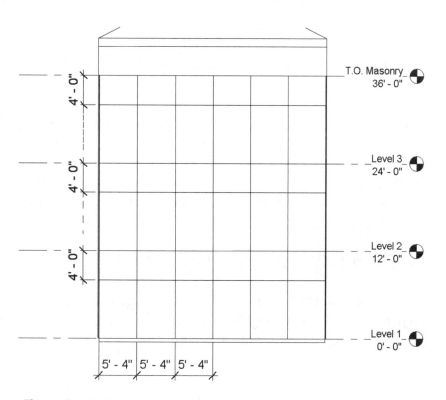

Figure 7-5.1 South Temp view – curtain grid added

If a curtain grid line did not land in the correct place, you can select it and adjust the dimensions that will appear on the screen. To select the grid you need to place your cursor over the grid line and press the Tab key until the curtain grid is highlighted, and then click to select.

5.   Select the *Curtain Grid* tool and then click on the **One Segment** option on the *Options Bar* (Figure 7-5.2).

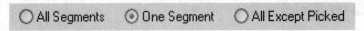

Figure 7-5.2 Options Bar for Curtain Grid tool

6.   Draw two vertical lines to set up the main entry door location. (Figure 7-5.3) *You do not need to draw the dimensions shown.*

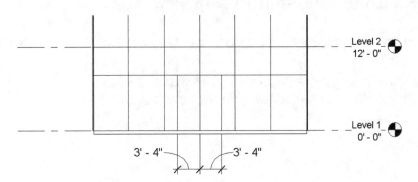

Figure 7-5.3 Curtain grid for door location

Notice that the One Segment option limits the grid to the "cell" you clicked in, rather than extending from top to bottom as the others did.

Next, you will set up the curtain grid lines around the corners. This can be done from the east or west views, similar to the previous steps. However, this can also be accomplished in a 3D view.

7.   Click on the **3D** icon on the *View* toolbar.

8.   Using the **Curtain Grid** tool, add the grid lines shown in **Figure 7-5.4**. Starting at the outside corner, space the grids 5'-4" (the last space will be smaller).

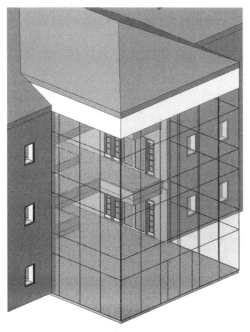

As you move the cursor, while placing the horizontal grids, you should see the grid "snap" to the grid around the corner; that is when you click the mouse.

Drag your cursor on the ViewCube to see your project from different views. Clicking the "Home" icon (visible when your cursor is over the ViewCube) will reset the view.

Figure 7-5.4 Curtain grid – 3D view

Adding Doors:

9. Switch back to **South Temp** view and select one of the 3'-4" wide cells; place your cursor over the cell [edge] and press the *Tab* key until that cell is highlighted and then click to select.

10. With the cell selected, pick **Curtain Wall Sgl Glass** from the *Type Selector* on the *Options Bar*. (Figure 7-5.5)
    If that type is not loaded, click on Properties and then Load. Load the style from the Doors folder.

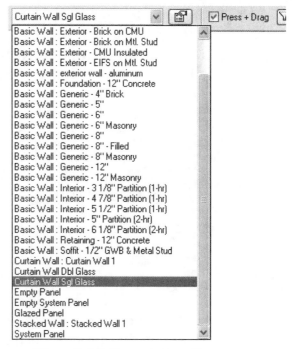

Figure 7-5.5 Type selector with curtain wall cell selected

11. Repeat the previous two steps for the other 3'-4" wide cell. (Figure 7-5.6)

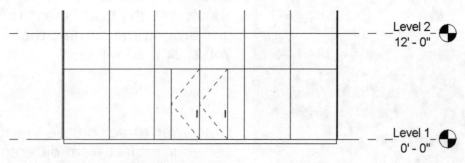

Figure 7-5.6 Curtain grid with doors added

Adding Curtainwall Mullions:

Thus far you have simply setup the spacing for the curtainwall mullions. Next you need to place the curtainwall mullions. This involves selecting a size for the mullion, as they typically come in many shapes and sizes. (The depth is usually related to the height of the curtainwall, as the mullion acts as the structure for the glass wall.)

12. Switch to the **3D** view.

13. Select the **Mullion** tool from the *Modeling* tab.

14. Select **Rectangular Mullion – 2.5" x 5" rectangular** from the type selector (Figure 7-5.7).

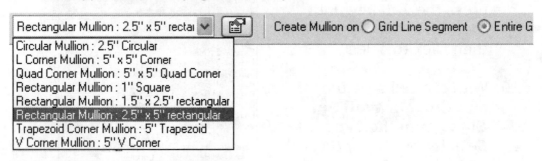

Figure 7-5.7 Type selector for Mullion tool

15. Select all the grid lines you previously placed and the perimeter (excluding the outside corners and the bottom horizontal member on the south face).

Next, you will add the horizontal mullion at the bottom, on the south side. You need to place this mullion so it does not extend through the door openings.

16. With the Mullion tool selected, click **Grid Line Segment** from the *Options Bar* (Figure 7-5.7).

17. Click on the bottom edge of the six cells (skipping the two door openings), to place the horizontal mullion (Figure 7-5.8).

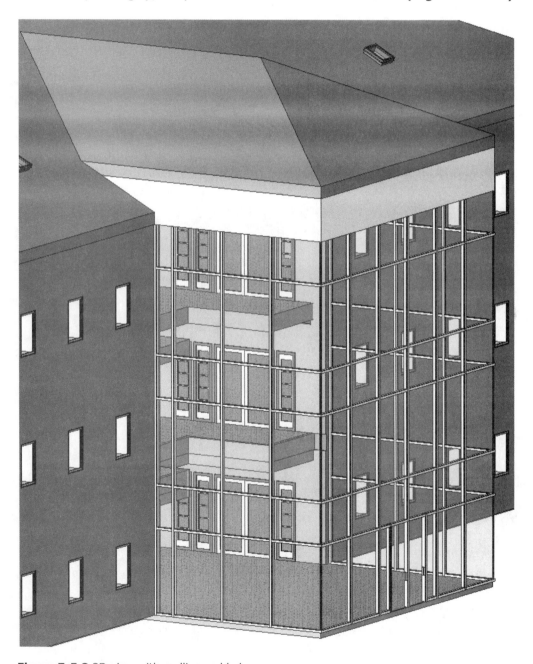

Figure 7-5.8 3D view with mullions added

18. Click on the two verticals next to each door to place a mullion. (Figure 7-5.8)

In this example, you will not place a corner mullion. This will be a butt-joint condition where the two panes of glass are held together with silicon in the corner.

All views will now be updated to show the curtainwall mullions.

19. Switch to the **Level 1** plan view to see the added curtainwall mullions and doors (Figure 7-5.9).

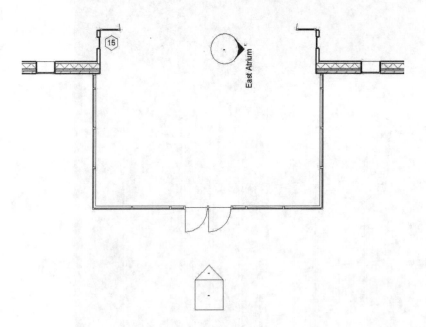

Figure 7-5.9 Level 1 plan view with curtainwall mullions

20. **Save** your project as **ex7-5.rvt**.

Exercise 7-6:
Design Options

This exercise will explore a feature called *Design Options*. This feature allows you to present two or more options for a portion of your design without having to save a copy of your project and end up having to maintain more than one project until the preferred design option is selected.

Design Options Overview:

A Revit project can have several design option studies at any given time. You might have an (A) entry canopy options study, (B) an executive board room options study, and a (C) toilet room layout options study in a project. Each of these studies can have several design options associated with them. For example, the entry canopy study might have three options: 1. flat roof, 2. gable roof, and 3. sloped glass roof.

A particular study of an area within your project is called a *Design Option Set*, and the different designs associated with a *Design Options Set* are called *Options*. Both the *Design Options Set* and the *Options* can be named.

One of the *Options* in a *Design Option Set* is specified as the *Primary* option (the others are called *Secondary* options); this is the option that is shown by default in all new and existing views. However, you can adjust the *Visibility* of a *View* to show a different option. Typically you would duplicate a *View*, adjust the *Visibility*, and *Rename* it to have each option at your finger-tips.

When the preferred design is selected, by you and/or the owner, you set that *Option* to *Primary*. Finally, you select a tool called *"Accept Primary"* which deletes the *Secondary Options* and the *Design Option Set*, leaving the *Primary Option* as part of the main building model.

Design Option Set

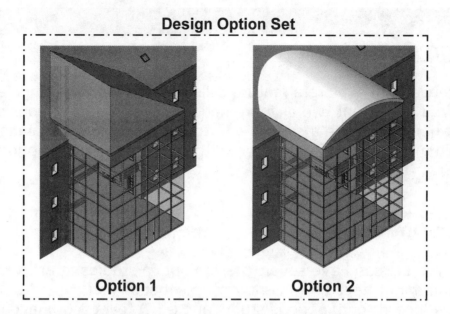

Option 1   Option 2

The following image (Figure 7-6.1) is an overview of the Design Options Dialog:

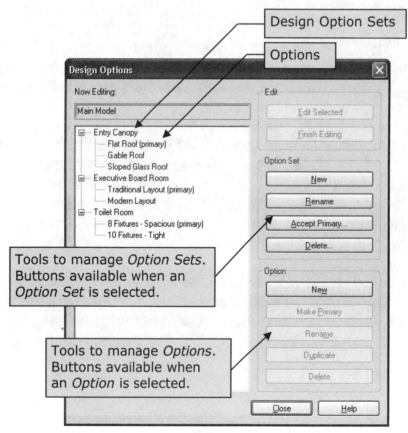

Figure 7-6.1 Design Options Dialog; Modern Layout Option selected

Notes about the Design Options dialog box:

Edit buttons:
You can edit a *Design Option* by selecting an *Option* (in the window area on the left) and then clicking the *"Edit Selected"* button. Next you add, move and delete elements in that Design Option.

When finished editing a *Design Option*, you reopen the *Design Options* dialog and click the *"Finish Editing"* button.

If you are currently in an Option Editing mode, the *Now Editing* area in the *Design Options* dialog displays the *Option* name being modified; otherwise it displays "Main Model".

Option Set buttons:
The *New* button is always available. You can quickly set up several *Option Sets*. Each time you create a new *Option Set*, Revit automatically creates a *Primary Option* named "Option 1".

The other buttons are only available when an Option Set label is highlighted (i.e., selected) in the window list on the left.

The *Accept Primary* button causes the Primary option of the selected Set to become a normal part of the building model and deletes the Set and Secondary Options. This is a way of "cleaning house", by getting rid of unnecessary information which helps to better manage the project and keeps the file size down.

Option buttons:
These buttons are only available when an *Option* (primary or secondary) is selected within an *Option Set*. You can quickly set up several *Options* without having to immediately add any content (i.e., walls, components, etc.) to them.

The *Make Primary* button allows you to change the status of a *Secondary Option* to *Primary*. As previously mentioned, the *Primary Option* is the *Option* that is shown by default in existing and new views.

The *Duplicate* button will copy all the elements in the selected Option into a new Option (this makes the file larger because you are technically adding additional content to the project). You can then use the copied elements (e.g., walls, furniture, etc.) as a starting point for the next design option. This is handy if the various options are similar.

Now you will put this knowledge to use!

Setting up a Design Option Set:

In this exercise you will create two Design Option Sets; one for the curtainwall and another for the roof area above the curtain wall. You will create an alternate roof and curtainwall design for the office building project.

You could just create one Design Option Set and have two design options total. However, by placing the curtainwall options in one Option Set and the roof in another, you actually get a total of four design options. You can mix and match the curtainwall and roof options.

Setting up Design Options in your project:

First you will setup the Option Sets and Options.

    1.   Open ex7-5.rvt and **Save As ex7-6.rvt**.

    2.   Select *Design Options* → **Design Options...** from the *Tools* pull-down menu.

You are now in the Design Options dialog box (Figure 7-6.2). Unless you have modified your template file to have Option Sets, your dialog will look like this one.

    3.   In the *Option Set* area click **New**.

Figure 7-6.2 Design Options Dialog; initial view

Notice an *Option Set* named <u>Option Set 1</u> has been created. Revit also automatically created the *Primary Option* named <u>Option 1</u> (Figure 7-6.3). Next you will rename the Option Set to something that is easier to recognize.

Figure 7-6.3 Design Options Dialog; new option set created

4. (See warning below.) Select the *Option Set* currently named <u>Option Set 1</u> and then click the **Rename** button in the *Option Set* area.

    WARNING! Be sure you are not renaming the *Option* but, rather, the *Option Set.*

5. In the *Rename* dialog type: **Curtainwall**. (Figure 7-6.4)

6. Click **OK** to rename.

Giving the *Option Set* a name that is easy to recognize helps in managing the various options later, especially if you have several.

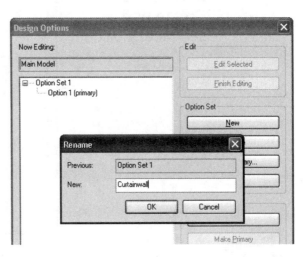

Figure 7-6.4 Rename Option Set Dialog; enter Curtainwall

Next you will create a *Secondary Option* for the *Curtainwall* Option Set.

7. With the *Curtainwall Option Set* selected (or any option in that set), click **New** in the *Option* area.

Notice a secondary Option was created and automatically named Option 2. If you have descriptive names for the options in a set, you should apply them. In this example you can leave them as they are.

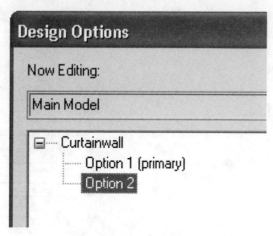

Figure 7-6.5 Design Options Dialog;
secondary option created

8. Create an *Option Set* for the roof: (Figure 7-6.6)

    a. Name the set: **Atrium Roof**;
    b. Create one secondary option.

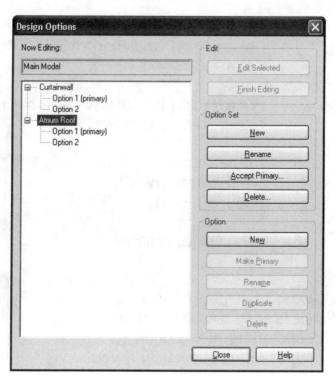

Figure 7-6.6 Design Options Dialog

The basic thinking with the *Design Options* feature is that you set up the *Option Set* and *Option*s and then start drawing the elements related to the current *Option*. So, you create the *Options* and then click "Edit Selected" in the *Design Options* dialog, close the dialog, make the additions and modifications relative to that *Design Option*, and finally go back into the *Design Option* dialog and click the "Finish Editing" button.

However, in your case, you want to move content already drawn to *Option 1*. Revit has a feature that allows you to move content to a *Design Option Set,* which means the content gets copied to each *Option* in the *Set* you select. This option will work for the curtainwall because the second option will be similar to the first one.

Curtainwall Design Option:

You are now ready to setup the different design options.

9. Switch to the **Default 3D view**.

10. Select the three curtainwall sections (three major areas around the atrium) and the three short walls above the curtainwalls.
    TIP: *Make sure you click when the entire curtainwall area is selected, not just an individual mullion or cell. You may need to use the Tab key to cycle through the available options below your cursor.*

11. From the *Tools* pull-down menu, select *Design Options* → **Add to Design Option Set**.

12. Select *Curtainwall* from the dialog and then click **OK** (Figure 7-6.7)

The selected items are now in both *Option 1* and *Option 2* under the *Option Set: Curtainwall*.

From this point forward you can only modify the curtainwall when in *Option 1* or *Option 2* "edit mode" (in which case the tables are turned and you cannot edit the main building model; this is because "exclude options" is selected on the *Options Bar*).

Figure 7-6.7 Design Options Dialog

13. In the **Design Options** dialog, select Curtainwall:Option 2 (i.e., Option Set: *Curtainwall*; Option: *Option 2*).

14. Click the **Edit Selected** button (Figure 7-6.6).

15. Click **Close** to close the *Design Options* dialog.

Now you should notice that the main building model is slightly grey and not editable. (It is not editable because "active option only" is selected on the *Options Bar*).

16. Zoom in on the curtainwall area in your 3D view.

17. Using the **Curtain Grid** tool on the *Modeling Tab*, select horizontal lines equally spaced between the larger vertical spaces as shown in Figure 7-6.8 (You should be able to place all the grid lines from this one view angle).
    TIP: Use the "All except picked" setting on the Option Bar when placing the grid on either side of the doors on Level 1.

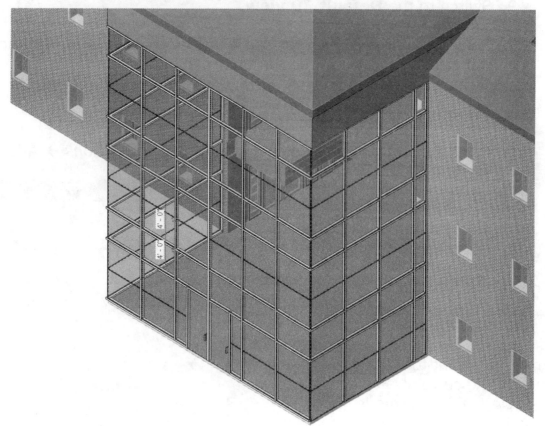

Figure 7-6.8 3D View: horizontal curtain grid lines added

18. Select the **Mullion** tool from the *Modeling tab*.

19. Select **Rectangular Mullion – 2.5" x 5" rectangular** from the type selector (Figure 7-6.8).

20. Select each one of the gird lines to place the horizontal mullions (Figure 7-6.9).

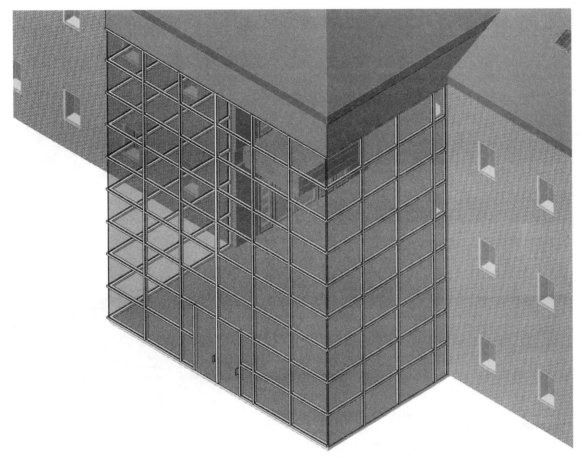

Figure 7-6.9 3D View: horizontal mullions added

21. Open the *Design Options* dialog and click the **Finish Editing** button.

22. Click OK to close the dialog box.

It now appears like all your changes disappeared, right? Well, if you recall from the introduction to this exercise, the *Primary Option* is displayed by default for all new and existing views. So when you finished editing _Curtainwall:Option 2_ the *Default 3D View* switched back to the Primary Option (which is currently set to Option 1).

Next you will create a new view and adjust its *Visibility* to display _Option 2_ of the _Curtainwall_ Options Set.

First you will create a duplicate copy of the 3D view.

23. In the Project Broswer, under 3D Views, right-click on the **{3D}** label.

24. Select **Duplicate View → Duplicate** from the pop-up menu.

You now have a copy of the 3D view named *Copy of {3D}*.

25. **Rename** the new view to **Curtainwall Option 2**.

26. Switch to your new view (if required).

27. From the *View* pull-down menu, select **Visibility/Graphics.**
    TIP: *Or just type* VV *on the keyboard (but do not press Enter).*

28. Click on the **Design Options** tab at the top of the dialog.

29. Change the *Design Option* parameter for *Curtainwall* to *Option 2* (Figure 7-6.10).

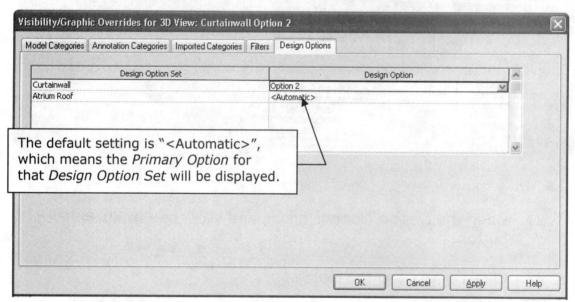

Figure 7-6.10 Visibility/Graphic Overrides dialog: modified Curtainwall design option visibility

30. Click **OK** to close the dialog.

Now, with the *{3D}* view and the *Curtainwall:Option 2* view, you can quickly switch between design options. Both views could be placed on the same sheet and printed out for a design critique.

Atrium Roof Design Option:

Similar to getting things ready to create the second option for the curtainwall, you will do the same for the atrium roof. However, the second roof option is totally different from the first option so it does not make sense to move the current roof to each option in the *Atrium Roof Option Set*; you would end up completely deleting the roof from *Atrium Roof:Option 2* (deleting the roof would be no problem in this case, but another scenario might have hundreds of entities that need to be moved to Option 1, which would be more difficult to delete from Option 2). Next you will explore the how to move content to just one *Option* in an *Option Set*.

To do this you simply *Cut* the content to the clipboard and then *Paste* it back in when *Atrium Roof:Option 1* editing is enabled.

31. Switch to the **Default 3D view**.

32. Select the roof area over the atrium/curtainwall.

33. Select **Cut** from the *Edit* pull-down menu (or Ctrl+X).

The roof is now temporarily removed from the project (Figure 7-6.11). You will paste it back in shortly.

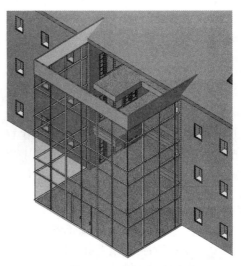

34. In the *Design Options* dialog, highlight **Option 1 (primary)** under the *Atrium Roof* Option Set.

Figure 7-6.11 Default 3D view: roof Cut to clipboard

35. Click the **Edit Selected** button.

36. Click **Close** to close the *Design Options* dialog.

37. From the *Edit* pull-down menu, select **Paste Aligned → Same Place**.

The roof is now back in the project as part of *Atrium Roof:Option 1*.
TIP: Be careful not to Copy or Cut anything else to the clipboard until you Paste the roof back in. When you Copy something, you overwrite whatever is currently in the Clipboard.

38. Click **Finish Editing** in the *Design Options* dialog.

You are now ready to start creating the second roof option.

39. Select **Option 2** under *Atrium Roof Option Set*.

40. Click the **Edit Selected** button.

41. Click **Close** to close the *Design Options* dialog.

Your view should now look similar to Figure 7-6.11. The roof is gone because *Atrium Roof:Option 2* does not currently have a roof in it.

42. Switch to the **South** elevation view.

43. Zoom in to the area above the curtainwall.

Next, you will create an in-place Family to represent a curved roof option over the atrium area. Basically, you will create a solid by specifying a depth and then drawing a profile of the curved roof with lines.

44. Click **Create...** on the *Modeling* Tab.

Immediately, you are prompted to select a Family Category. This allows Revit to understand how other elements should interact with the object(s) you are about to create.

45. Select **Roofs** from the *Family Category* list (Figure 7-6.12).

46. Click **OK**.

Now you are prompted to provide a name for the new *Family*.

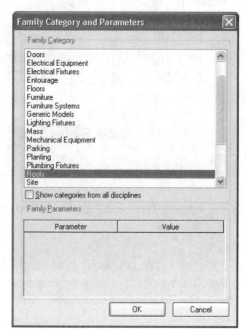

Figure 7-6.12
Family Category and Parameters dialog

47. For the *Family* name, type **Atrium Roof** (Figure 7-6.13).

Figure 7-6.13 Family name prompt

You are now in a mode where you draw the Atrium Roof. Notice that the *Design Bar* has changed to just have a Family tab (Figure 7-6.14) which has all the tools available to create a Family. You are continuously in the Family edit mode until you select Finish Family or Quit Family from the *Design Bar*.

48. Click **Solid Form>>** on the *Design Bar*.

You are now prompted to select the type (or form) of solid you wish to create.

49. Select **Solid Extrude** from the fly-out menu. (Figure 7-6.15)

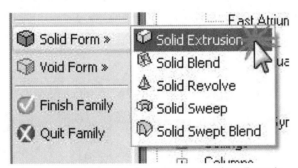

Figure 7-6.15 Form fly-out menu; select Extrude

Figure 7-6.14
Family tab
(*Design Bar*)

Finally, you are prompted to select a plane in which to start drawing the profile of the solid to be extruded. Even though the view is a 2D representation of a 3D model, Revit needs to know where you want the 3D Solid created. You will select the wall above the curtainwall as a reference surface to establish a working plane.

50. Select **Pick a Plane** and click **OK** (Figure 7-6.16).

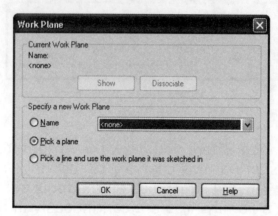

Figure 7-6.16 Work Plane dialog; select Pick a Plane

51. Move the cursor over the upper edge of the wall above the curtainwall and press the Tab key until a dashed line appears around the perimeter of the wall, and then click the mouse to select (Figure 7-6.17).

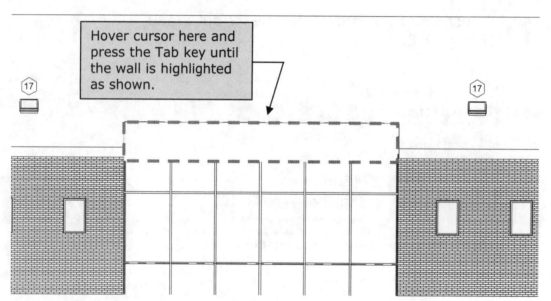

Figure 7-6.17 South Elevation; select wall to establish work plane

Next you will draw an arc to specify the bottom edge of the curved roof design option.

Notice the *Design Bar* changed again to show tools related to drawing an extruded solid (Figure 7-6.18).

52. On the *Options Bar*, enter **-40'-0"** for the **Depth** (Figure 7-6.18). ***FYI:*** *A positive number for the depth would cause the solid to project out from the curtainwall rather than back over the atrium.*

53. Click **Lines** from the *Design Bar* (Figure 7-6.18).

54. Click the **Arc** icon from the *Options Bar* (the icon on the left with an arc passing through three points).

55. Pick the three points shown in Figure 7-6.18 to draw the arc. The angle 71.847° is not critical; get as close as possible.
    TIP: *Zoom in on each arc endpoint to accurately select the corners.*

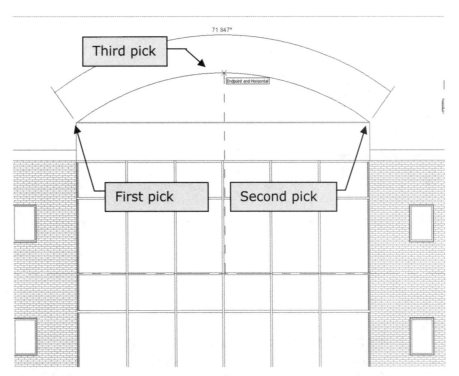

Figure 7-6.18 South Elevation; drawing arc to define roof

Now you will draw another arc 1'-0" above the previous one.

56. On the *Options Bar*, enter **1'-0"** for the *Offset*.

57. Pick the same three points shown in Figure 7-6.18.

Notice that an arc is drawn offset 1'-0" from the points you picked. If you pick the first two points in the other direction, the arc would be offset in the other direction (downward in this case).

Next, you will draw two short lines to connect the endpoints of the two arcs. This will create a closed area which is required before finishing the sketch. Think of it this way: you need to completely specify at least two dimensions before Revit and extrude to create the third.

58. Click the "straight" line icon on the *Options Bar*. This will switch you from drawing arcs back to drawing straight line segments.

59. Zoom in and draw a short line on each end of the arc as shown in Figure 7-6.19. (Make sure "Offset" is set back to zero.)

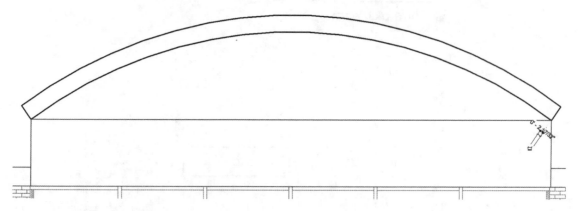

Figure 7-6.19 South Elevation; two arcs and two short lines define roof profile

60. Click **Finish Sketch** from the *Design Bar*.
    TIP: If you get any warnings, it may be because one or more of the profile's corners do not create a perfect intersection. Zoom in to see and use the Trim tool to close the corners.

You are still in the Create Family mode. Before you finish you will apply a material to the roof element.

61. Click the roof to select it.

62. Click the **Properties** icon on the *Options Bar*.

63. Click in the *Material* value field and then click the "**...**" icon that appears.

The Material dialog opens.

64. Select **Metal–Roofing** from the list of predefined *Materials* and then click OK.
    FYI: *Notice the rendering material is set to "Aluminum Anodized Dark Bronze" for Metal – Roofing on the Render Appearance tab.*

65. Click **OK** to close the *Properties* dialog.

You are now ready to finish the Family.

66. From the *Design Bar* click **Finish Family**.

You are now also ready to finish editing the current design option for the time being.

67. In the *Design Options* dialog click **Finish Editing**.

68. Click **Close** to close the dialog.

As before, the Option you were just working on was not the *Primary Option* in the *Atrium Roof Design Set*, so the current view reverted back to *Atrium Roof:Option 1* (which is the Primary view).

You will create a 3D view that has *Option 2* set to be visible for both the *Curtainwall* Option Set and the *Atrium Roof* Option Set.

69. Right-click on the **Default 3D view** and click **Duplicate**.

70. Rename the duplicated view to **Atrium – Option 2**.

71. Switch to the new view (Atrium – Option 2).

72. Click **Visibility/Graphics...** from the *View* menu.

73. On the *Design Options* tab, set both *Option Sets* to **Option 2** in the *Design Option* column.

74. Click **OK** to close the dialog.

You can now see a 3D view of your new roof option. However, you realize that the walls above the curtainwall need to be modified based on the roof option; so it would make more sense to have the walls in the Atrium Roof Option Set rather than the Curtainwall Option Set.

Next, you will make this change and then modify the wall to conform to the curved roof option.

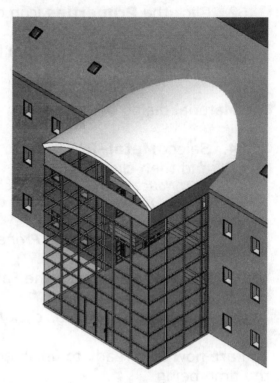

Figure 7-6.20 Atrium – Option 2 view

75. In the Default 3D View: open each of the two *Options* (i.e., enter edit mode) in the *Curtainwall* Option Set and **Cut** the three walls above the curtainwall to the clipboard.

76. Now open each of the two *Options* for the *Atrium Roof* Option Set and **Paste** the three walls using *Paste Aligned\Same Place*.

The three walls should now exist in the *Atrium Roof:Option 1* set and the *Atrium Roof:Option 2* set. Next you will modify the *Option 2* walls.

77. Enter edit mode for *Atrium Roof:Option 2.*

78. In your newly created 3D view "Atrium Option 2", zoom in to the south wall above the curtainwall that needs to be extended up to the curved roof.

79. Click on the wall to select it.

80. Click the **Attach** button, next to Top/Bottom, from the *Options Bar* (Figure 7-6.21).

:ive Option Only | Edit Profile | Top/Base: Attach | Detach

Figure 7-6.21 Options Bar with wall selected

This feature allows you to *Attach* a wall to another object. In this example you will pick the curved roof which will cause the wall to extend up and conform to the underside of the curved roof.

The *Edit Elevation Profile* button (Figure 7-6.21) would allow you to achieve the same results. Using that tool you sketch a new perimeter for the wall in an elevation or 3D view. This is particularly handy if you do not have another object to conform to; you simply want the top of the wall to do something unusual.

81. Hover the cursor over the curved roof until it highlights, and then click to select it.

Immediately the wall is modified; it should look similar to Figure 7-6.22.

82. In the *Design Options* dialog, click **Finish Editing**.

83. **Save** you project as **ex7-6.rvt**.

Figure 7-6.22 Atrium – Option 2 view; Wall attached to curved roof

TIP: *The Design Options feature can also be used to manage alternates, where both the base bid and the alternate(s) need to be drawn.*

Self-Exam:

The following questions can be used as a way to check your knowledge of this lesson. The answers can be found at the bottom of this page.

1. The plan is updated automatically when an elevation is modified, but not the other way around. (T/F) *F*

2. You can use the Elevation tool to place both interior and exterior elevations. (T/F) *T*

3. You can rename elevation views to better manage them. (T/F) *T*

4. You have to resize the Level tags and annotations after changing a view's scale. (T/F) *F*

5. How do you enter 5 ½" without entering the foot or inch symbol? *#0 5.5*

   _____

Review Questions:

The following questions may be assigned by your instructor as a way to assess your knowledge of this section. Your instructor has the answers to the review questions.

1. The visibility of the crop window can be controlled. (T/F) *T*

2. You have to manually adjust the lineweights in the elevations. (T/F) *F*

3. As you move the cursor around the building, during placement, the elevation tag turns to point at the building. (T/F) *T*

4. There is only one part of the elevation tag that can be selected. (T/F) *F*

5. You cannot adjust the "extent of view" (width) using the crop window. (T/F) *F*

6. What is the first thing you should do after placing an elevation tag?
   _____ *rename the elevation* label

7. In addition to the Window tool, if one window is already placed, you can use the ____*copy or align*____ tool to place additional instances of that window.

8. With the elevation tag selected, you can use the ____*rotation control*____ to adjust the tag orientation to look at an angled wall.

9. You need to adjust the ____*control lines*____ to see objects, in elevation that are a distance back from the main elevation.

10. What feature allows you to develop different ideas? ___*design options*___

Lesson 8
Office Building: SECTIONS::

Sections are one of the main communication tools in a set of architectural drawings. They help the builder understand vertical relationships. Architectural sections can occasionally contradict other drawings, such as mechanical or structural drawings. One example is a beam shown on the section is smaller than what the structural drawings call for; this creates a problem in the field when the duct does not fit in the ceiling space. The ceiling gets lowered and/or the duct gets smaller, ultimately compromising the design to a certain degree.

Revit takes great steps toward eliminating these types of conflicts. Sections, like plans and elevations, are generated from the 3D model. So it is virtually impossible to have a conflict between the architectural drawings. The final step will be to get the engineers working on the same 3D model; this would eliminate conflicts and redundancy in drawing.

Exercise 8-1:
Specify section cutting plane in plan view

Similar to elevation tags, placing the reference tags in a plan view actually generates the section view. You will learn how to do this next.

Placing section tags:

1. Open ex7-6.rvt and **Save As ex8-1.rvt**.

2. Switch to **Level 1** view.

3. Select the **Section** tool from the **Basics** tab on the *Design Bar*.   ⬦ Section

4. Draw a Section tag as shown in Figure 8-1.1. Start on the left side in this case. Use the Move tool if needed to accurately adjust the section tag after insertion. The section should go through the doors in the stair shaft (Figure 8-1.1).

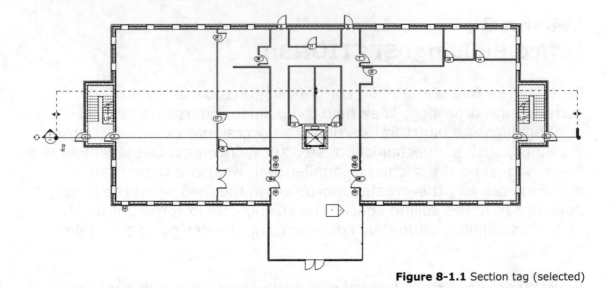

Figure 8-1.1 Section tag (selected)

Figure 8-1.1 shows the section tag selected. The section tag features are very similar to the elevation tags covered in the previous lesson. You can adjust the depth of view (*Far Clip Plane*) and the width of the section with the *Adjustment Grips*.

Section views are listed under that heading in the *Project Browser*. Similar to newly created elevation views, you should name section views as you create them.

5. Rename the new section view to: **Longitudinal Section**.

6. Switch to the **Longitudinal Section** view (Figure 8-1.2).

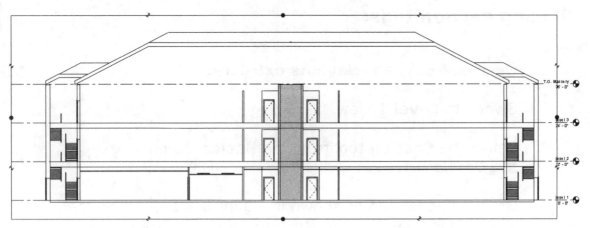

Figure 8-1.2 Longitudinal section view

You can see that the stairs are cut off on the back side because of the *Far Clip Plane* location in the plan view (Figure 8-1.1). Also, you can see the roof is shown in section exactly where the section line is shown in plan. Figure 8-1.2 also shows the *Crop Region*.

7. Adjust the *Far Clip Plane* in plan view so the entire stair shows and the *Crop Region* is not visible (Figure 8-1.3).

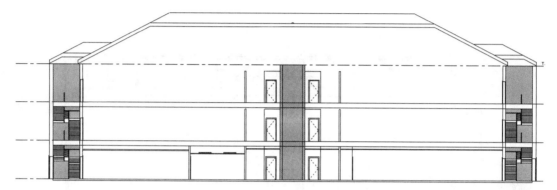

Figure 8-1.3 Longitudinal view - updated

8. Change the view *Properties* so the **Detail Level** is set to **Medium**. *(Notice how the walls change to show more detail.)*

9. Switch back to the section and zoom in to the elevator shaft area as shown in **Figure 8-1.4**.

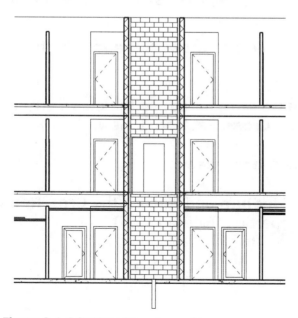

Figure 8-1.4 Section view – zoomed in

You should notice an added level of detail in the section view. For example, the concrete hatch in the floor and the CMU joint lines in the elevator shaft. This added detail helps the drawing read better.

Next you will add a cross sectional view.

10. Create a **Section** as shown in **Figure 8-1.5**.
   TIP: You can use the control arrows to make the section look the other direction.

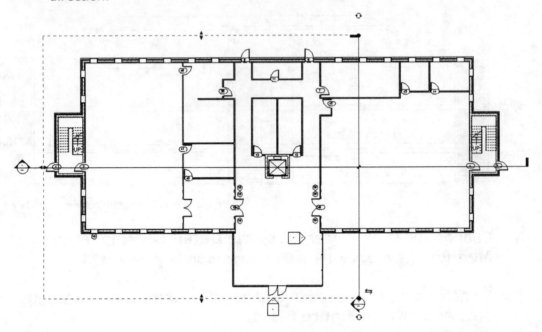

Figure 8-1.5 Level 1 view; Section tag (selected)

11. Rename the new section view to **Cross Section 1** in the *Project Browser*.

12. Adjust the **Far Clip Plane** (if required) so the entire atrium roof will be visible in the **Cross Section 1** view.

13. Switch to the **Cross Section 1** view.

14. Set the *Detail Level* to **Medium** and turn off the **Crop Region** visibility in the View Properties (Figure 8-1.6).

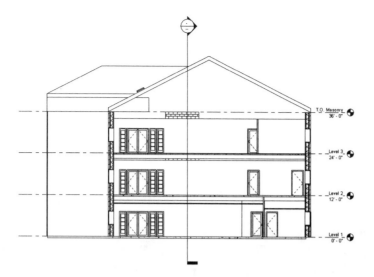

Figure 8-1.6 Cross Section 1 view

Revit automatically displays lines heavier for objects that are in section than for objects beyond the cutting plane and shown in elevation.

Also, with the Detail Level set to medium, the walls and floors are hatched to represent the material in section.

Notice that the Longitudinal Section tag is automatically displayed in the Cross Section 1 view. If you switch to the Longitudinal Section view you will see the Cross Section 1 tag. Keeping with Revit's philosophy of change anything anywhere, you can select the section tag in the other section view and adjust its various properties, like the Far Clip Plane.

15. **Save** your project as **ex8-1.rvt**.

FYI:

In any view that has a Section Tag in it, you can double-click on the round reference bubble to quickly switch to that section view.

Exercise 8-2:
Modifying the project model in section view

Again, similar to elevation views, you can modify the project model in section view. This includes adjusting door locations and ceiling heights.

Modifying doors in section view:

In this section you will move a door and delete a door in section view.

1. Open ex8-1.rvt and **Save As ex8-2.rvt**.

2. Open **Cross Section 1** view.

3. On **Level 2**, move the *Single Glass* door **5'-0"** to the north and **delete** the door added in a previous lesson, see modified section view Figure 8-2.1. (See Figure 8-1.6 for an unmodified view.)

4. Adjust the **ceiling height** in the lower right room to be **9'-0"** above Level 1 (Figure 8-2.1).
   TIP: Select the ceiling and simply change the temporary dimension that appears.

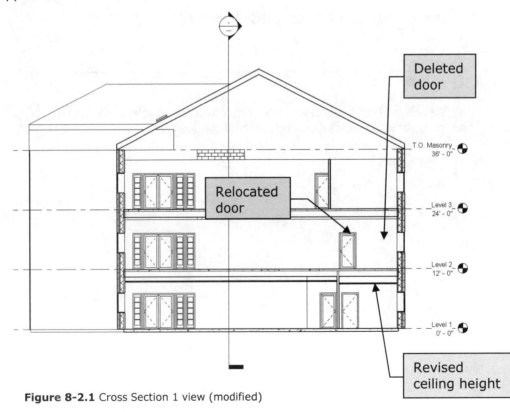

Figure 8-2.1 Cross Section 1 view (modified)

5. Switch to the **Level 2** view (Figure 8-2.2).

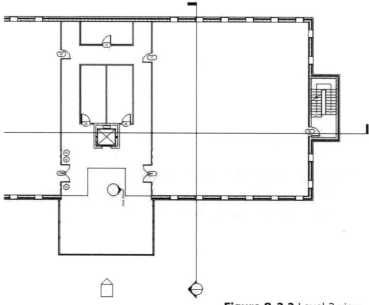

Figure 8-2.2 Level 2 view

You should see the door in its new location and the other door has been deleted.

6. Switch to the **East Atrium** view (Figure 8-2.3).

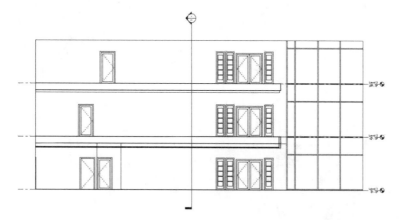

Figure 8-2.3 East Atrium view

You can see the changes here as well. Compare this elevation with Figure 7-4.1 from lesson 7. Also, notice that the section mark was automatically added to the elevation. Remember, you can double-click on the section bubble to switch to that view.

7. Save your project as **ex8-2.rvt**.

Exercise 8-3:
Wall Sections

So far in this lesson you have drawn building sections. Building sections are typically 1/16" or 1/8" scale and light on the detail and notes. Wall sections are drawn at a larger scale and have much more detail. You will look at setting up wall sections next.

Setting up the Wall Section view:

1. Open ex8-2 and **Save As ex8-3.rvt**.

2. Switch to the **Cross Section 1** view.

3. From the *View* tab on the *Design Bar*, select the **Callout** tool.

4. Place a **Callout** tag as shown in Figure 8-3.1. ***TIP:*** *Pick in the upper left and then in the lower right (don't drag) to place the Callout tag.*
   a. Select **Section: Wall Section** from the *Type Selector*.

5. Use the *Control Grips* for the *Callout* tag to move the reference bubble as shown in Figure 8-3.1.

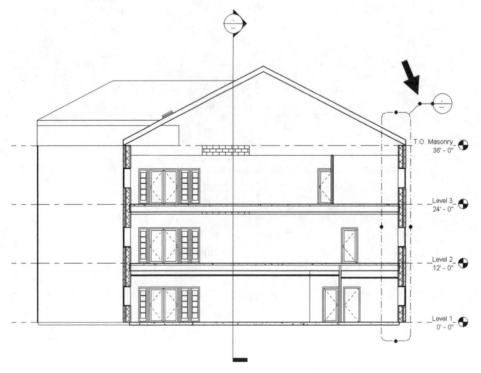

Figure 8-3.1 Cross Section 1 view with Callout added

Notice that a view was added in the *Sections* category of the *Project Browser*. Because *Callouts* are detail references off of a section view, it is a good idea to keep the section view name similar to the name of the callout.

Additionally, *Callouts* differ from section views in that the callout is not referenced in every related view. This example is typical, in that the building sections are referenced from the plans and wall sections are referenced from the building sections. The floor plans can get pretty messy if you try to add too much information to them.

6. Double-click on the reference bubble portion of the *Callout* tag to open the **Callout of Cross Section 1** view (Figure 8-3.2).

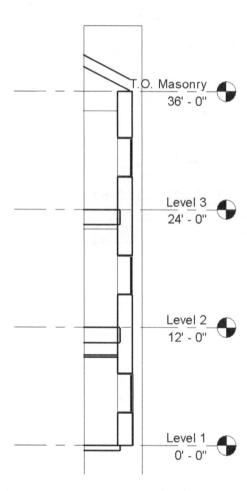

Figure 8-3.2 Callout of Cross Section 1

7. In the View properties, set the *View Scale* to **¾" = 1'-0"** and the *Detail Level* to **Fine** (Figure 8-3.3).

    Notice the Level tags size changed as well as the Detail Level (Figure 8-3.4).

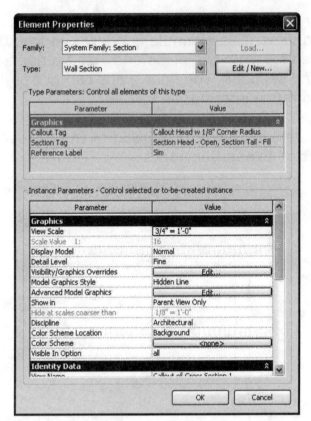

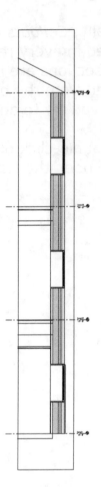

Figure 8-3.3 View properties

Figure 8-3.4 Revised Detail Level and view scale

If you zoom in on a portion of the *Callout* view, you can see the detail added to the view. The wall's interior lines (i.e., veneer lines) are added and the materials in section are hatched (Figure 8-3.5).

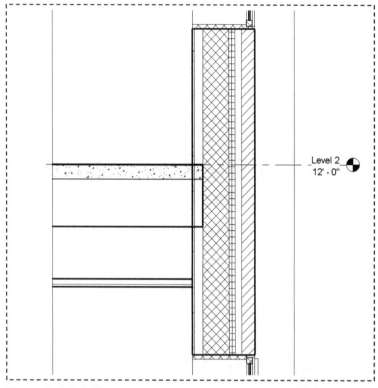

Level 2
12' - 0"

Figure 8-3.5 Callout view (zoomed in)

You can use the **Join Geometry** tool to clean up the floor to wall condition shown above. Simply click the icon and the two objects you want to join (this works on many things). See Figure 8-3.6 for a "joined" condition; every view is updated!

You can use the **Detail Lines** tool to add more detailed information to the drawing. For example, you could show the masonry coursing, window trim, brick vents/weeps and flashing.

As before, you can turn off and adjust the crop region.

8. **Save** your project as **ex8-3.rvt**.

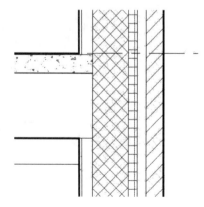

Figure 8-3.6 Joined wall/floor

Exercise 8-4:
Annotation

This exercise will explore adding notes and dimensions to your wall section.

Add notes and dimensions to Callout of Cross Section 1:

1. Open ex8-3.rvt and **Save As ex8-4.rvt**.

2. Switch to **Callout of Cross Section 1** view.

3. Adjust the view properties so the crop region is not visible.

4. Add two dimensions and adjust the Level tag location as shown in **Figure 8-4.1**.
   TIP: Dimension to the masonry opening.

These dimensions are primarily for the masons laying up the CMU and Brick. Typically, when an opening is dimensioned in masonry, the dimension has the suffix M.O. This stands for Masonry Opening, clearly representing that the dimension identifies an opening in the wall. You will add the suffix next.

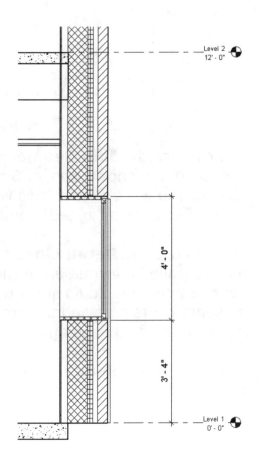

5. Select the dimension at the window opening and pick the **Blue text** (i.e., 4'-0").

6. Type **M.O.** in the Suffix field. (Figure 8-4.2)

7. Click **OK**.

Figure 8-4.1 Added dimensions

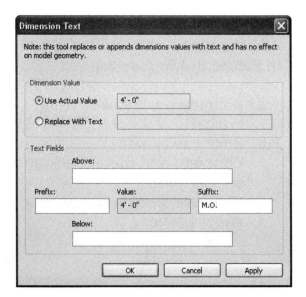

Figure 8-4.2 Selected dimension properties

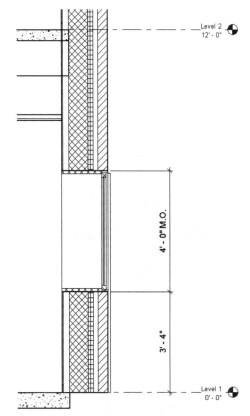

Figure 8-4.3 Dimension with suffix

Figure 8-4.3 shows the dimension with the added suffix.

8. Add the additional dimensions shown in **Figure 8-4.4**; be sure to add the suffixes.

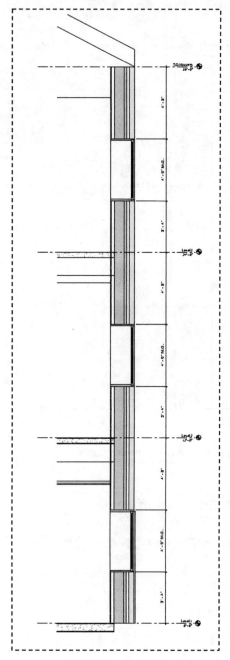

Figure 8-4.4 All dimensions added

9. Add the notes with leaders shown in Figure 8-4.5. *(See step 10.)*

    a. Aluminum window system, typical
    b. Brick cavity wall
    c. Concrete and metal deck and stl. bar joists
    d. Concrete slab on grade over vapor barrier

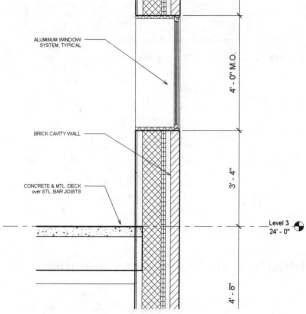

Figure 8-4.5 Notes added

10. The text style should be set to **3/32" Arial**; it may still be set to the last text style you used (¼" Outline Text, in this book).

11. Select the text and use the grips and the justification buttons to make the text look like **Figure 8-4.5**.

FYI:
Architectural text is typically all uppercase.

2D Detail Components:

Autodesk Revit Building has a large array of 2D detail components that can be used to create details. These components allow for efficient detail drafting and design. Not every detail in Revit is generated from the 3D model; the amount of modeling required to make this happen is restricted by time and file size.

- To create a 2D detail one would create a **Drafting View** via *View > New*, and then provide a name and select a scale.
- Once the *Drafting View* has been created **Detail lines** (via the Drafting tab) can be added.
- In Addition to *Drafting Lines*, one can insert pre-drawn items from the <u>Detail Library</u>.
  i. Select **Detail Components** from the *Drafting* tab.
  ii. Select **Load** from the *Options Bar*.
  iii. Click **Imperial Detail Library** from the shortcut bar on the left of the *Open* dialog.
  iv. **Browse** to the specific "CSI organized' folder; for example, *Div 5-Metals→052100- Steel Joists Framing → K-Series Bar Joist-Side.rfa*.
  v. Click **Open** to place the component.
  vi. Add notes and dimensions.

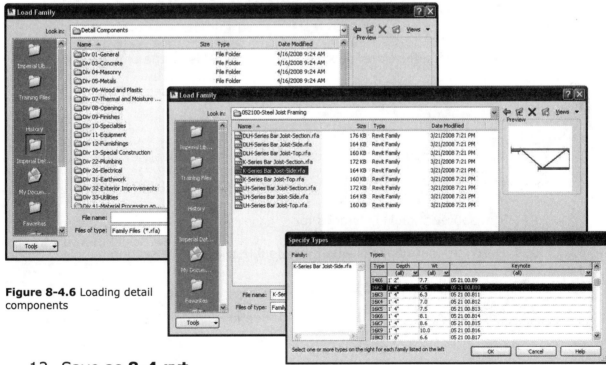

Figure 8-4.6 Loading detail components

12. Save as **8-4.rvt**.

Self-Exam:

The following questions can be used as a way to check your knowledge of this lesson. The answers can be found at the bottom of this page.

1. The controls for the section mark (when selected) are similar to the controls for the elevation mark. (T/F) *T*

2. In large-scale elevations (and areas elevated within a section), Revit displays the masonry coursing. (T/F) *T*

3. In large-scale sections (i.e., wall sections), Revit displays the masonry coursing in addition to the material hatching. (T/F) *F*

4. The "Crop Region" is represented by a red line in the section view. (T/F) *T*

5. Use the _____ tool to reference a larger section off a building section. *callout*

Review Questions:

The following questions may be assigned by your instructor as a way to assess your knowledge of this section. Your instructor has the answers to the review questions.

1. The visibility of the crop window can be controlled. (T/F) *T*

2. It's not possible to draw a leader (line with arrow) with out placing text. (T/F) *T*

3. When a section mark is added to a view, all the other related views automatically get a section mark added to it. (T/F) *T*

4. It is possible to modify objects (like doors, windows and ceilings) in section views. (T/F) *T*

5. You cannot adjust the "depth of view" (width) using the crop window. (T/F) *F*

6. What is the first thing you should do after placing a section tag?

    _____ *rename the new tag* _____

7. If the text appears to be excessively large in a section view, the views

    _____ *text* _____ *style* _____ is probably set incorrectly.

8. The abbreviation M.O. stands for _____ *masonry* _____ *opening* _____.

9. Describe what happens when you double-click on the section bubble:

    _____ *you switch to that view* _____.

10. Revit provides __*4*__ different leader options within the text command.

Lesson 9
Office Building: FLOOR PLAN FEATURES::

This lesson explores the various "features," if you will, of a floor plan, such as toilet room layouts (i.e., fixtures and partitions), cabinets and casework (e.g., reception counters and custom cabinets). Additionally, you will look at placing pre-drawn furniture into your project.

Exercise 9-1:
Toilet room layouts

Toilet room layouts involve placing water closets (toilets), toilet partitions and sinks. These rooms have many code issues related primarily to handicapped accessibility. These codes vary from state to state (and even city to city).

You will start this exercise by loading several components to be placed into your project.

1. Open ex8-4.rvt and **Save As ex9-1.rvt**.

2. Select the **Component** tool and load the following items into the current project:

> **Local Files** *(i.e., on your hard drive)*
> a. Plumbing Fixtures**Toilet-Comercial-Wall-3D.rfa**
> b. Plumbing Fixtures**Urinal-Wall-3D**
>
> **Online Files** *(i.e., Revit's Web Library on internet)*
> c. Plumbing Fixtures**Sink-Wall-Rectangular**
> d. Specialty Equipment\Toilet Room Specialties**Grab Bar-3D**
> e. "   "**Toilet Stall-Accessible-Front-Braced-3D**
> f. "   "**Toilet Stall-Braced-3D**
> g. "   "**Urinal Screen-3D**

These files represent various predefined families that will be used to design the toilet room. It is possible to create custom families for non-typical conditions.

Figure 9-1.1 shows an example of the various families available for Toilet Stalls on Autodesk Revit's web site.

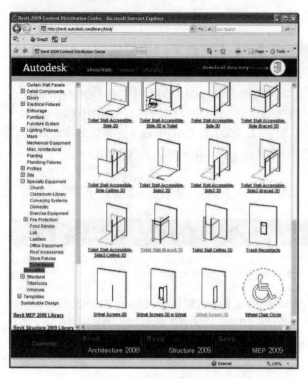

Figure 9-1.1 Toilet stalls online

3. Switch to **Level 1** view.

The next step will be to place the toilet stalls.

4. With the **Component** tool selected, pick **Toilet Stall-Accessible-Front-Braced-3D: 60" x 60" Clear** from the type selector.

5. Zoom in to the toilet rooms (north of the elevator).

6. **Place** the toilet stall as shown and then move into place using the **Move** tool and your snaps (Figure 9-1.2).

Once you move the toilet stall north, you will have your first stall in place.

Next, you will place two standard size toilet stalls.

7. Place two toilet stalls (**Toilet Stall-Braced-3D: 36" x 60" Clear**) as shown in Figure 9-1.3.

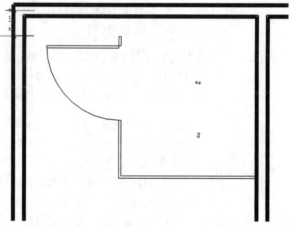

Figure 9-1.2 Accessible Toilet stall

As with most projects, you will need to modify the model as you develop the design. In this case we notice that toilets that are back-to-back and stacked on each floor will require a thicker wall to accommodate the fixture brackets (W.C.'s are not hung on the wall by light gauge metal studs) and larger piping. You will make this adjustment next.

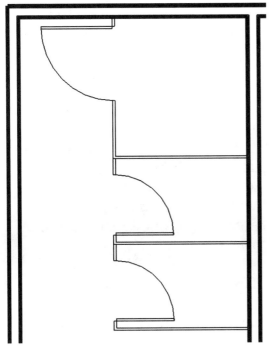

Figure 9-1.3 Toilet stalls placed

8. Select the middle wall and the west wall and **Move** them **6"** to the west.

9. **Move** the far east wall (of the two toilet rooms) **6"** to the east.

10. Add an additional **4⅞"** gyp. bd. wall as shown in **Figure 9-1.4**.
    TIP: *Make sure wall height and base offset are correct.*

11. Modify the north wall of the elevator shaft to have furring and gyp. bd. on the toilet room side.
    TIP: *Use the wall type you created for the stair shafts.*

12. Add the additional components as shown in **Figure 9-1.4**.

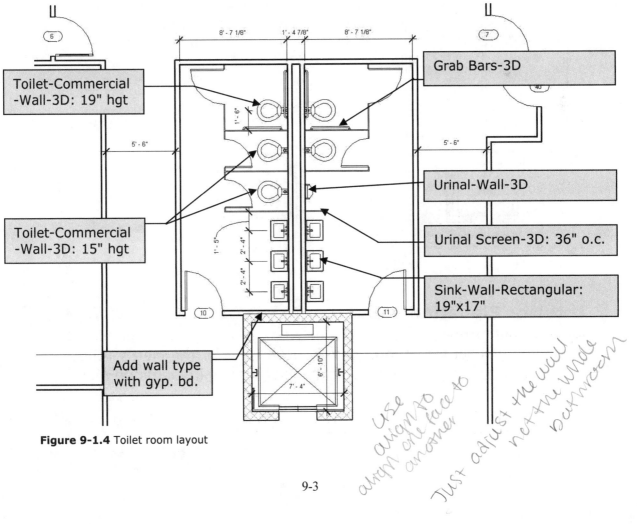

Figure 9-1.4 Toilet room layout

As mentioned previously, building codes vary by location. The toilets in the accessible stall area are typically mounted higher than the typical fixtures. When a room has more than one urinal, one is usually required to be mounted lower for accessibility. Another example is that Minnesota requires a separate vertical grab bar above the horizontal grab bar on the wall next to the toilet.

You will now copy the revised walls and toilet room layout to the other levels. The elevator shaft extends through each floor, so you will not have to copy that wall. Looking at the upper levels you can see the revised elevator shaft wall and the old wall layout (Figure 9-1.5). It will be easier to delete the stud walls rather than modify the existing walls.

13. Delete the walls, per **Figure 9-1.6**, for Levels 2 and 3.

14. **Copy** the walls and toilet room layout to the clipboard and **Paste Aligned** to Levels 2 and 3.

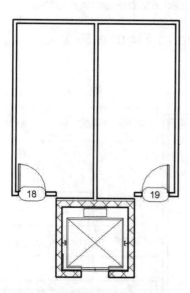

Figure 9-1.5 Walls on upper levels

Figure 9-1.6 Walls deleted

Interior Elevation view:

Next, you will set up an interior elevation view for the Men's Toilet Room. You will also add a mirror above the sinks in elevation view.

15. Switch to **Level 1** and Place an [Interior] **Elevation** bubble looking towards the wet wall (wall with fixtures on it); see Figure 9-1.7.

16. Rename the new view to: **Men's Toilet – Typical** in the *Project Browser*.

17. Switch to the new view. Adjust the Crop Region so the concrete slab is not visible. Your view should look like Figure 9-1.8.

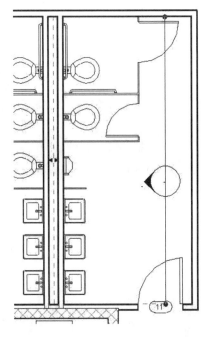

You may see the building section reference as shown in Figure 9-1.8. This would not typically be shown in an interior elevation view, especially because it does not intersect the elevation view. You will remove the reference in the next step. You cannot simply delete it, because that will remove it from all views and delete the section.

Figure 9-1.7 Elevation tag added

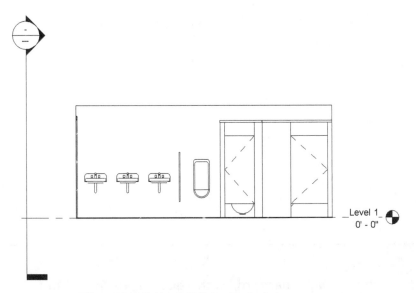

Figure 9-1.8 Men's Toilet – Typical view

18. If you see the building section mark, click on the section reference to select it and then right-click and pick **Hide in View → Elements** from the pop-up menu (Figure 9-1.9).

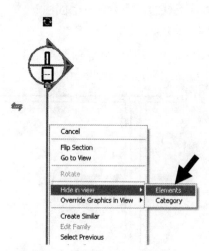

Figure 9-1.9 Hide annotation

19. Load component *Specialty Equipment\Toilet Room Specialties* **Mirror.rfa** from the Online Revit library.

20. While in the interior elevation view, place a **72" x 48" Mirror** on the wall above the sinks. Use the *Align* tool to align the mirror with the middle sink. (Figure 9-1.10)

21. Add the notes and dimensions shown in Figure 9-1.10. Adjust the heights and locations of the fixtures/ components as required.

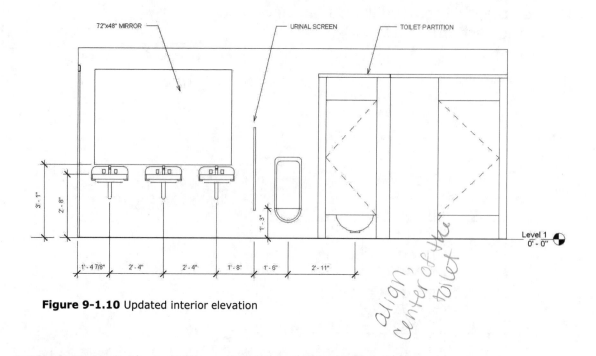

Figure 9-1.10 Updated interior elevation

FYI:

Keep in mind that many of the symbols that come with Revit (or any program for that matter) are not necessarily drawn or reviewed by an architect. The point is that the default values, such as mounting heights, may not meet ADA, national, state or local codes. Items like the mirror have a maximum height off the floor to the reflective surface that Revit's standard components may not comply with. However, as you apply local codes to these families, you can reuse them in the future.

Adjusting the Reflected Ceiling Plan:

Because you added a wall in the east toilet room, the definition of the room that the reflected ceiling plan uses is incorrect. You will adjust that next. You will have similar problems on Levels 2 and 3 because you deleted walls and then pasted new walls.

22. Switch to **Level 1 RCP** (Figure 9-1.11).

23. Hide the Interior Elevation tag from this view.

24. Delete the ceiling in the Men's Toilet room.

25. Place a new ceiling to fit within the room.

26. Select the ceiling grid in the atrium, and then pick **Edit Sketch** to adjust the reference lines for the perimeter of the ceiling grid in the atrium area (Figure 9-1.12).
    FYI: *You could have used this method for steps 24/25 as well.*

27. Correct the ceilings on Levels 2 and 3.

28. **Save** your project as **ex9-1.rvt**.

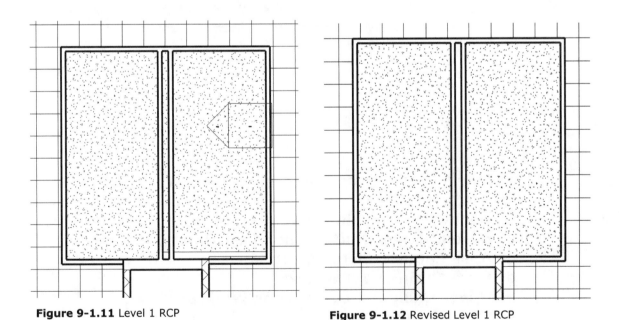

Figure 9-1.11 Level 1 RCP   **Figure 9-1.12** Revised Level 1 RCP

Exercise 9-2:
Cabinets

In this exercise you will look at adding cabinets and casework to your project. As usual, Revit provides several pre-defined families to be placed into the project.

Placing cabinets:

You will add base and wall cabinets in a break room on Level 1.

1. Open ex9-1.rvt and **Save As ex9-2.rvt**.

2. Switch to **Level 1** view and zoom into the area shown in **Figure 9-2.1**.

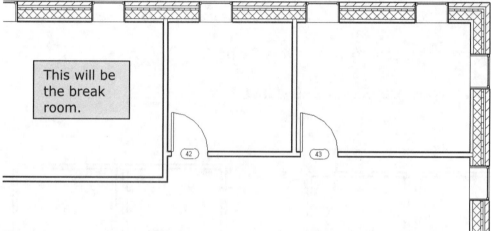

Figure 9-2.1 Level 1 – north-east corner

3. *Load* the following components into the project
   (*all local files – Casework\Domestic Kitchen*):
   a. **Counter Top w Sink Hole**
   b. **Base Cabinet-Double Door Sink Unit**
   c. **Base Cabinet-Single Door**
   d. **Base Cabinet-4 Drawers**
   e. **Upper Cabinet-Double Door-Wall**
   f. **Sink Kitchen-Single**
   g. **Refrigerator**

You are now ready to place the cabinets into your floor plan.

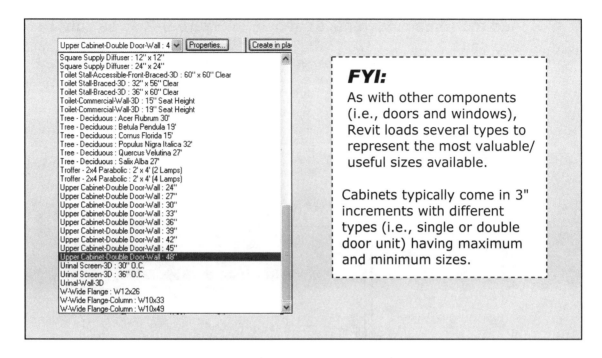

Upper Cabinet-Double Door-Wall : 4 ▾   [Properties...]   [Create in pla]

Square Supply Diffuser : 12'' x 12''
Square Supply Diffuser : 24'' x 24''
Toilet Stall-Accessible-Front-Braced-3D : 60'' x 60'' Clear
Toilet Stall-Braced-3D : 32'' x 56'' Clear
Toilet Stall-Braced-3D : 36'' x 60'' Clear
Toilet-Commercial-Wall-3D : 15'' Seat Height
Toilet-Commercial-Wall-3D : 19'' Seat Height
Tree - Deciduous : Acer Rubrum 30'
Tree - Deciduous : Betula Pendula 19'
Tree - Deciduous : Cornus Florida 15'
Tree - Deciduous : Populus Nigra Italica 32'
Tree - Deciduous : Quercus Velutina 27'
Tree - Deciduous : Salix Alba 27'
Troffer - 2x4 Parabolic : 2' x 4' (2 Lamps)
Troffer - 2x4 Parabolic : 2' x 4' (4 Lamps)
Upper Cabinet-Double Door-Wall : 24''
Upper Cabinet-Double Door-Wall : 27''
Upper Cabinet-Double Door-Wall : 30''
Upper Cabinet-Double Door-Wall : 33''
Upper Cabinet-Double Door-Wall : 36''
Upper Cabinet-Double Door-Wall : 39''
Upper Cabinet-Double Door-Wall : 42''
Upper Cabinet-Double Door-Wall : 45''
Upper Cabinet-Double Door-Wall : 48''
Urinal Screen-3D : 30'' O.C.
Urinal Screen-3D : 36'' O.C.
Urinal-Wall-3D
W-Wide Flange : W12x26
W-Wide Flange-Column : W10x33
W-Wide Flange-Column : W10x49

FYI:
As with other components (i.e., doors and windows), Revit loads several types to represent the most valuable/ useful sizes available.

Cabinets typically come in 3" increments with different types (i.e., single or double door unit) having maximum and minimum sizes.

4.   With the *Component* tool selected, pick **Base Cabinet-4 Drawers: 24"** from the *Type Selector* on the *Options Bar*.

5.   Place the cabinet as shown in **Figure 9-2.2**. *TIP: The control arrows are on the front side of the cabinet; the cursor is on the back. Press the spacebar to rotate while placing (i.e., before picking).*

6.   Place the other two base cabinets as shown in **Figure 9-2.3**, with a 24" single door base cabinet in the middle and a 48" sink base to the north end.

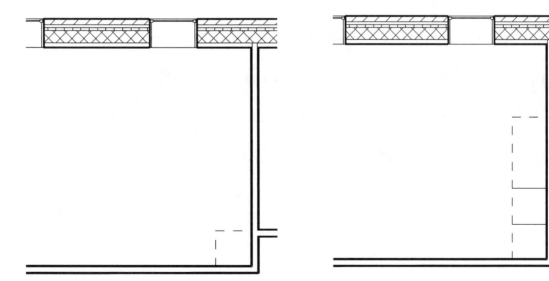

Figure 9-2.2 First cabinet placed   **Figure 9-2.3** Three base cabinets placed

7. Add the remaining items as shown in Figure 9-2.4; be sure to use snaps.
    (E.g., place sink to one side, use move and snap to a mid-point of the sink bowl, and then to the mid-point of the same line representing the hole in the countertop).

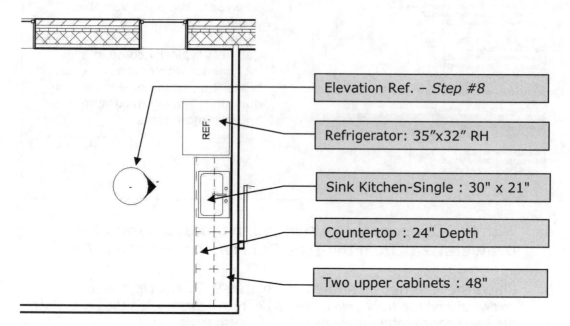

Figure 9-2.4 Completed plan view

8. Add an [interior] elevation tag to setup the interior elevation view. (Figure 9-2.4)

9. Rename the new elevation view to **Break Room (east)**.

10. Switch to the new view, **Break Room (east)**.

11. Adjust the **Crop Region** so the slab on grade is not visible.

12. Your drawing should look like **Figure 9-2.5**.

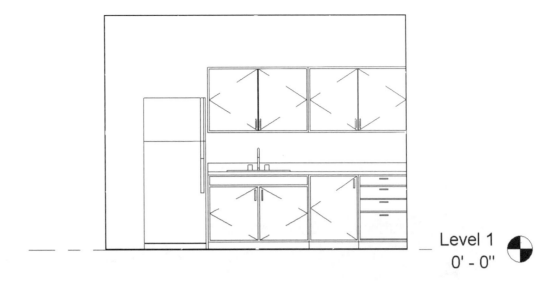

Figure 9-2.5 Interior elevation

You will add notes and dimensions to the elevation. You can also add 2D line work to the elevation.

13. Set the view scale to **½" = 1'-0"**.

14. Add the notes and dimensions per **Figure 9-2.6**.

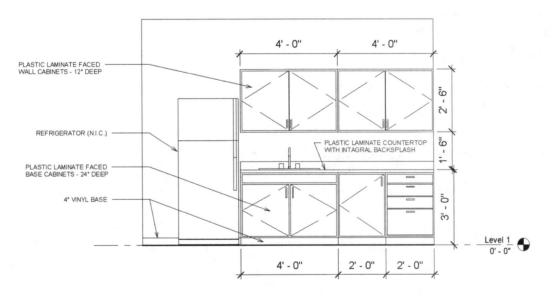

Figure 9-2.6 Interior elevation with annotations

15. Use the **Lines** tool, on the *Basics* tab, to draw the line on the wall behind the refrigerator, indicating the vinyl base.

When you select the **Lines** tool, Revit will ask you what plane you want to draw on (Figure 9-2.7). This will allow Revit to restrict all your line work to a particular plane. Otherwise you would not know exactly at what depth the lines would be drawn on.

16. Select **Pick a Plane** (Figure 9-2.7) and then pick the wall in the elevation view (use the TAB key and make sure the tool tip lists the wall before picking the plane).
    TIP: If you are prompted to switch to a different view, you selected the wrong plane. Click cancel and try again.

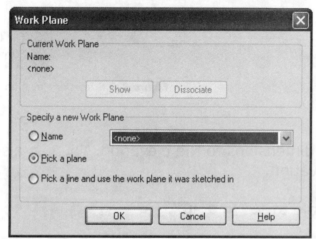

Figure 9-2.7 Work Plane prompt

FYI:

The main difference between the *Lines* tool on the Basics tab and the *Detail Lines* tool on the Drafting tab is this: any linework drawn with the *Lines* tool will show up on other views that see that surface. On the other hand, any linework drawn with the *Detail Lines* tool will only show up in the view in which they were created in.

So in this example, you may want to draw the lines using the Detail Line tool so the base does not show up in building and wall sections.

---

17. Draw the line, snap to the endpoint of the base cabinet toe kick.

18. Select the line and in the Type Selector, change the *Line Style* to **Thin Lines**.

19. **Save** your project as **ex9-2.rvt**.

Exercise 9-3:
Furniture

This lesson will cover the steps required to lay out office furniture. The processes are identical to those previously covered for toilets and cabinets.

Loading the necessary families:

1. Open ex9-2.rvt and **Save As ex9-3.rvt**.

2. Select the Component tool and load the following items into the current project:

    Local Files *(i.e., on your hard drive)*
    a. **Work Station Cubicle.rfa** (Furniture System)
    b. **Work Station Desktops** (Furniture System)
    c. **Sofa-Pensi** (Furniture)
    d. **Chair-Breuer** (Furniture)
    e. **Chair-Executive** (Furniture)
    f. **Chair-Task Arms** (Furniture)
    g. **Table-Round** (Furniture)

    Online Files *(i.e., Revit's Web Library on internet)*
    h. Specialty Equipment\Office Equipment**Copier-Floor**

These files represent various predefined families that will be used to design the offices.

TIP:

You can set the View mode for the Open dialog box (which is displayed when you click *Load from Library*. One option is Thumbnail mode; this displays a small thumbnail image for each file in the current folder. This makes it easier to see the many symbols and drawings that are available for insertion.

Above: View set to List mode

Right: View set to Thumbnail mode

Designing the office furniture layout:

3. Switch to the **Level 3** view.

4. Place the furniture as shown in Figure 9-3.1.
   TIP: *Use snaps to assure accuracy; use rotate and mirror as required.*

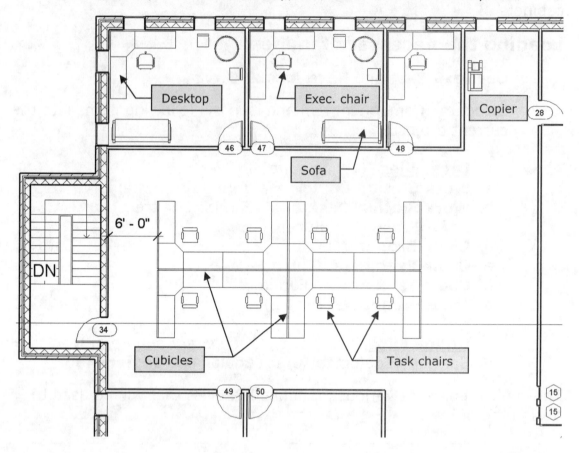

Figure 9-3.1 Level 3 – furniture layout

The cubicles in the open office area should be centered in the north-south direction. The cubicle partitions should overlap so only one partition is visible. The items not labeled in Figure 9-3.1 should be compared to the families listed in step 2; it will be obvious as to what the items are.

3D view of office layout:

Next you will look at a 3D view of your office area. This involves adjusting the visibility of the roof and skylights.

5. Switch to the **Default 3D** view.

6. Right click anywhere in the drawing window and select **View Properties** from the pop-up list.

7. Click **Edit** next to the *Visibility* parameter.

8. Uncheck the *Roof* category and click **OK** twice.

The roof should not be visible now. However, you should still see the skylights floating in space. You will make those disappear next.

9. Select one of the skylights floating above the office area.

10. Click the **Temporary Hide/Isolate** from the *View Control Bar*.

You should see the menu shown in **Figure 9-3.2** show up next to the *Temporary Hide/Isolate* icon. This allows you to isolate an object (so it's the only thing on the screen) or hide it (so the object is temporarily not visible).

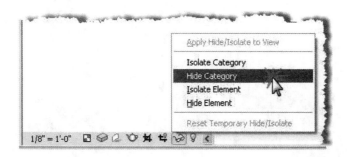

Figure 9-3.2 Hide/Isolate popup menu

11. Click **Hide Category** in the menu. (Figure 9-3.2)
    FYI: This makes all the skylights hide; you could leave it at "Hide Element" and select each skylight.

12. Adjust your 3D view to look similar to **Figure 9-3.3** by clicking and dragging your mouse on the ViewCube.

You will now restore the original visibility settings for the 3D view.

13. Click the Hide/Isolate icon and then select **Reset Temporary Hide/Isolate** from the popup up menu.

    NOTE: The Temporary Hide/Isolate feature is just meant to be a temporary control of object visibility while you are working on the model. If you want permanent results, you can click the "Apply Hide/Isolate to View" option. Also, to the right of the Hide/Isolate icon is the Reveal Hidden Elements icon (the light bulb icon), which will clearly show any elements that have been previously hidden.

14. Reset the 3D view's visibility settings so the roof is visible.

15. **Save** your project as **ex9-3.rvt**.

    Notice the furniture and toilet rooms are represented in 3D.

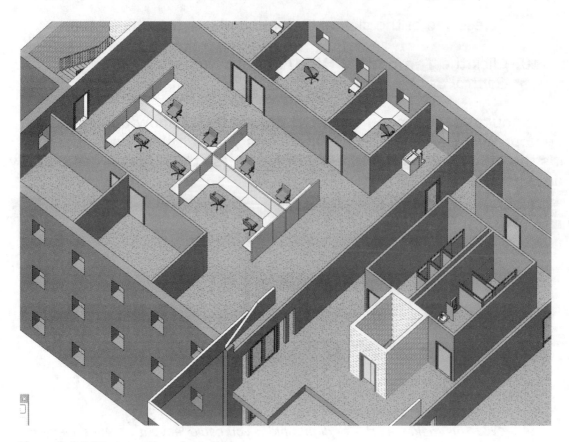

Figure 9-3.3 3D view with roof not visible

Online Content:

A few locations on the internet provide additional content for use in Revit. Some are free and some are not. Hopefully product manufacturers will start providing content based on the products they make; making it easier for people to include that manufacturer's product in their project (both the virtual and real projects).

You have already spent a little time looking at Revit's online content library (revit.autodesk.com/library/html/). You should spend some more time there so you know what is generally available. This will help you to reduce duplicated effort.

The Modern Medium 2009 Library, available on Revit's content library, has a ton of furniture you can use in your project. (see sample screen shot below).

The following sites also contain content that can be downloaded:
- www.revitcity.com
- www.augi.com
- www.revitdrop.com

You should occasionally search the internet to see if additional content becomes available. You can do a Google search for "revit content", make sure to include the parentheses. The rendering content, such as that offered by www.archvision.com, will be covered in chapter 11.

Exercise 9-4:
Adding Guardrails

This lesson will cover the steps required to lay out guardrails. The steps are similar to drawing walls; you select your style and draw its path.

Adding a guardrail to the Atrium:

1. Open ex9-3.rvt and **Save As ex9-4.rvt**.

2. Switch to Level 2 view.

3. From the *Modeling* tab select **Railing**.

4. **Zoom** into the Atrium area (south of the elevator).

At this point you will draw a line representing the path of the guardrail. The railing is offset to one side of the line, similar to Walls. However, you do not have the *Loc Line* option as you do with the Wall tool, so you have to draw the railing in a certain direction to get the railing to be on the floor and not hovering in space just beyond the floor edge.

5. Draw a line along the edge of the floor as shown in **Figure 9-4.1**.
    TIP: *Select Chain from the Options Bar to draw the railing with fewer picks.*

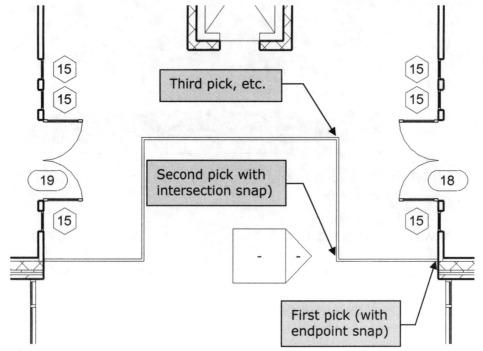

Figure 9-4.1 Adding guardrail – Level 2

6. Click **Finish Sketch** from the *Design Bar*.

The railing has now been drawn. In the next step you will switch to a 3D view and see how to quickly change the railing style. This will also involve changing the height of the railing. Most building codes require the railing height be 42" when the drop to the adjacent surface is more than 30"; this is called a guardrail.

7. Switch to the **Default 3D** view.

8. Zoom into the railing shown on Level 2, looking at it through the curtainwall. (Notice the railing style – Figure 9-4.2.)

Figure 9-4.2 Added railing – 3D view

9. Select the railing. You may have to use the Tab key to cycle through the various selection options.

10. With the railing selected, select the various railing types available in the *Type Selector* on the *Options Bar*. When finished make sure **Railing: Guardrail – Pipe** is selected. (Figure 9-4.3)

Figure 9-4.3 Options for selected railing

Your railing should now look like Figure 9-4.4. Notice that a handrail was added to the railing. You should also notice that the handrail is on the wrong side of the guardrail. You will adjust that next.

Figure 9-4.4 Railing with new style

11. Switch to the **Level 2** plan view and select the railing.

12. Click on the **Control Arrows** to flip the railing orientation. (See the *FYI* box below for additional information.)

13. You can switch back to the **3D view** to see the change.

14. Finally, from the Level 2 plan view, **Copy** the railing to the clipboard and **Paste** it into the Level 3 view.

15. **Save** your project as **ex9-4.rvt**.

FYI:

The last modification, using the control arrows, flipped the railing about the sketch lines, so the railing is now hanging out in space. You can fix this by selecting the railing, clicking "edit" on the *Options Bar*, and then moving the sketch lines in to compensate.

Make sure to examine the railing sample file available on Revit's online content library (revit.autodesk.com/library/html/). You can download this file, open it, select a railing and view its properties to see how it works.

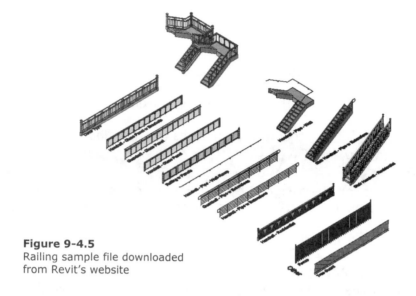

Figure 9-4.5
Railing sample file downloaded from Revit's website

You can Copy/Paste a railing style from this drawing into one of your project files. Then you select your railing and pick the newly imported one from the *Type Selector*. This process was done to achieve the image below (Figure 9-4.6). Notice the glass railing with brackets.

Figure 9-4.6 Optional railing configuration

Self-Exam:

The following questions can be used as a way to check your knowledge of this lesson. The answers can be found at the bottom of this page.

1. The toilet room fixtures are preloaded in the template file. (T/F)

    F

2. You do not need to be connected to the internet when you click on the *Load from Web* button in the Load from Library dialog box. (T/F)

    F

3. The Revit items are not always in compliance with codes. (T/F)

    T

4. You can draw 2D lines on the wall in an interior elevation view. (T/F)

    T

5. Use the _____ tool to copy fixtures to other floors

    Copy to clipboard

Review Questions:

The following questions may be assigned by your instructor as a way to assess your knowledge of this section. Your instructor has the answers to the review questions.

1. Revit provides several different styles of toilet stalls for placement. (T/F)

    T

2. Most of the time Revit automatically updates the ceiling when walls are moved, but occasionally you have to manually make revisions. (T/F)

    T

3. It is not possible to draw dimensions on an interior elevation view. (T/F)

    F

4. Cabinets typically come in 6" increments. (T/F)

    F

5. Base cabinets automatically have a countertop on them. (T/F)

    F

6. What can you adjust so the concrete slab does not show in section?

    ~~temporarily hide element~~ *crop region*

7. How does Revit determine where to place 2D line in an elevation view (based on the example in this lesson)?

    by selecting ~~pick a plane~~ 2D work plane

    will do on test

8. What is the current size of your Revit Project?

    Big   4 or 5 meg

9. What should you use to assure accuracy when placing furniture?

    Snaps

10. You use the *hide /isolate* tool to make various components temporarily invisible.

Lesson 10
Office Building: SCHEDULES::

You will continue to learn the powerful features available in Revit. This includes the ability to create parametric schedules; you can delete a door number on a schedule and Revit will delete the corresponding door from the plan.

Exercise 10-1:
Room and Door Tags

This exercise will look at adding room tags and door tags to your plans. As you insert doors, Revit adds tags to them automatically. However, if you copy or mirror a door you can lose the tag and have to add it.

Adding Room Tags:

You will add a Room Tag to each room on your Level 1 floor plan.

1. From the *Basics* tab on the *Design Bar*, select **Room**.

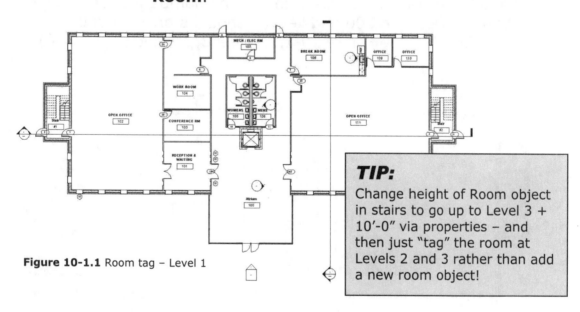

Figure 10-1.1 Room tag – Level 1

TIP:
Change height of Room object in stairs to go up to Level 3 + 10'-0" via properties – and then just "tag" the room at Levels 2 and 3 rather than add a new room object!

Placing a room/room tag is similar to placing a ceiling in the reflected ceiling plan; as you move your cursor over a room, the room (perimeter) highlights. When the room you want to place a room name tag in is highlighted, you click to place the tag in that room.

2. Place your cursor within the atrium area, which will also automatically place a room tag.(Figure 10-1.1)

By default, Revit will simply label the space 'Room' and number it '1.' You will change these to something different.

3. Press **Esc** or select **Modify** to cancel the Room command.

4. Click on the *Room Tag* you just placed to select it.

5. Now click on the room name label to change it; enter **Atrium**.

6. Now click on the room number to change it; enter **100**.

7. Add *Room Tags* (using the **Room** tool) for each room on Level 1, incrementing each room number by 1 (Figure 10-1.1).

The stair shafts typically are numbered Stair #1, Stair #2, etc. The same number is then placed on each level. This is because stair shafts are really one tall room and the finishes would apply to the entire shaft, not each floor. When you try to place a tag with the same name and number, Revit will warn you; you can click OK to ignore.

8. Add Room Tags to Levels 2 and 3. The numbering for Level 2 should start with 200 and Level 3 should start with 300. (For Level 2, see Figure 10-1.2; Level 3, see Figure 10-1.3.)

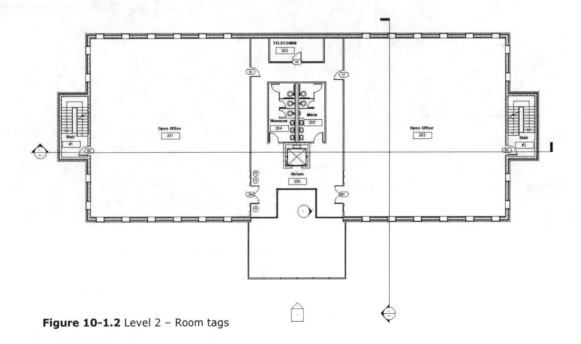

Figure 10-1.2 Level 2 – Room tags

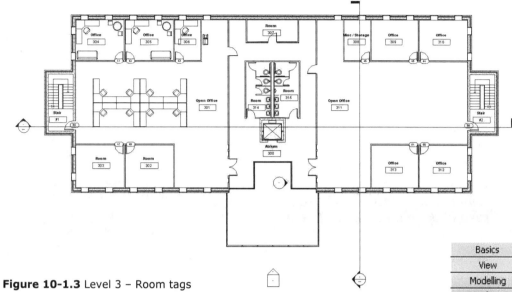

Figure 10-1.3 Level 3 – Room tags

Adding Door Tags:

Next you will add Door Tags to any doors that are missing them. Additionally, you will adjust the door numbers to correspond to the room numbers.

Revit numbers the doors in the order they are placed into the drawing. This would make it difficult to locate a door by its door number if door number 1 was on Level 1 and door number 2 was on Level 3, etc. Typically, a door number is the same as the room the door swings into. For example, if a door swung into an office numbered 304, the door number would also be 304. If the office had two doors into it, the doors would be numbered 304A and 304B.

9. Switch to **Level 1** view.

10. Click the **Tag >>** button on the *Drafting* tab. (Figure 10-1.4), and then **By Category**.

Notice as you move your cursor around the screen Revit displays a tag, for items that can have tags, when the cursor is over it. When you click the mouse is when Revit actually places a tag.

Figure 10-1.4 Drafting tab

11. **Uncheck** the **Leader** option on the *Options Bar*.

12. Place a door tag for each door that does not have a tag, do this for each level.

13. Renumber all the door tags to correspond to the room they open into; do this for each level.
    (Figure 10-1.5)
    Remember to click Modify, select the Tag and then click on the number to edit it.

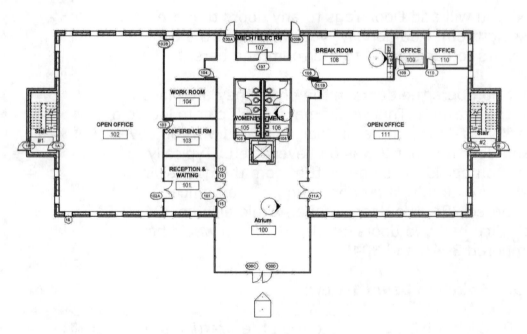

Figure 10-1.5 Level 1 – door tags (scale changes to make tags larger on this page)

14. **Save** your project as **ex10-2.rvt**.

Exercise 10-2:
Generate a Door Schedule

This exercise will look at creating a door schedule based on the information currently available in the building model (i.e., the tags).

Create a Door Schedule view:

A door schedule is simply another view of the building model. However, this view displays numerical data rather than graphical data. Just like a graphical view, if you change the view it changes all the other related views. For example, if you delete a door number from the schedule, the door is deleted from the plans and elevations.

1. Open ex10-1.rvt and **Save As ex10-2.rvt**.

2. Select the **Schedule/Quantities** button from the *View* tab on the *Design Bar*.

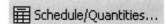

3. Select **Doors** under *Category* and then click **OK**. (Figure 10-2.1)

Figure 10-2.1 New Schedule dialog

You should now be in the *Schedule Properties* dialog where you specify what information is displayed in the schedule, how it is sorted and the text format.

4. On the **Fields** tab, add the information you want displayed in the schedule. Select the following (Figure 10-2.2):
    a. Mark *TIP: Click the **Add** → button each time.*
    b. Width
    c. Height
    d. Frame Material
    e. Frame Type
    f. Fire Rating

As noted in the dialog, the fields added to the list on the right are in the order they will be in the schedule view. Use the *Move Up* and *Move Down* buttons to adjust the order.

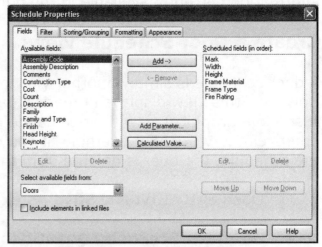

Figure 10-2.2 Schedule Properties – Fields

5. On the **Sorting/Grouping** tab, set the schedule to be sorted by the Mark (i.e., door number) in ascending order. (Figure 10-2.3)

TIP:

The Formatting and Appearance tabs allow you to adjust how the schedule looks. The formatting is not displayed until the schedule is placed on a plot sheet.

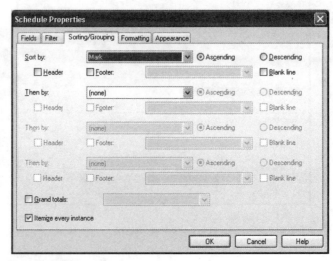

Figure 10-2.3 Schedule Properties – Sorting

6. Click the **OK** button to generate the schedule view.

You should now have a schedule similar to Figure 10-2.4.

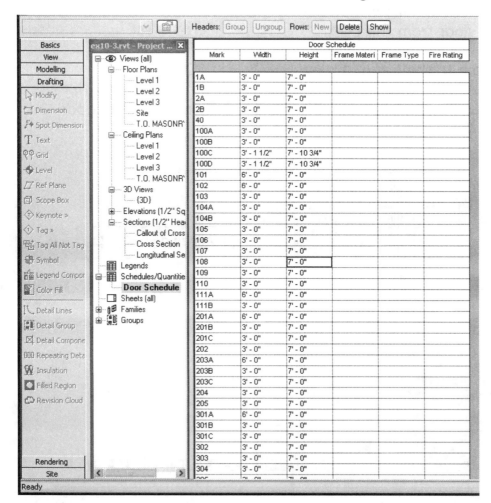

Figure 10-2.4 Door schedule view

TIP:

From the **File** menu you can select **Export → Schedule...** to create a text file
(*.txt) that can be used in other programs like MS Excel.

Next you will see how adding a door to the plan automatically updates the door schedule. Likewise, deleting a door number from the schedule deletes the door from the plan.

7. Switch to the **Level 1** view.

8. Add a door as shown in **Figure 10-2.5**; number the door **111C**.

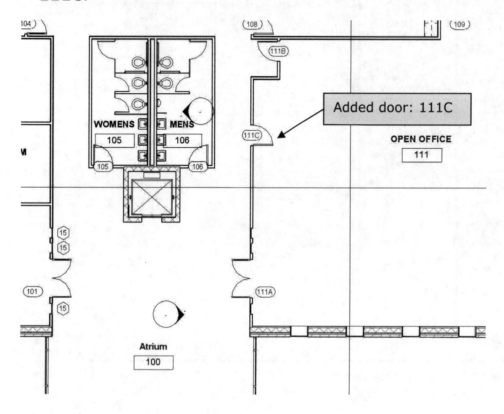

Figure 10-2.5 Level 1 – door added

9. Switch to the **Door Schedule** view, under Schedules/Quantities in the *Project Browser*. Notice door 111C was added. (Figure 10-2.6)

109	3' - 0"	7' - 0"
110	3' - 0"	7' - 0"
111A	6' - 0"	7' - 0"
111B	3' - 0"	7' - 0"
111C	3' - 0"	7' - 0"
201A	6' - 0"	7' - 0"
201B	3' - 0"	7' - 0"

Figure 10-2.6 Updated door schedule

Next you will delete door 111C from the door schedule view.

   10. Click in the cell with the number **111C**.

   11. Now click the **Delete** button from the *Options Bar*.
       (Figure 10-2.7)

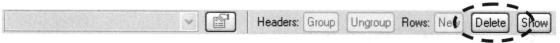

Figure 10-2.7 *Options Bar* for the door schedule view

You will get an alert. Revit is telling you that the actual door will be
deleted from the project model (Figure 10-2.8).

   12. Click **OK** to delete the door (Figure 10-2.8).

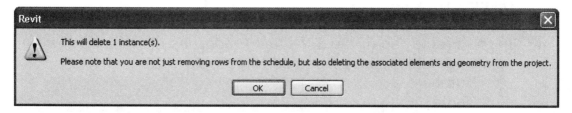

Figure 10-2.8 Revit alert message

   13. Switch back to the **Level 1** view and notice that door 111C has
       been deleted from the project model.

   14. **Save** your project as **ex10-3.rvt**.

> **TIP:**
> You can also change the door number in the schedule and the even the size;
> however, changing the size actually changes the door family which affects all the
> doors that size and style.

Exercise 10-3:
Generate a Room Finish Schedule

In this exercise you will create a Room Finish schedule. The process is similar to the previous exercise. You will also create a color-coded plan based on information associated with the *Room* object.

Create a Room Finish Schedule:

1. Open ex10-2.rvt and **Save As ex10-3.rvt**.

2. Select the **Schedule/Quantities** button from the *View* tab on the *Design Bar*.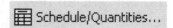

3. Select **Room** under *Category* and then click **OK**. (Figure 10-3.1)

4. In the **Fields** tab of the *Schedule Properties* dialog, add the following fields to be scheduled (Figure 10-3.2):
    a. Number
    b. Name
    c. Base Finish
    d. Floor Finish
    e. Wall Finish
    f. Ceiling Finish
    g. Area

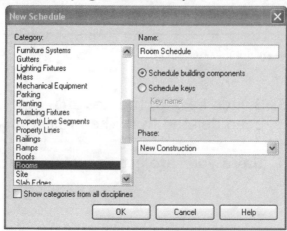

Figure 10-3.1 New Schedule dialog

Area is not typically listed on a room finish schedule. However, you will add it to your schedule to see the various options Revit allows.

5. On the **Sorting/Grouping** tab set the schedule to be sorted by the **Number** field.

6. On the **Appearance** tab, select **Bold** for the header text (Figure 10-3.3).

7. Select **OK** to generate the **Room Schedule**.

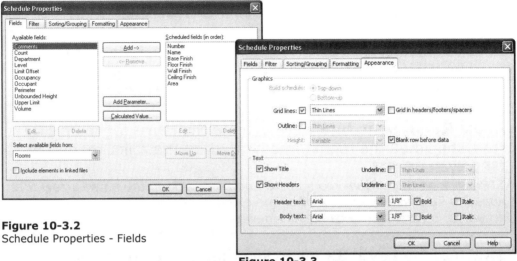

Figure 10-3.2
Schedule Properties - Fields

Figure 10-3.3
Schedule Properties - Appearance

Place cursor here to resize the column

		Room Schedule				
Number	Name	Base Finish	Floor Finish	Wall Finish	Ceiling Finish	Area
#1	Stair					168 SF
#2	Stair					168 SF
100	Atrium					1805 SF
101	RECEPTIO					313 SF
102	OPEN OFFI					1977 SF
103	CONFERE					204 SF
104	WORK RO					437 SF
105	WOMENS					161 SF
106	MENS					161 SF
107	MECH / EL					131 SF
108	BREAK R					389 SF
109	OFFICE					104 SF
110	OFFICE					143 SF
111	OPEN OFFI					2309 SF
200	Atrium					1759 SF
201	Open Offi					3000 SF
202	TELECOM					131 SF
203	Open Offi					3000 SF
204	Womens					161 SF
205	Mens					161 SF
300	Atrium					1759 SF
301	Open Offi					1870 SF
302	Room					240 SF
303	Room					243 SF
304	Office					232 SF
305	Office					229 SF
306	Office					125 SF
307	Room					131 SF
308	Misc / Stor					125 SF
309	Office					229 SF
310	Office					232 SF
311	Open Offi					1870 SF
312	Office					243 SF
313	Office					240 SF
314	Room					161 SF
315	Room					161 SF

Figure 10-3.4 Room Schedule view

Your schedule should look similar to the one to the left. (Figure 10-3.4)

8. Resize the Name column so all the room names are visible. Place the cursor between the Name and Base Finish and drag to the right until all the names are visible. (Figure 10-3.4)

The formatting (i.e., Bold header text) will not show up until the schedule is placed on a plot sheet.

Modifying and Populating a Room Schedule:

Like the door schedule, the room schedule is a tabular view of the building model. So you can change the room name or number on the schedule or in the plans.

9. In the **Room Schedule** view, change the name for room **307** (this should be the room directly north of the toilet rooms) to **MECH/ELEC RM**.
    TIP: Click on the current room name and then click on the down-arrow that appears. This gives you a list of all the existing names in the current schedule; otherwise you can type a new name.

10. Switch to the **Level 3** view to see the updated room tag.

You can quickly enter finish information to several rooms at one time. You will do this next.

11. In the Level 3 plan view, select the Rooms (not the room tags) for all private offices – 9 total (Figure 10-3.5).
    REMEMBER: Hold the Ctrl key down to select multiple objects.
    TIP: Move the cursor near the room tag but not over it to select the room – the large "X" will appear when the Room is selectable (see image below).

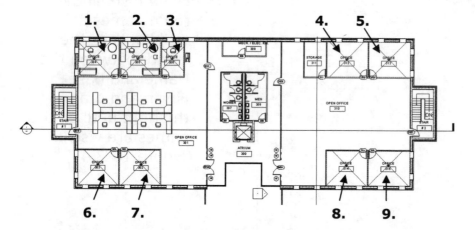

Figure 10-3.5 Level 3 – selected room tags

12. Click the **Properties** button on the *Options Bar*.

The Parameters listed here are the same as the Fields available for display in the room schedule. When more than one tag is displayed and a parameter is not the same (e.g., different names), that value field is left blank. Otherwise, the values are displayed for the selected tag. Next you will enter values for the finishes.

13. If the *Name* field is blank enter **OFFICE**, so the nine rooms are labeled office.

14. Enter the following for the finishes (Figure 10-3.6):
    a. Base Finish: **Wood**
    b. Ceiling Finish: **ACT 1**   *(ACT = acoustic ceiling tile)*
    c. Wall Finish: **VWC 1**   *(VWC = vinyl wall covering)*
    d. Floor Finish: **Carpet 1**

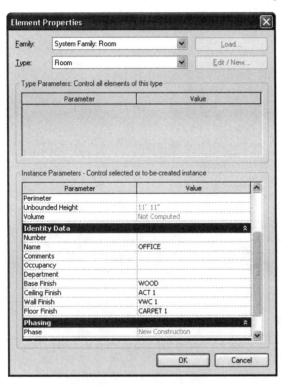

Figure 10-3.6 Element Properties – Room Tags

15. Click **OK**.

16. Switch back to the **Room Schedule** view to see the automatic updates (Figure 10-3.7).

You can also enter data directly into the Room Schedule view.

17. Enter the following data for the Men's and Women's toilet rooms:
    a. Base: **COVED CT**
    b. Ceiling: **Gyp. Bd.**
    c. Wall: **CT**
    d. Floor: **CT**

Hopefully, in the near future, Revit will be able to enter the finishes based on the wall, floor and ceiling type previously created!

TIP:

You can add fields and adjust formatting anytime by right-clicking on the schedule view and selecting View Properties. This gives you the same options that were available when you created the schedule.

204	WOMENS					161 SF
205	MENS					161 SF
300	Room					1786 SF
302	OFFICE	Wood	Carpet 1	VWC 1	ACT 1	229 SF
303	OFFICE	Wood	Carpet 1	VWC 1	ACT 1	232 SF
304	OPEN OFFICE					1896 SF
305	OFFICE	Wood	Carpet 1	VWC 1	ACT 1	232 SF
306	OFFICE	Wood	Carpet 1	VWC 1	ACT 1	229 SF
307	OFFICE	Wood	Carpet 1	VWC 1	ACT 1	125 SF
308	MECH / ELEC RM					98 SF
309	WOMENS					161 SF
310	MEN					161 SF
311	MISC. / STORAGE					125 SF
312	OFFICE	Wood	Carpet 1	VWC 1	ACT 1	229 SF
313	OFFICE	Wood	Carpet 1	VWC 1	ACT 1	232 SF
314	OPEN OFFICE					1896 SF
315	OFFICE	Wood	Carpet 1	VWC 1	ACT 1	232 SF
316	OFFICE	Wood	Carpet 1	VWC 1	ACT 1	229 SF
# 1	STAIR					168 SF

Figure 10-3.7 Partial Room Schedule with new data

Setting up a color-coded floor plan:

With the Rooms in place you can quickly set up color-coded floor plans. These are plans that indicate (with color) which rooms are Offices, Circulation, Public, etc., based the room name in our example.

18. Switch to **Level 3** view.

19. From the *Drafting* tab select **Color Scheme Legend**.

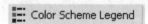

20. Click just below the floor plan on the right side.

21. Click select **Name** and then **OK** to the following prompt (Figure 10-3.8).

You now have a color-coded plan where the colors are assigned by room name; e.g., all the rooms named "Office" have the same color (Figure 10-3.9).

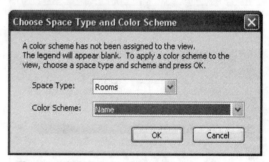

Figure 10-3.8 Color fill warning

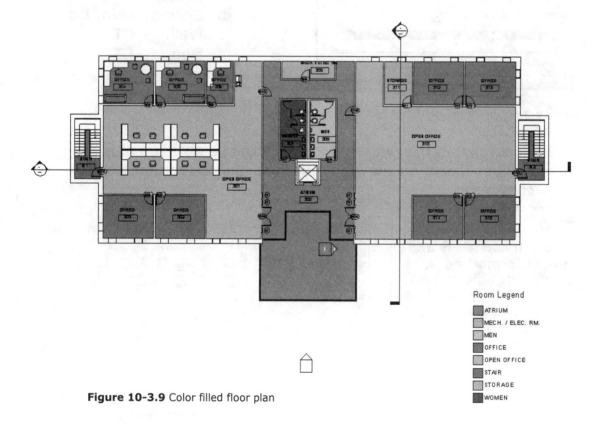

Figure 10-3.9 Color filled floor plan

Room Legend

- ATRIUM
- MECH. / ELEC. RM.
- MEN
- OFFICE
- OPEN OFFICE
- STAIR
- STORAGE
- WOMEN

22. Select the *Room Legend* shown in **Figure 10-3.9**.

23. Click **Edit Color Scheme...** on the *Options Bar*. (Figure 10-3.10)

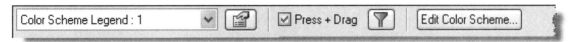

Figure 10-3.10 Options Bar – Color Legend key selected

Each unique room name will get a different color. Before you finish you will change one *Color* and one *Fill Pattern*.

24. Click on the *Color* for the **Atrium**.

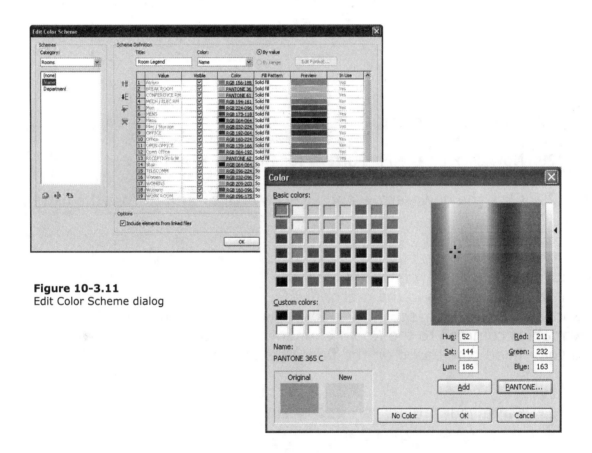

Figure 10-3.11
Edit Color Scheme dialog

Figure 10-3.12 Color selector

25. Click the **PANTONE...** button to select a standard Pantone color. (Figure 10-3.12)

26. Type **365** in the *Find Color* area and press enter. (Figure 10-3.13)

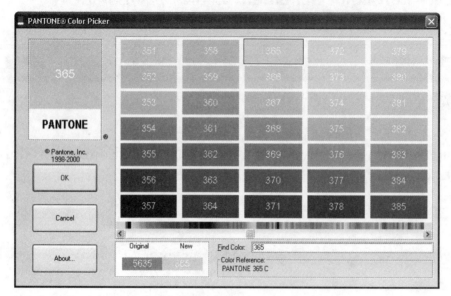

Figure 10-3.13 PANTONE Color selector

27. Click **OK** to accept.

28. Now click on the *Fill Pattern* for the **MECH /ELEC RM**.

29. Click the down-arrow and select **Vertical-small** from the list.

30. Click **OK**.

Your plan should now have the new color you selected for the Atrium and a hatch pattern in the mechanical room. The color legend can also sort by *Department* (see Figure 10-3.11) in addition to many other variables common to the *Room* element. (Interior Designers can create a color filled plan based on the floor finishes for example.)

31. **Save** your project as **ex10-4.rvt**.

Self-Exam:

The following questions can be used as a way to check your knowledge of this lesson. The answers can be found at the bottom of this page.

1. Revit is referred to as a Building Information Modeler (BIM). (T/F) *T*

2. The area for a room is calculated when a room tag is placed. (T/F) *T*

3. Revit can tag all the doors not currently tagged on a given level with the "Tag All Not Tagged" tool. (T/F) *T*

4. You can add or remove various fields in a door or room schedule. (T/F) *T*

5. Use the _____ _____ tool to add color to the rooms in a plan view. *colorfill*

Review Questions:

The following questions may be assigned by your instructor as a way to assess your knowledge of this section. Your instructor has the answers to the review questions.

1. You can add a door tag with a leader. (T/F) *T*

2. You can export your schedule to a file that can be used in MS Excel. (T/F) *T*

3. A door can be deleted from the door schedule. (T/F) *T*

4. The schedule formatting only shows up when you place the schedule on a plot sheet. (T/F) *T*

5. It is not possible to add the finish information (i.e., base finish, wall finish) to multiple rooms at one time. (T/F) *F*

6. When setting up a color scheme, you can adjust the color and the _Fill_ pattern in the Edit Color Scheme dialog.

7. Use the _element Properties_ dialog to adjust the various fields associated with each room tag in a plan view.

8. Most door schedules are sorted by the _Mark_ field.

9. Revit provides access to the industry standard _Pantone_ color library.

schedule is live to the model — change it here, you change it in the drawing

based on human perception

gama control – matching plot color to monitor color

Notes:

Lesson 11
Office Building: Photo-Realistic Rendering::

You will take a look at Revit's photo-realistic rendering abilities. Rather than reinventing the wheel, Revit chose to use an established architectural rendering program called Mental Ray. Autodesk makes several high-end rendering programs like *Autodesk 3D Studio Max*, *Autodesk Maya* and *Mental Ray*, which work with Revit models in various ways. (The options improve with each new release.)

Exercise 11-1:
Creating an exterior rendering

The first thing you will do is set up a view. You will use the *Camera* tool to do this. This becomes a saved view that can be opened at any time from the Project Browser.

Creating a Camera view:

1. Open the **Level 1** view and **Zoom All to Fit**, so you can see the entire plan.

2. From the *View* tab, select **Camera**.

3. Click the mouse in the lower right corner of the screen to indicate the camera eye location.
   NOTICE: *Before you click, Revit tells you it wants the eye location first on the Status Bar.*

4. Next click near the atrium curtainwall; see Figure 11-1.1.

Revit will automatically open a view window for the new camera. Take a minute to look at the view and make a mental note of what you see and don't see in the view (Figure 11-1.2).

5. Switch back to the **Level 1** plan view.

6. Adjust the camera, using its grips, to look similar to Figure 11-1.3. **TIP:** *If the camera is not visible in plan view, right click on the 3D view name in the Project Browser (3D View 1) and select Show Camera.*

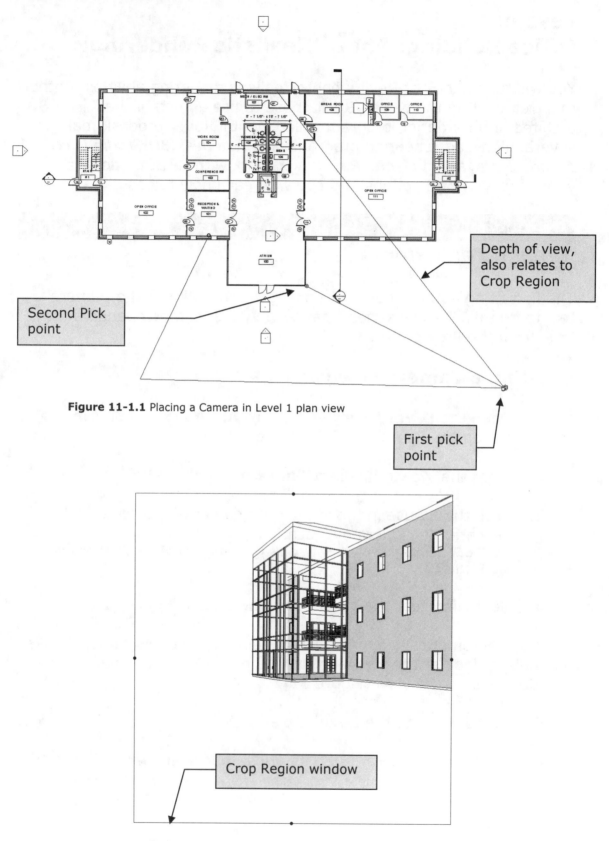

Figure 11-1.1 Placing a Camera in Level 1 plan view

Depth of view, also relates to Crop Region

Second Pick point

First pick point

Crop Region window

Figure 11-1.2 Initial Camera view

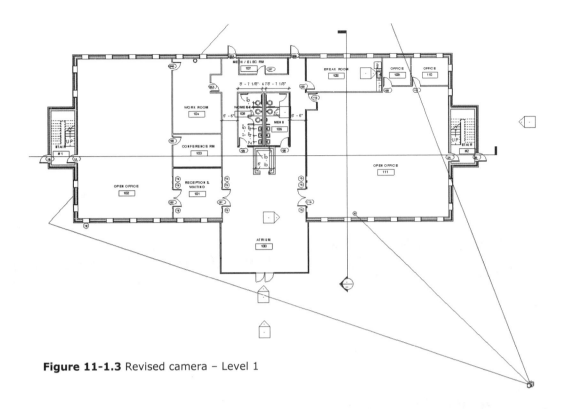

Figure 11-1.3 Revised camera – Level 1

7. Now switch to 3D View 1 and adjust the **Crop Region** to look similar to **Figure 11-1.4**.

This will be the view we render later in this exercise.

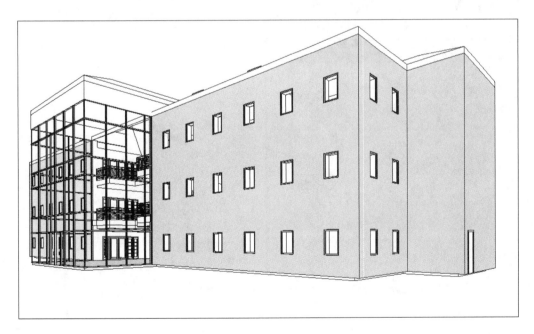

Figure 11-1.4 Revised camera – 3D View 1

Assigning materials to objects:

Materials are scanned images or computer generated representations of the materials your building will be made of.

Typically materials are added while the project is being modeled. For example, when you create a material (using the *Materials...* command under the *Settings* menu), you can assign a material at that time. Of course, you can go back and add or change it later. Next you will change the material assigned for the exterior brick wall.

8. Switch to **Level 1** plan view.

9. Select an exterior wall somewhere in plan view.

10. Click **Properties** from the *Options Bar*.

11. Click **Edit/New** and then click **Edit** *structure*.

12. Notice the material selected for the exterior finish is **Masonry – Brick**; click in that cell (Figure 11-1.5).

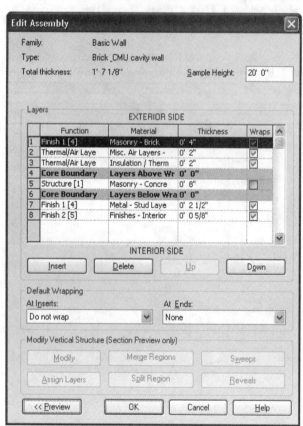

13. Click the "**...**" icon to the right of the label **Masonry – Brick**.

Now you will take a look that the definition of the material Masonry – Brick.

TIP: You can also get here via: From the Settings menu select **Materials...**

You are now in the *Materials* dialog. You should notice that a material is already selected. Next you will select a different brick material.

Figure 11-1.5 Exterior wall assembly

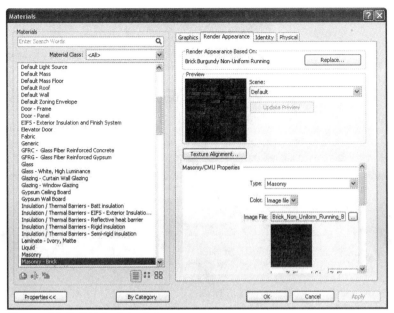

Figure 11-1.6 Materials dialog

14. On the *Render Appearance* tab click **Replace**.

You will now see Revit's *Material Library* dialog. The current material will be selected and displayed (Figure 11-1.7).

You can browse through the list and select any material in the list to be assigned to the *Masonry – Brick* material in Revit. The material does not have to be brick but would be confusing if something else where assigned to the *Masonry – Brick* material.

15. Scroll down in *Brick* [class] and select **Brick Red Non-uniform Running**, and then click **OK**.

Notice the material listed is now updated.

16. Click **OK** to close the *Materials* dialog.

Now, when you render, any object (wall, ceiling, etc.) that has the material *Masonry – Brick* associated with it, will have the Red brick on them.

If you need more than one brick color, you assign that material to another wall type.

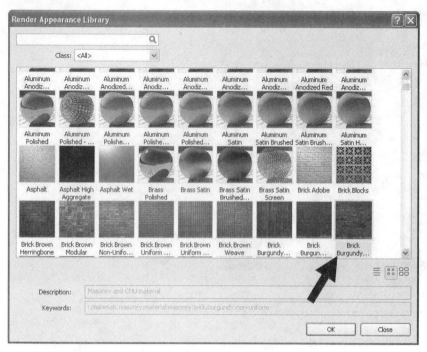

Figure 11-1.7 Revit's Material Library dialog

Sun and Shadow Settings:

The first step in preparing a rendering is to define the sun and shadow settings. You will explore the various options available.

17. Select **Sun and Shadow Settings...** from the *Settings* menu.

18. Make the following changes (Figure 11-1.8)

   a. Place: **Minneapolis, MN** (or pick your city)
   b. **Uncheck** *Ground Plane at Level*

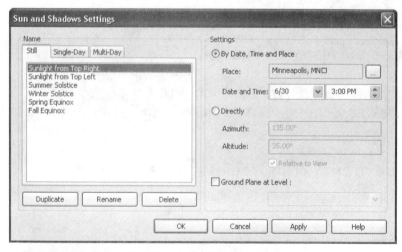

Figure 11-1.8 Sun and Shadows Settings dialog

19. Click **OK** to close the dialog.

The previous sun and show settings apply to the entire project, not just the current view, which is the intent for the *Settings* menu.

Setting up the Environment:

You have limited options for setting up the building's environment. If you need more control than what is provided directly in Revit you will need to use another program like Autodesk 3DS Design 2009 which is designed to work with Revit and can create extremely high quality renderings and animations; it even has day lighting functionality that helps to validate LEED® (Leadership in Environmental and Energy Design) requirements. You can adjust the lighting and the background. *You modified the Sun related settings in the previous steps*. You will review these options next.

20. Switch to your camera view:
    3D View 1.

21. Select the **Show Rendering Dialog** icon on the *View Control Bar*; it looks like a teapot (Figure 11-1.9).

    FYI: *This icon is only visible when you are in a 3D view, the same as the SteeringWheels and ViewCube.*

The *Rendering* dialog box is now open (Figure 11-1.10). This dialog box allows you to control the environmental settings you are about to explore and actually create the rendering (which you will do soon!).

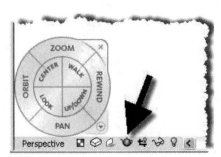

Figure 11-1.9 Scene Selection dialog

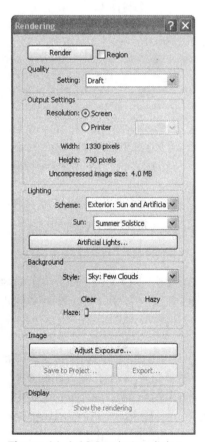

Figure 11-1.10 Rendering dialog

22. In the *Lighting* section, click the down-arrow next to *Scheme* to see the options. Select **Exterior Sun and Artifical** when finished (Figure 11-1.11).

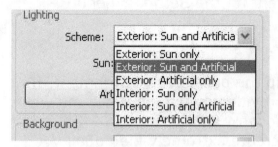

Figure 11-1.11 Lighting options

The lighting options are very simple choices: is your rendering an interior or exterior rendering and is the light source Sun or Artificial – or both? You may have artificial lights (i.e., light fixtures like the ones you placed in the office) but still only desire a rendering solely based on the light provided by the sun.

23. In the *Lighting* section, set the *Sun* to **Sunlight from Top Right**.

FYI: *In the Sun and Shadow Settings dialog box, Revit lets you set up various "scenes" which control time of day. Two examples would be:*
- *Daytime, summer*
- *Nighttime, window*

Looking back at Figure 11-1.8, you would click *Duplicate* and provide a name. This name would then be available from the *Sun* drop-down list in the *Render* dialog box.

24. Click on the **Artificial Lighting** button (Figure 11-1.12).

You will now see a dialog similar to the one shown to the right (Figure 11-1.12).

You will see several 2x4 light fixtures. The light fixtures relate to the fixtures you inserted in the reflected ceiling plans. It is very convenient that you can place lights in the ceiling plan and have them ready to render whenever

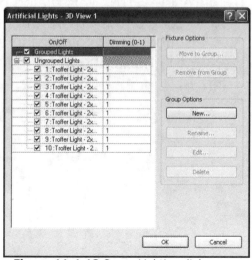

Figure 11-1.12 Scene Lighting dialog

you need to (i.e., render and cast light into the scene!). Here you can group lights together so you can control which ones are on (e.g., exterior and interior lights).

25. Click **Cancel** to close the *Artificial Lighting* dialog.

26. Click the down-arrow next to *Style* in the *Background* area (Figure 11-1.13).

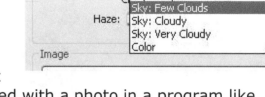

27. Select **Sky: Few Clouds**.

Notice that one option for the background is color. This can be set to a unique color that can be replaced with a photo in a program like Adobe PhotoShop.

Next you will place a few trees into your rendering. You will adjust their exact location so they are near the edge of the framed rendering, so as not to cover too much of the building.

28. Switch to Level 1 plan view and select **Component** from the *Design Bar. (Close the Render dialog if it is still open.)*

29. Pick **RPC Tree – Deciduous : Largetooth Aspen 25'** from the *Type Selector* on the *Design Bar*.
    FYI: *If the tree is not listed in the type selector, click Load from Library and load the Deciduous tree family from the Plantings folder.*

30. Place three trees as shown in **Figure 11-1.14**. (You will make one smaller in a moment.)

Figure 11-1.13 Background style

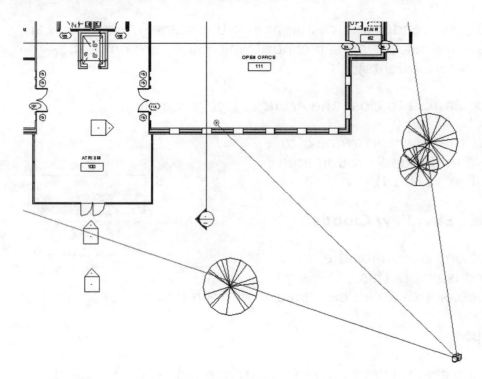

Figure 11-1.14 Level 1 with trees added

31. Adjust the trees in plan view, reviewing the effects in the 3D View 1 view, so your 3D view is similar to Figure 11-1.15.

32. In the Level 1 plan view, select the tree that is shown smaller in **Figure 11-1.14**.

33. Select *Properties* on the *Options Bar*, and then click *Edit/New*. Click **Duplicate** and enter the name: **RPC Tree – Deciduous : Largetooth Aspen 18'**.

34. Change the *Plant Height* to **18'** (from 25') and then click **OK** to close the open dialog boxes.

The previous three steps allow you to have a little more variety in the trees being placed. Otherwise, they would all be the same height, which is not very natural.

Figure 11-1.15 3D View 1 – with trees

35. Open the **3D View 1** camera view.

36. Open the Rendering dialog.

37. Make sure the *Quality* is set to **Draft**.

> **FYI:** *The time to process the rendering increases significantly as the quality level is raised.*

38. Click **Render** from the *Rendering* dialog box.

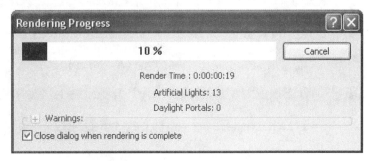

You will see a progress bar while Revit is processing the rendering (Figure 11-1.16).

Figure 11-1.16 Rendering progress

After a few minutes, depending on the speed of your computer, you should have a rendered image similar to Figure 11-1.17 below. You can increase the quality of the image by adjusting the quality setting in the *Render* dialog. However, these higher settings require substantially more time to generate the rendering. The last step before saving the Revit project file is to save the rendered image to a file.

FYI: Each time you make changes to the model (that are visible from that view), you will have to re-render the view to get an updated image.

Depending on exactly how your view was setup, you may be able to see light from one of the light figures in the office off the Atrium. Also, notice the railing through the curtainwall; Revit has the glazing in windows set to be transparent!

Figure 11-1.17 Rendered view

39. From the *Rendering* dialog select **Export**.

   FYI: The 'Save to Project' button saves the image within the Revit Project for placement on Sheets. This is convenient but does make the project size larger so you should delete old ones!

40. Select a *location* and provide a *file name*.

41. Set the *Save As* type: to **JPEG**.

42. Click **Save**.

The image file you just saved can now be inserted into MS Word or Adobe Photoshop for editing.

Exercise 11-2:
Rendering an isometric in section

This exercise will introduce you to a view tool called *Section Box*. This tool is not necessarily related to renderings, but the two tools together can produce some interesting results.

Setting up the 3D view:

1.   Open file ex11-1.rvt and **Save As ex11-2.rvt**.

2.   Switch to the *Default* **3D** view via the 3D icon on the toolbar *(not the 3D View 1 from Exercise 11-1)*.

3.   *Right-click* in the drawing area and select **View Properties**.

4.   Activate the **Section Box** parameter and then click **OK**.

You should see a box appear around your building, similar to Figure 11-2.1. When selected, you can adjust the size of the box with its grips. Anything outside the box is not visible. This is a great way to study a particular area of your building while in an isometric view. You will experiment with this feature next.

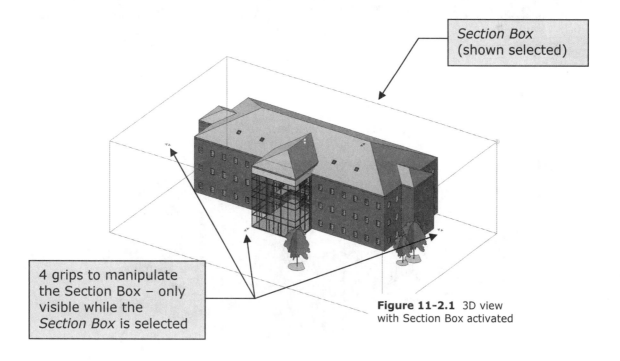

Section Box
(shown selected)

4 grips to manipulate the Section Box – only visible while the *Section Box* is selected

Figure 11-2.1 3D view with Section Box activated

5. To practice using the **Section Box**, drag the grips around until your view looks similar to **Figure 11-2.2**.
    TIP: This will require the Dynamically Modify View tool as well.

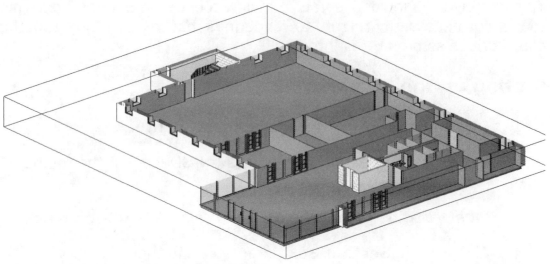

Figure 11-2.2 3D view with adjusted Section Box

This creates a very interesting view of the Level 1 – West Wing. What client would have trouble understanding this drawing?

6. Now re-adjust the **Section Box** to look similar to **Figure 11-2.3**.

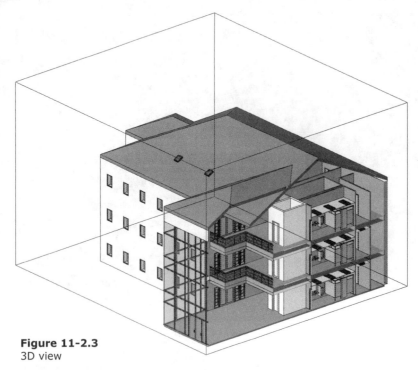

Figure 11-2.3
3D view

7. From the *Settings* menu, select **Sun and Shadow Settings** and change the following *Sun* settings (Figure 11-2.4):
    a. Click **Duplicate** (name: 28 February 8am)
    b. Month: **2** (February)
    c. Day: **28**
    d. Clock Time: **8:00am**

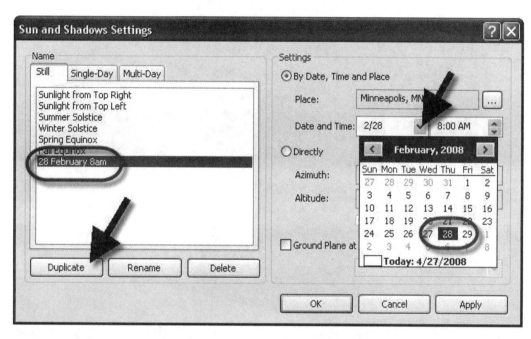

Figure 11-2.4 Modified Sun settings

8. Select the **Render** icon, select the *Scheme*: **Exterior: Sun only**, and then set *Sun* to: **23 February 8am**.

9. Set the *Background Style* to: **Sky: Very few clouds**

10. Select the **Region** option and then adjust the "render region crop" that appears to indicate the area to be rendered.

    TIP: This tool is nice for checking a material before rendering the entire building, which takes longer.

The image will take a few minutes to render (again, depending on the speed of your computer). When finished it should look similar to **Figure 11-2.5**. The image looks much better on the screen or printed in color.

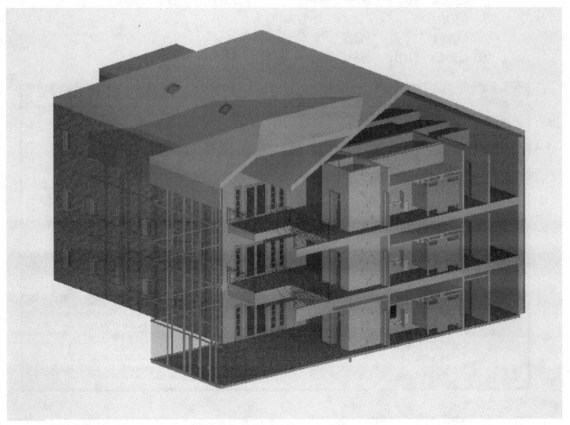

Figure 11-2.5 Rendered isometric view

Adjusting an object's material:

As previously mentioned, most objects already have a material assigned to them. This is great because it allows you to quickly render your project to get some preliminary images. However, they usually need to be adjusted. You will do this next.

11. Switch to **Level 1** plan view and zoom in on the toilet rooms.

12. Select one of the toilet partitions.

13. Click the **Properties** button from the *Options Bar*.

14. Click the **Edit/New**... button.

Notice the Toilet Partition material is set to **Toilet Partition**. This value is a material; you will change this next (Figure 11-2.6).

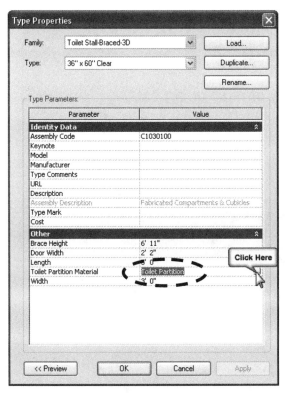

Figure 11-2.6 Toilet Partition properties

15. **Click** on the Toilet Partition value (which will cause a "**...**" icon to display to the right), click the icon.

You are now in the *Materials* dialog box, where you can create and edit *Materials*.

16. Select **Toilet Partition** from the *Name* drop-down.

17. Change the Accurender material to: **Granite, Black Polished** (Figure 11-2.7).

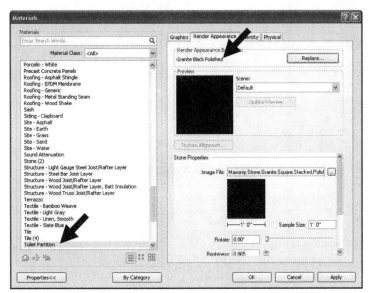

Figure 11-2.7 Material selector

18. Click **OK** to close the open dialog boxes.

19. You can now re-render the 3D view and see the results.

20. **Save** your project as ex **11-2.rvt**.

Exercise 11-3:
Creating an interior rendering

Creating an interior rendering is very similar to an exterior rendering. This exercise will walk through the steps involved in creating a high quality interior rendering.

Setting up the camera view:

1. Open ex11-2.rvt and **Save As ex11-3.rvt**.

2. Open **Level 2** view.

3. From the *View* tab, select **Camera**.

4. Place the *Camera* as shown in **Figure 11-3.1**.

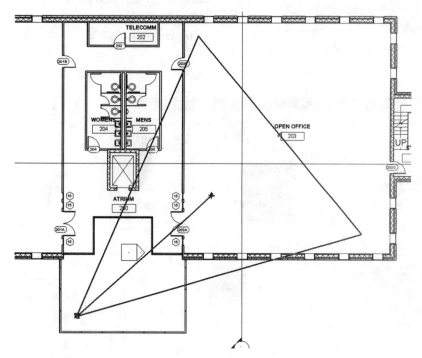

Figure 11-3.1 Camera placed – Level 2 view

Revit uses default heights for the camera and the target. These heights are based on the current level's floor elevation. These reference points can be edited via the camera properties.

Revit will automatically open the newly generated camera view. Your view should look similar to **Figure 11-3.2**.

FYI: *Make sure you created the camera on Level 2 and picked the points in the correct order.*

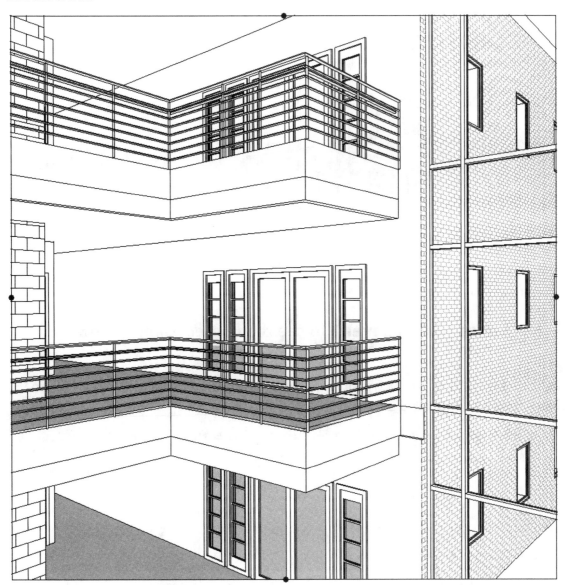

Figure 11-3.2 Initial interior camera view

5. Using the **Crop Region** rectangle, modify the view to look like **Figure 11-3.3**.

    TIP: *You will have to switch to plan view to adjust the camera's depth of view to see the trees.*

    REMINDER: *If the camera does not show in plan view, right-click on the camera view label in the project browser and select Show Camera. If you did not add a ceiling to the third floor lobby previously, you should do that now.*

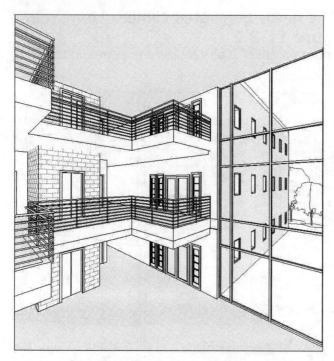

Figure 11-3.3 Modified interior camera

6. Switch back to **Level 2** to see the revised *Camera* view settings.

Notice the field of view triangle is wider based on the changes to the Crop Region (Figure 11-3.4).

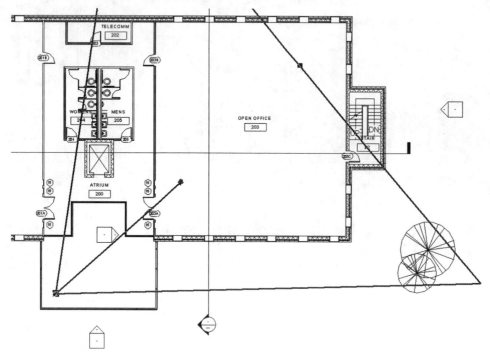

Figure 11-3.4 Modified camera – Level 2

7. Select the *Camera* and click the **Properties** button on the *Option Tab* (Figure 11-3.5).

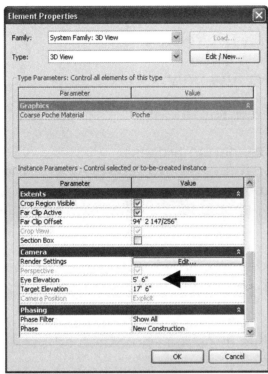

Figure 11-3.5 Camera properties

8. Change the **Eye Elevation** to **5'-6"**.

9. Click **OK**.

Your interior camera view should now look similar to **Figure 11-3.6**. This would be a person standing on Level 1 looking up. The vertical lines are distorted due to the wide field of view (crop region). This is similar to what a camera with a 10-15mm lens would get in the finished building.

FYI: A ceiling was added at the second and third levels in this image to "clean" things up for the rendering.

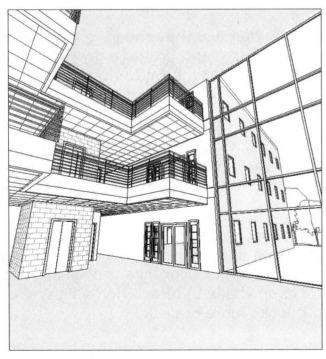

Figure 11-3.6 Interior camera view

Creating the rendering:

Next you will render the view.

10. Select **Render** from the *View Control Bar.*

11. Set the *Scheme* to **Interior: Sun only**.

12. Set the *Sun* to **Sunlight from Top Right**.

13. Click **Render** to being the rendering process.

This will take several minutes depending on the speed of your computer. When finished, the view should look similar to Figure 11-3.7.

14. Click **Export** from the *Rendering* dialog box to save the image to a file on your hard drive. Name the file **Atrium.jpg** (jpeg file format).

You can now open the *Atrium.jpg* file in Adobe Photoshop or insert into a MS Word type program to manipulate or print.

To toggle back to the normal hidden view, click **Show the Model** from the *Rendering* dialog box.

There are many things you can do to make the rendering look even better. You can add interior light fixtures and props (e.g., pictures on the wall, items on the counter top, and lawn furniture on the lawn). Once you add interior lights, you can adjust the Sun setting to nighttime and then render a night scene.

TIP: *Setting the output to Printer rather than Screen allows you to generate a higher resolution image. Thus, between the Quality setting and the output setting you can create an extremely high quality rendering, but it might take hours, if not days, to process!*

Revit also gives you the ability to set a material to be self-illuminating. This will allow you to make a button on the dishwasher look like it is lit up or, if applied to the glass on the ranger door, like the light in the oven is on! You can also set a lamp shade to glow when a light source has been defined under it so it looks more realistic.

Figure 11-3.7 Rendered view

FYI:

The rendered image above has ceilings and lights added to each floor in the Atrium that were not added by any previous lesson, unless your instructor assigned that task as extra work for Lesson 6. You should quickly add this information prior to rendering the view. This will make the rendering look much better.

Rendering a night scene:

One more variation we will look at is rendering the interior atrium view at nighttime. This involves adjusting the sun settings so the Sun is below the horizon and making sure you have the correct number of light fixtures to light the space being rendered.

15. Add Ceilings and light fixtures to Levels 2 and 3 per steps covered in previous chapters.

16. Open the *Rendering* dialog box.

17. Make the adjustments shown in the image to the left. Make sure Scheme is set to **Interior: Artificial Only**.

18. While in the camera view for the Atrium, click on the **Render** button.

When the rendering is completed you will have a night view of your interior atrium. This clearly shows the effect the 2x4 light fixtures have on the rendering, as they are the primary light source for this rendering. Your image should look similar to **Figure 11-3.8**.

You can also try this (especially if you have placed light fixtures for the entire building) on your exterior camera view. Nighttime renderings can be very dramatic.

Figure 11-3.8 Rendered nighttime view

You will learn how to add people in the next lesson!

Notice you can see reflections in the curtainwall glass. Revit accurately renders reflective surfaces like glass and shiny or polished metal (like the elevator doors). This creates a more realistic rendering.

19. **Save** your project as **11-3.rvt**.

Exercise 11-4:
Adding people to the rendering

Revit provides a few RPC people to add to your renderings. These are files from a popular company that provides 3D photo content for use in renderings (http://www.archvision.com). You can buy this content in groupings (like college students) or per item. In addition to people, they offer items like cars, plants, trees, office equipment, etc.

Loading content into the current project

1. Open ex11-3.rvt and **Save As 11-4.rvt**.

2. Switch to **Level 2** view.

3. Select the **Component** tool from the *Rendering* tab.

4. Click the **Load** button on the *Options Bar*.

5. Browse to the **Entourage** folder and select both the **RPC Male** and **RPC Female** files (using the Ctrl key to select both at once) and click **Open**.

6. Place one **Male** and one **Female** as shown in **Figure 11-4.1**.

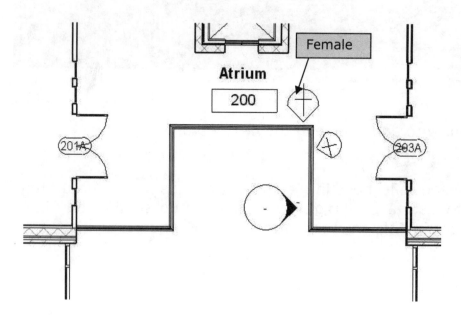

Figure 11-4.1 Level 2 – RPC people added

The line in the circle (Figure 11-4.1) represents the direction a person is looking. You simply Rotate the object to make adjustments.

7. Switch to **Level 1** view.

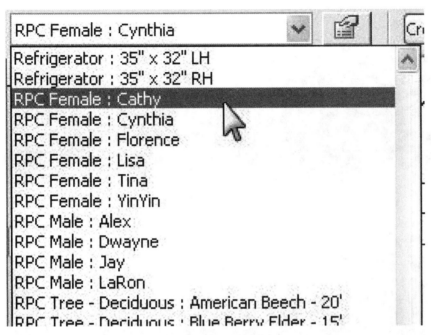

Figure 11-4.2 Type Selector – Options Bar

8. Place a few of the other people available (similar to Fig. 11-4.3)

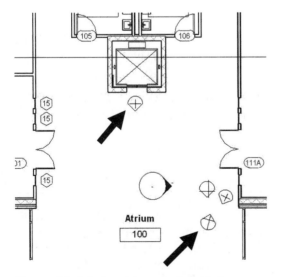

9. Switch to your interior atrium camera view.

10. Render the Atrium view with the daytime settings previously used.

Figure 11-4.3 Level 1 – people added

Your rendering should now have people in it and look similar to **Figure 11-4.4**.

Figure 11-4.4 Interior Atrium view with people added

Adding people and other "props" gives your model a sense of scale and makes it look a little more realistic. After all, architecture is for people. These objects can be viewed from any angle. Try a new camera view from a different angle to see how the people adjust to match the view and perspective, maybe from the third floor looking down to Level 1.

11. **Save** your project as **ex11-4.rvt**.

> **FYI:**
> As with other families and components, the more you add to your project, the bigger your project file becomes. It is a good idea to load only the items you need and delete the unused items via the Project Browser. Your project should be about 5.6MB at this point in the tutorial.

Self-Exam:

The following questions can be used as a way to check your knowledge of this lesson. The answers can be found at the bottom of this page.

1. Creating a camera adds a view to the Project Browser list. (T/F)
   _T_

2. Materials are defined in Revit's Materials dialog box. (T/F)
   _T_

3. After inserting a light fixture, you need to adjust several setting before rendering and getting light from the fixture. (T/F)
   _F_

4. You can adjust the season, which affects how the trees are rendered. (T/F)
   _F_

5. Use the _____ _____ tool to remove a large portion of the model.
   section Box

Review Questions:

The following questions may be assigned by your instructor as a way to assess your knowledge of this section. Your instructor has the answers to the review questions.

1. You cannot pick a material for the ground plane. (T/F)
   _F_

2. You cannot get accurate lighting based on day/month/location. (T/F)
   _F_

3. Adding components and families to your project does not make the project file bigger. (T/F)   _F_

4. Creating photo-realistic renderings can take a significant amount of time for your computer to process. (T/F)
   _T_

5. The RPC people can only be viewed from one angle. (T/F)
   _F_

6. The RPC components do not cast shadows (T/F).
   _F_

7. Adjust the _Crop Region_ to make more of a perspective view visible.

8. You use the _Component_ tool to load and insert RPC people.

9. You can adjust the Eye Elevation of the camera via the camera's

   _____ _properties_.

10. What is the file size of (completed) Exercise 11-4? _Big_____ MB

Notes:

Lesson 12
Office Building: Construction Documents Set::

This lesson will look at bringing everything you have drawn thus far together onto sheets. The sheets, once set up, are ready for plotting. Basically, you place the various views you have created on sheets. The scale for each view is based on the scale you set while drawing that view (which is important to have set correctly because it affects the text and symbol sizes. When finished setting up the sheets, you will have a set of drawings ready to print, individually or all at once.

Exercise 12-1:
Setting up a sheet

Creating a Sheet view:

1. Open ex11-5.rvt and **Save As** 12-1.rvt.

2. Select **Sheet...** from the *View* tab. ☐ Sheet...

Next Revit will prompt you for a Titleblock to use. The template file you started with only has one; that's the one you will use (Figure 12-1.1).

3. Click **OK** to select the **E1 30x42 Horizontal** titleblock.

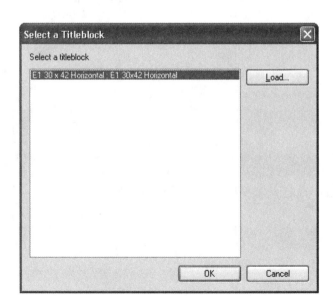

> **NOTICE:** *A new view shows up in the Project Browser under the heading: Sheets. Once you get an entire CD set ready, this list can be very long.*

Figure 12-1.1 Select a Titleblock

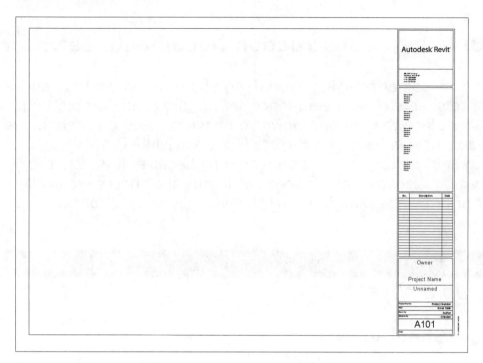

Figure 12-1.2 Initial Titleblock view

4. **Zoom** into the sheet number area (lower right corner).

5. Adjust the text to look similar to **Figure 12-1.3**.

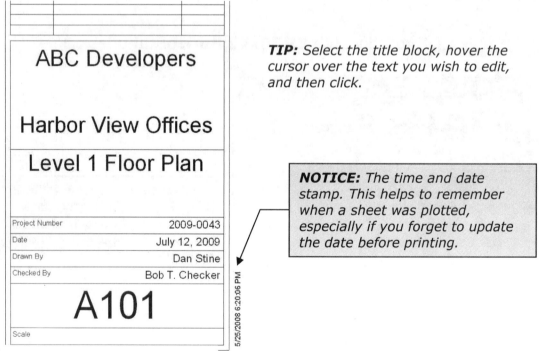

TIP: Select the title block, hover the cursor over the text you wish to edit, and then click.

NOTICE: The time and date stamp. This helps to remember when a sheet was plotted, especially if you forget to update the date before printing.

Figure 12-1.3 Revised Titleblock data

6. **Zoom out** so you can see the entire sheet.

7. With the sheet fully visible, click and drag the **Level 1** label (under floor plans) from the *Project Browser* onto the sheet view.

You will see a red box that represents the extents of the view you are placing on the current sheet.

8. Move the cursor around until the box is somewhat centered on the sheet (this can be adjusted later at any time).

Your view should look similar to **Figure 12-1.4**.

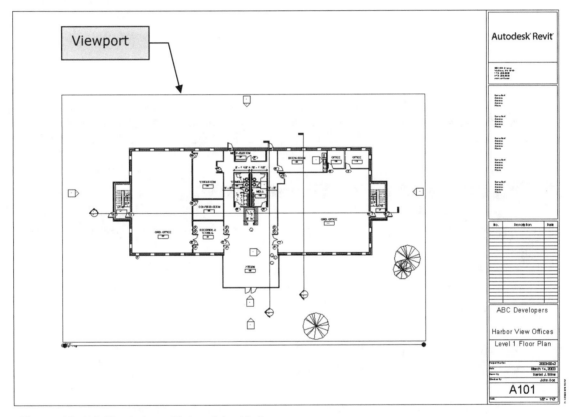

Figure 12-1.4 Sheet view with Level 1 added

9. Click the mouse in a "white" area (not on any lines) to deselect the Level 1 view. Notice the red box goes away.

10. **Zoom In** on the lower left corner to view the drawing identification symbol that Revit automatically added. (Figure 12-1.5)

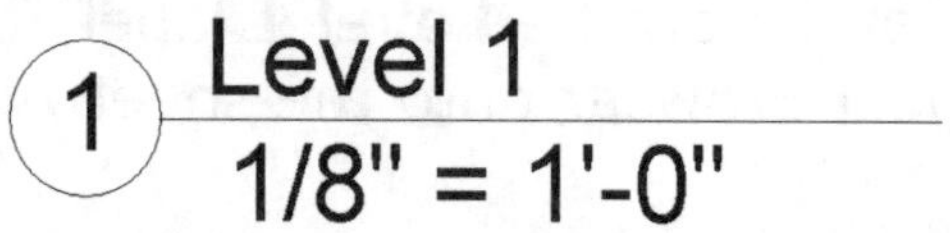

NOTICE:
The drawing number for this sheet is added. The next drawing you add will be number 2.

The view name is listed. This is another reason to rename the elevation and section views as you create them.

Also notice that the drawing scale is listed. Again, this comes from the scale setting for the Level 1 view.

① Level 1
1/8" = 1'-0"

Figure 12-1.5 Drawing ID tag

11. **Zoom Out** to see entire sheet again.

12. Add two more sheets and set up Levels 2 and 3 on them:
    a. Sheet A102 → Level 2 Floor Plan
    b. Sheet A103 → Level 3 Floor Plan

NOTICE: *When you create a new sheet, most of the titleblock is filled in and the number has increased by 1. This pre-entered info can be changed if needed.*

Setting up the Exterior Elevations:

Next you will set up the exterior elevations on the A200 series sheets.

13. Create a new Sheet and adjust the title block data:
    a. Sheet Title: Exterior Elevations
    b. Sheet Number: A200

14. Drag the **South** elevation view onto the sheet. Place the drawing near the lower right.

15. Drag the **North** elevation view onto the same sheet. Place the drawing so that the drawing title tag is aligned. (Revit will snap to this position vertically.)

Your drawing should look similar to Figure 12-1.6.

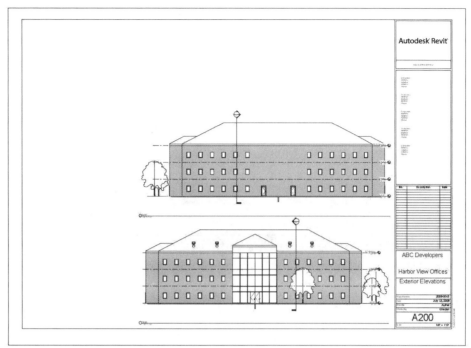

Figure 12-1.6 North and South exterior elevations

Next you will turn off the trees in the south view. Normally you would turn them off in all views. However, you will only turn them off in the south view to show that you can control visibility per view on a sheet.

16. Click near the edge of the drawing to select the viewport of the south elevation (reference Figure 12-1.4).

17. Now **Right-Click** and select **Activate View** from the pop-up menu.

At this point you are in the viewport and can make changes to the project model to control visibility, which is what you will do next.

18. Right-click in the "white space" and select **View Properties...**

19. Click the **Edit** button next to *Visibility*.

20. In the Visibility dialog **Uncheck Planting**.

21. Close the open dialog boxes.

22. Right-click anywhere in the drawing area and select **Deactivate View** from the pop-up menu.

Now the trees are turned off for the South Elevation but not the North.

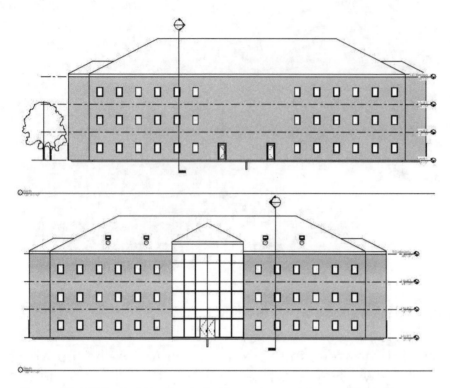

Figure 12-1.7 North & South exterior (trees removed from south view)

23. Create another Sheet for the other two exterior elevations (East and West); the sheet should be number **A201**.

Now you will stop for a moment and notice that Revit is automatically referencing the drawings as you place them on sheets.

24. Switch to **Level 1** (see Figure 12-1.8).

Notice in Figure 12-1.8 that the number A200 represents the sheet number that the drawing can be found on. The number one (1) is the drawing number to look for on sheet A200.

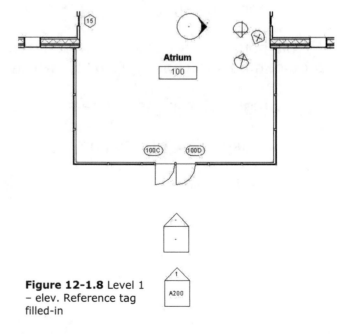

Figure 12-1.8 Level 1 – elev. Reference tag filled-in

Setting up Sections:

25. Create a sheet numbered **A300** and titled **Building Sections**.

26. Add a cross section, in plan view, through the atrium area.

27. Add the three building sections as shown in **Figure 12-1.9**.

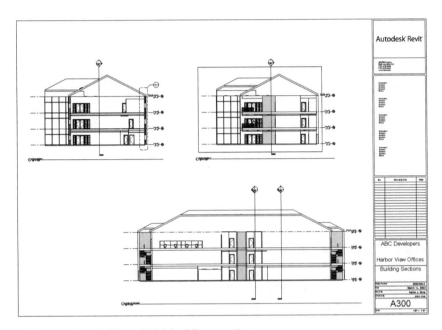

Figure 12-1.9 Sheet A300 building sections

28. Switch to *Level 1* plan view and zoom into the area shown in Figure 12-1.10.

Notice, again, that the reference bubbles are automatically filled in when the referenced view is placed on a sheet. If the drawing is moved to another sheet, the reference bubbles are automatically updated.

You can also see in Figure 12-1.9 (above) that the reference bubbles on the building sections are filled in.

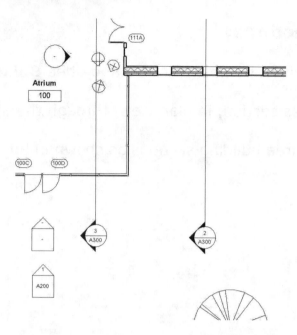

Figure 12-1.10 Level 1 – Section ref's filled in

Set up the remaining sheets:

Next you set up sheets for the remaining views that have yet to be placed on a sheet (except for the 3D views).

Create the following sheets and place the appropriate views on them:
- A111   Level 1 Reflected Ceiling Plan
- A112   Level 2 Reflected Ceiling Plan
- A113   Level 3 Reflected Ceiling Plan
- A400   Wall Sections
- A500   Interior Elevations
- A800   Schedules

Question: On a large project with hundreds of views, how do I know for sure if I have placed every view on a sheet?

Answer: Revit has a feature called *Browser Organization* that can hide all the views that have been placed on a sheet. You will try this next.

29. Take a general look at the *Project Browser* to see how many views are listed. (See Figure 12-1.12 on page 12-10.)

30. From the *Settings* pull-down menu select **Browser Organization...**

31. On the *Views* tab, click the check-box next to **not on sheets**. (Figure 12-1.11)

Figure 12-1.11 Project Browser

32. Click **OK**.

33. Notice the list in the *Project Browser* is now smaller. (See Figure 12-1.13 on *page* 12-10.)

The Project Browser now only shows drawing views that have not been placed onto a sheet. Of course, you could have a few views that do not need to be placed on a sheet, but this feature will help eliminate errors.

Next you will reset the Project Browser.

34. Open *Browser Organization* again and check the box next to **all** and click **OK** to close the dialog box (Figure 12-1.11).

Notice that the new sheets, just created, can be found under *Sheets (all)* on the *Project Browser* (Figure 12-1.14).

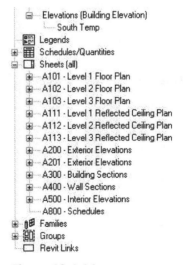

Figure 12-1.14
Project Browser; Sheets (all)

Figure 12-1.12
Project Browser; Views (all)

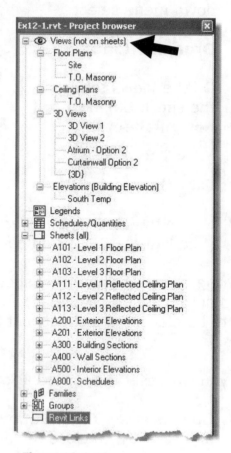

Figure 12-1.13
Project Browser; Views (not on sheets)

Sheets with Design Options:

Finally, you will setup a sheet to show two of the atrium Design Options.

35. Create a *Sheet* named **Atrium Options** and number it **A900**.

36. Open both *Atrium – Option 2* and *Curtainwall Option 2 view* and change the scale to **⅛" = 1'-0"**.

37. Place the two views, mentioned above, on sheet A900.
    (See Figure 12-1.15.)

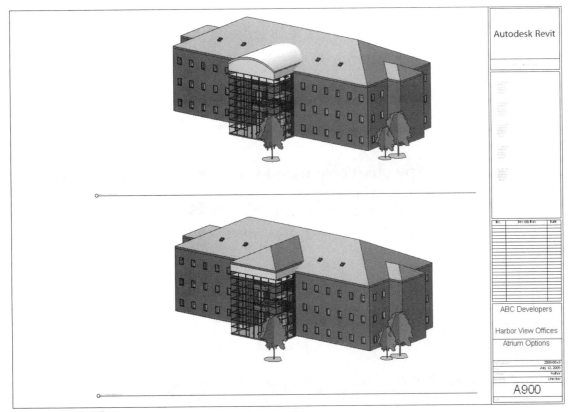

Figure 12-1.15
Atrium Options Sheet; two views with Design Options added

38. **Save** your project as **ex12-1.rvt**.

Exercise 12-2:
Sheet Index

Revit has the ability to create a sheet index automatically. You will study this now.

Creating a Sheet List View

1. Open ex12-1.rvt and **Save As** ex12-2.

2. From the *View* pull-down menu select **New → Drawing List...**

You are now in the Drawing List dialog box. Here you specify which fields you want in the sheet index and how to sort the list.
(Figure 12-2.1)

3. Add **Sheet Number** and **Sheet Name** to the right *(click Add →)*.

4. Click **OK**.

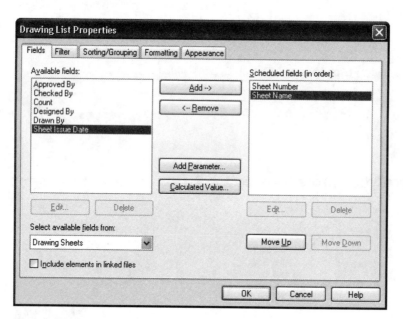

Figure 12-2.1
Drawing List Properties Dialog; sheet number and name "added"

Now you should notice that the *Sheet Names* are cut off because the column is not wide enough. You will adjust this next.

5.   Move your cursor over the right edge of the *Drawing List* table and click-and-drag to the right until you can see the entire name (Figure 12-2.2).

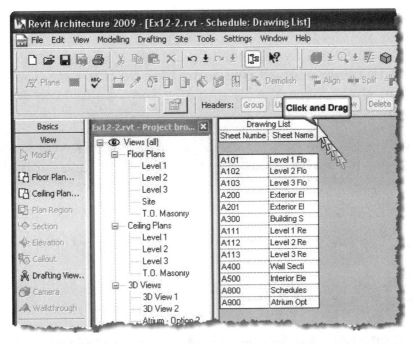

Figure 12-2.2
Drawing List view; notice sheet names are cut off in right column

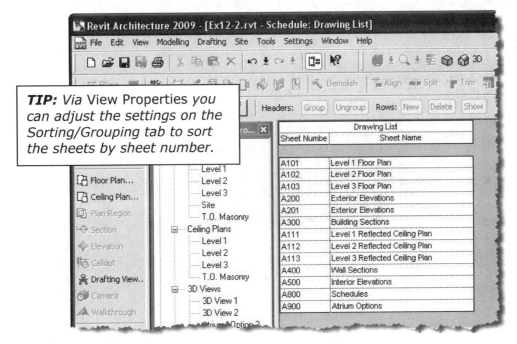

TIP: Via View Properties *you can adjust the settings on the Sorting/Grouping tab to sort the sheets by sheet number.*

Figure 12-2.3
Drawing List view; sheet names are now visible

Setting up a Title Sheet

Now you will create a title sheet to place your sheet index on.

6. Create a new Sheet:
   a. Number: **T001**
   b. Name: **Title Sheet**

7. From the *Schedules/Quantities* category of the *Project Browser*, place the view named **Drawing List** on the *Title Sheet*. Once on the sheet, drag the "triangle" grip to adjust the column width.

Next you will place one of your rendered images that you saved to file (raster image). If you have not created a raster image, you should refer back to Lesson 11 and create one now (otherwise you can use any BMP or JPG file on your hard drive if necessary).

8. From the *File* pull-down menu select **Import/Link → Image...**

9. Browse to your JPG or BMP raster image file, select it and click **Open** to place the Image.

10. Click on your Title Sheet to locate the image.

Your sheet should look similar to Figure 12-2.4.

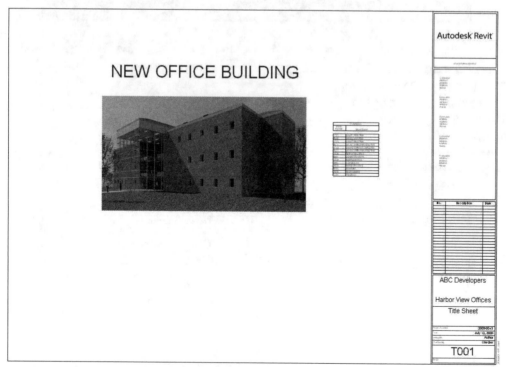

Figure 12-2.4 Sheet View: Title Sheet with drawing list, text and image added

11. Use the **Text** command to add the title shown in Figure 12-2.4.

When you have raster images in you project, you can manage them via the Raster Images dialog.

12. From the *File* menu, select **Raster Images...**

You are now in the Raster Image dialog which gives you a little information about the image and allows you to delete it from the project (Figure 12-2.5).

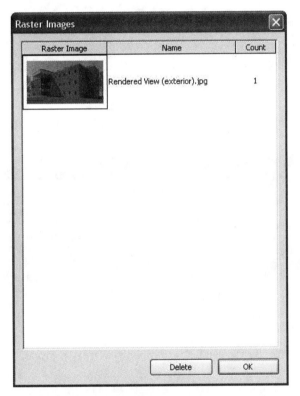

Figure 12-2.5 Raster Image dialog

13. Click OK to close the Raster image dialog.

14. **Save** your project as **ex12-2.rvt**.

Exercise 12-3:
Printing a set of drawings

Revit has the ability to print an entire set of drawings, in addition to printing individual sheets. You will study this now.

Printing a set of drawings

1. **Open ex12-2.rvt**.

2. Select **Print...** from the *File* pull-down menu.

3. In the *Print range* area, click the option **Selected views/ sheets** (Figure 12-3.1).

4. Click the **Select...** button within the *Print range* area.

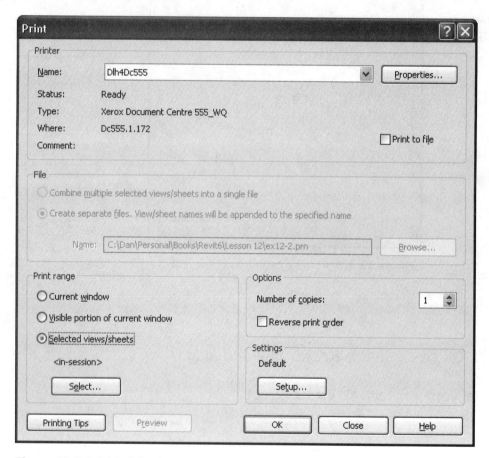

Figure 12-3.1 Print dialog box

You should now see a listing of all views and sheets (Figure 12-3.2).

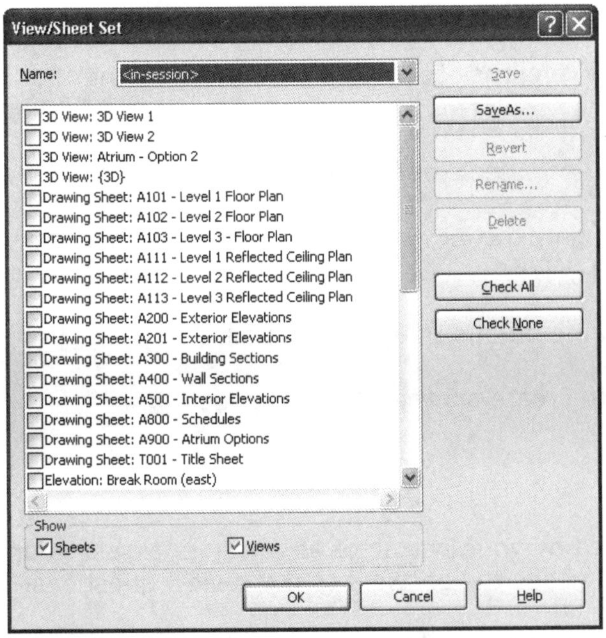

Figure 12-3.2 Selecting tool for printing

Notice at the bottom you can **Show** both **Sheets** and **Views**, or each separately. Because you are printing a set of drawings you will want to see only the sheets.

5. **Uncheck** the **Views** option.

The list is now limited to just sheets set up in your project.

6. Select all the Drawing Sheets.

FYI:

Once you have selected the sheets to be plotted you can click Save. This will save the list of selected drawings to a name you choose. Then, the next time you need to print those sheets, you can select the name from the drop-down list at the top (Figure 12-3.2).

On very large projects (e.g., 20 floor plan sheets) you could have a Plans list saved, a Laboratory Interior Elevations list saved, etc.

---

7. Click **OK** to close the **View/Sheet Set** dialog.

8. IF YOU ACTUALLY WANT TO PRINT A FULL SET OF DRAWINGS, you can do so now by clicking OK. Otherwise click **Cancel**.

9. You do not need to save the file at this time.

[End of Exercise 12-3]

You should now have a basic understanding of the Autodesk Revit Architecture software. **Gook luck with your future Revit projects!**

Self-Exam:

The following questions can be used as a way to check your knowledge of this lesson. The answers can be found at the bottom of this page.

1.   You have to manually fill in the reference bubbles after setting up the sheets. (T/F) *F*

2.   You cannot control the visibility of objects per viewport. (T/F) *F*

3.   It is possible to see a listing of only the views that have not been placed on a sheet via the Project Browser. (T/F) *T*

4.   You only have to enter your name on one titleblock, not all. (T/F) *F*

5.   Use the _____ tool to create another drawing sheet. *sheet*

Review Questions:

The following questions may be assigned by your instructor as a way to assess your knowledge of this section. Your instructor has the answers to the review questions.

1.   You need to use a special command to edit text in the titleblock. (T/F) *F*

2.   The template you started with has several titleblocks to choose from. (T/F) *F*

3.   You only have to enter the project name on one sheet, not all. (T/F) *T*

4.   The scale of a drawing placed on a sheet is determined by the scale set in that view's properties. (T/F) *T*

5.   You can save a list of drawing sheets to be plotted. (T/F) *T*

6.   Use the _activate view_ tool to edit the model from a sheet view. ~~view properties~~

7.   The reference bubbles will not automatically update if a drawing is moved to another sheet. (T/F) *F*

8.   On new sheets, the sheet number on the titleblock will increase by one from the previous sheet number. (T/F) *T*

Index

Video Index

Videos are located on the DVD that came with this book.

*See DVD for Bonus Videos

Notes:

Notes:

Notes:

Notes:

Notes:

Notes:

Notes:

Notes:

Notes:

Notes: